Photograph: Jonathan Cosgrove

Amanda Sinclair is Foundation Professor of Management Diversity and Change at Melbourne Business School, the University of Melbourne. She is the author of several books on gender and leadership, including *Trials at the Top* (1994) and *Doing Leadership Differently* (1998), and co-author of a book on leadership and diversity, *New Faces of Leadership* (2002). She consults to organisations and senior management teams, is a regular contributor to the business press, and also teaches yoga. A mother of four, Amanda brings to all her work a strong interest in leadership that supports well-being and growth.

Praise for *Leadership for the Disillusioned*:

'*Leadership for the Disillusioned* is a true gem among the avalanche of books published each year on leadership. In a very different voice, Amanda Sinclair provides us with deep insights in her search for a different type of leader. Valuing reflective thinking, experiential learning and critical theory, she truly liberates us from the shadow side of the leader within.'

Professor Manfred Kets de Vries, Director, INSEAD Global Leadership Center and author of The Leader on the Couch

'This is a marvellous book, one of the best I have ever read on leadership. Its critical analysis of leadership discourses, of power relations, identity work, spirituality and the egoistic preoccupations with self are all very important. Beautifully written, clear and concise, it is also personal, experiential and empowering. For theorists and practitioners interested in the liberating possibilities of a different kind of leadership, this is a "must-read".'

David Collinson, Professor of Leadership and Organisation, The Centre for Excellence in Leadership, Lancaster University Management School

'At long last, Amanda Sinclair blows open leadership myths—hopefully saving us from the thousands of leadership courses teaching how you too can become one of the "chosen" and never questioning what leadership is for. *Leadership for the Disillusioned* is a must for all of us who want leadership to be about liberation and freedom.'

Rhonda Galbally, CEO, www.ourcommunity.com.au

AMANDA SINCLAIR

leadership
for the disillusioned

*Moving beyond myths and heroes
to leading that liberates*

ALLEN&UNWIN

First published in 2007

Allen & Unwin
83 Alexander Street
Crows Nest NSW 2065
Australia
Phone: (61 2) 8425 0100
Fax: (61 2) 9906 2218
Email: info@allenandunwin.com
Web: www.allenandunwin.com

National Library of Australia
Cataloguing-in-Publication entry:

Sinclair, Amanda, 1953- .
    Leadership for the disillusioned : moving beyond myths and
    heroes to leading that liberates.

    Bibliography.
    Includes index.
    ISBN 978 1 74175 100 0.

    1. Leadership. I. Title.

    158.4

Index by Russell Brooks
Set in 10/14 pt Syndor ITC by Midland Typesetters, Australia

10 9 8 7 6 5 4 3 2 1

contents

Contents

PART III **GOING DEEPER**

table, figure and images

Table and figure

Images

acknowledgments

First, thank you to the leaders who have generously allowed me to include parts of their leadership stories in the book—Mick Dodson, Lillian Holt, Christine Nixon, Chris Sarra, Cathy Walter and John Wilson.

I wrote a draft (which I thought was close to final) of (what I thought would be titled) *Liberating Leadership* while at the Judge Business School, Cambridge University, for three months in 2005. Being there was undoubtedly a highlight of my life and I wish to formally thank the sponsors of my Visiting Fellowship there, Deloitte & Touche. There are many people at the Judge whom I thank for their conversations, generosity and assistance, but there are three who made my visit particularly special: Chris Grey, John Roberts and Dame Professor Sandra Dawson.

Many other friends and colleagues will recognise in the book insights from our conversations and their suggestions. For their support of me and my leadership ideas I am grateful to many people, including Naomi Raab, Richard Searle, Sundhya Pahuja, Pat Seybolt (who also helped with research), Peter Gronn, Robert Burke and Valerie Wilson. My students at Melbourne Business School and my clients have been welcome fellow-travellers and teachers on the journey of writing this book. I would like to thank colleagues at MBS, especially the library staff who have gone way beyond the call of duty in research fossicking for me, and MBS Director, John Seybolt, for his belief in and support of my work on leadership. Special thanks go to my MBS yoga class for reminding me to take time out and enjoy the moment.

I would like to also acknowledge people outside 'work'. Jean-Alain and Elizabeth D'Argent have encouraged my development in yoga and as a yoga teacher, and supported me to deepen my understanding of the philosophies guiding this practice. I feel privileged to be part of the wonderful community that is Dharma Yoga.

Jackie Yowell has been an amazing editor, whose tact and commitment to creating the best book possible make her a legend. My thanks also go to the professional and friendly team at Allen & Unwin. Who could have thought that getting ideas into print could actually be a rewarding process?

It's not easy having an author in the family and to my darling children—to Huw (amazingly and unfailingly interested in the content), Charlie, Amy and James—and to my mother Barb (who also found the marvellous *Richard II* quote that follows), thank you for withstanding my obsessions and for all the ways you are yourselves.

Finally, and perhaps most importantly, I wish to thank my partner, Warwick Pattinson, for too many things to list here, but in particular his practical support, his tolerance, for standing up to me and getting me to stop writing (at times), his unstinting encouragement to put myself at the centre of the writing, his editorial help and his love.

Amanda Sinclair

Note: Parts of the book have been published elsewhere and are reproduced with permission. A version of Chapter 6 appeared in 2005 in *Leadership* 1(4): 387–406 and is adapted with permission from Sage.

What must the king do now? Must he submit?
The king shall do it. Must he be depos'd?
The king shall be contented. Must he lose
The name of king? o' God's name, let it go.
I'll give my jewels for a set of beads,
My gorgeous palace for a hermitage,
My gay apparel for an almsman's gown,
My figur'd goblets for a dish of wood,
My sceptre for a palmer's walking staff,
My subjects for a pair of carved saints,
And my large kingdom for a little grave,
A little, little grave, an obscure grave;
Or I'll be buried in the king's highway,
Some way of common trade, where subjects' feet
May hourly trample on their sovereign's head

William Shakespeare, *Richard II*, act 3, scene 3, lines 143–57

Introduction:
Leadership
for liberation

⅜

The process of becoming a leader is very much the same as becoming an integrated human being.

Warren Bennis (1989)

This leadership book is not about how to run a company. It is for those who are disillusioned by their encounters with leaders and leadership: with idealised heroic performances, impoverished theories and oversimplified templates. My desire is to explore how leadership can be a liberating force, an idea and a way of influencing that *frees* people.

Leadership, it seems, has become ubiquitous. Everyone is being encouraged to do it. From CEOs to public servants, community activists to sales assistants, footballers to schoolchildren—all are regularly exhorted to show leadership. Despite all this attention, there is little evidence that we are getting better at it.

Why might our appetite for leadership be a bad thing? In the first part of this book, I argue that we have often been seduced by ideas and practices of leadership. Leadership has become a panacea. People call for leadership, but what do they really mean? Often such a call is a concealed request for toughness, a particular performance of single-handed heroism. People call for leadership because they feel unable to do the difficult and challenging work of thinking about how to move forward together.

Despite the thousands of books on the topic, what's often missing from accounts of leadership is a more systemic or critical perspective. When we look at leadership critically, we ask questions like: How has leadership come to be such an influential idea? What shapes the models of leadership being promoted? Whose interests are they serving? I argue in this book that it is not until we apply and explore these critical perspectives that we unshackle ourselves from banal exhortations and release ourselves towards more thoughtful, complex and ultimately liberating ideas and practices of leadership.

SOME BACKGROUND

When I first starting thinking about leadership, I thought the answers to how to do it must lie in Harvard Business School cases. I teach at Melbourne Business School, and it is routine in such environments to have the heads of global companies wheeled out as exemplars of leadership. Dutifully, I watched and read about people like Jack Welch, ex-CEO of GE.

It didn't take me long to feel a bit restive. Where others were seeing leadership, I was seeing a sharp-talking manager, big on jargon, fond of basketball and baseball analogies. I wondered what he stood for—apart from making a lot of money for GE. And for himself, as it turned out: after retiring, he continued to be paid a staggering salary. He was a model of successful leadership, with the business media only briefly questioning excesses like maintaining a New York flat with daily fresh flowers just in case he ever needed to visit.

Why does this model of leadership remain so attractive? If you have ever been on a leadership development program, you may indeed have been exposed to the GE leadership recipe, or the Richard Branson one—or, if it was a few years ago, even the Enron one (which had a Harvard Business School case study written about it). Alternatively, you might have had heroes held up to you for study—the explorer Shackleton, great military commanders, or warriors like Sun Zsu. You may even have been encouraged to go on great adventures yourself—if not conquering the Antarctic or Everest (and there are some leadership development programs that do just this), at least scaling walls or taking on some whitewater rafting.

I am not saying these are not valuable exercises, or that some of these individuals have not delivered great leadership, or even that there are not things to be learned from them. However, my research and teaching have led me to the belief that much of what is undertaken in the name of leadership may be damaging and, at worst, enslaving. Leadership, as it is so often encouraged and

Introduction: Leadership for liberation

modelled today, may be bad for leaders, followers and organisations alike, not to mention the wider society. In this book, I present examples and evidence, from my work in the field over two decades, of a subtle but pervasive corruption in the thinking and practice of leadership.

But why does this matter?

All of us feel the consequences of bad leadership. Organisations and their leaders are gaining greater impact in a world where societies are increasingly ungovernable, certainly by traditional mechanisms of regulation and control. Leadership acquires powerful new relevance as a potential custodian of, and advocate for, values such as public good, community welfare, well-being, and sustainable development.

I have written this book because I see all around me—among friends, colleagues, leaders engaged in all sorts of important work—people struggling to find ways to do the work of leadership differently: more mindfully, more collaboratively, taking others with them in personally sustainable and satisfying ways.

How might leadership be reclaimed to guide those of us in organisations who seek to make them meaningful, valuable and happier places to be? My argument in this book is that leadership should be aimed at helping to free people from oppressive structures, practices and habits encountered in societies and institutions, as well as within the shady recesses of ourselves. *Good leaders liberate*. Further, we can liberate leadership thinking itself from its narrow instrumental confines, so it may reconnect with such ideals.

Drawing on my observation and analysis of leaders, I make the case for thinking about leadership as a way of being that is reflective and thoughtful about self; that values relationships and the present; that is connected to others and embodied; that is not narrowly striving or ego-driven; and that is liberating in its effects. This leadership is work almost all of us do at some time or another. This is not the 'captains of industry' type of leadership, but the work we do as role models—as teachers, parents, problem-solvers, activists, spokespeople and organisers. Some lead simply by scrutinising and questioning standards, such as reformers or whistleblowers; others do so by acting according to principles or values when those around them have opted for pragmatism. Because all of us are also sometimes followers, my argument is that we all have an interest in leadership. We shouldn't leave the thinking and writing about leadership to those who designate themselves 'experts'.

So, I have written this book for a broad audience, including:

○ people in corporations and other organisations who feel cynical about, and disaffected by, what they see going on around them under the heading of 'leadership', yet want to do a good job, find satisfaction in their work, and contribute to valuable purposes;[1]

○ people in community, not-for-profit or voluntary organisations who are seeking to lead in a connected and humane way, but feel under pressure to become more commercially focused and to emulate models of business leadership and practice;

○ professionals, directors and administrators in human services (such as principals, doctors, teachers and social workers) who find their time and energies increasingly consumed by directives to do more 'leadership', leaving less for the professional work for which they were trained and to which they are committed;

○ people who have done some leadership training and feel disturbed by what wasn't covered and what wasn't talked about;

○ people seeking more insight into leadership, but who find only unsatisfying books full of checklists and homilies from corporate chiefs;

○ teachers and academics in leadership and organisational studies who seek fresh inspiration for their research agendas and for classroom discussion;

○ people who work as trainers, coaches, mentors and developers of leaders who are looking for ways to broaden and deepen the dialogue they facilitate, perhaps into areas that resist discussion; and

○ students of leadership of all kinds and at all stages of their lives, from people reflecting back on a life of work to those starting out with an interest in, aspiration for or scepticism about leadership.

A *CRITICAL* UNDERSTANDING OF LEADERSHIP

Among the thousands of books written on the meaning of leadership, there is grudging agreement that leadership is a process of influence between leaders and followers. What distinguishes leadership from other forms of influence is that the leader draws on some form of authority, power or control. This does not mean that the only people who can lead must be in high-level jobs or political posts, nor that leadership is a position or role. Leadership is a relationship, in which leaders inspire or mobilise others to extend their capacity to imagine, think and act in positive new ways.

Almost all of us have some kind of power, access to certain types of authority and opportunities for leadership. Parents with teenagers have leadership opportunities, even though it may not feel like it. Teenagers, too, can show leadership with their parents—even though it may feel far from an inspiring experience for either party, at least in the short term.

Yet, if we turn to much of the literature on leadership, a more rigid understanding is in evidence. I go into this in more detail in the next two chapters, but in summary I am suggesting that leadership has come to be an imperative that:

○ requires an individual performance of heroic action, certainty and decisiveness;
○ assumes the job of the leader is to orchestrate change in others, not in oneself;
○ is aimed at organisationally mandated goals (like growth of market-share and shareholder wealth, winning clients or tenders, and achieving record performances of one kind or another); and
○ ignores longer-term and deeper questions of purpose (like *what is leadership for?*).

This traditional view of leadership rests on the flawed assumption that it is the job of leaders to change the behaviours, actions and beliefs of others. This assumption should be challenged as neither feasible nor morally defensible. To use one's role as a leader primarily to transform others is often to treat people as instruments—as a means to someone else's ends. In contrast, I argue that good leaders don't treat people as means to ends, as simply 'human resources' or 'human capital' to be deployed for business, the state or other assumed interests.[2]

So, if leaders can't and shouldn't set out to change people, where does this leave leadership? I argue for a critical understanding of leadership that questions the very intent and assumptions of most leadership thinking. A critical perspective begins by asking questions such as: What are the purposes to which leadership is being put? Who benefits from those purposes? Who or what may suffer or be adversely affected, perhaps in subtle and not immediately obvious ways?[3] Does leadership act to entrench (for leaders or followers) ways of working and living that are so pressured and materially focused that they are, in the end, unsustainable?

Leadership is not a job or a position, but a way of influencing others towards ends recognised as valuable and fulfilling. This may make leadership sound like a benign and uncontroversial activity, but it is far from that. Obstacles, conflict, risks and failure litter the ground around leadership. Some of the obstacles are internal, including protecting one's ego, self-doubt or inertia. Others lie in the structural conditions of organisations and institutional life, and include the ways in which leadership has traditionally been defined. One of the aims of this book is to support readers to identify these obstacles and to consider whether and how they might be overcome, or alternatively subverted or changed.

A more meaningful way to think about leadership is as *a form of being* (with ourselves and others): a way of thinking and acting that awakens and mobilises people to find new, freer and more meaningful ways of seeing, working and living. This form of leadership is anchored to personal self-awareness and mindfulness towards others.

I also question the contemporary assumption that all great leaders must have a great 'vision'[4]—that is, a view of the goal that is so clear, prescient and inspiring as to compel its following. Many undisputed leaders, such as Gandhi, built their leadership rather on some principles of living, and knew that the precise shape of transformation would emerge through collective effort. Martin Luther King, even in his iconic 'I have a dream' speech, did not overspecify his vision for equality for black Americans, nor the route that needed to be taken to get to it.[5]

Contrary to popular leadership rhetoric, good leaders don't always arrive at their intended destination. Instead, leaders may find themselves at unexpected places en route, and their leadership is demonstrated by the fact that they pause and recognise the importance of what is unanticipated. It is in working through opposition and difficulties—in stopping, listening and venturing again—that leadership is revealed.[6] Chinese philosopher Lao-tzu is quoted as saying that 'a good traveller has no fixed plans and is not intent on arriving'. Being too intent on arriving can blind leaders to new and important information, and prevent them from seeing the importance of existing conditions—fostering an 'end justifies the means' mentality.

This does not mean that there shouldn't be a capacity to imagine, hope or take risks in articulating and sharing possible futures. Indeed, initiating this discussion is often a key role for leaders. As organisational analyst Robert Denhardt has pointed out, leaders sometimes act as repositories for the collective fantasies of followers.[7] Problems occur where a leader is too attached to a vision, and in its pursuit shows inadequate flexibility, humility and respect for followers. The only visions that really work are those that resonate deeply with a group, organisation or society, and are available to be taken up and shaped by that community.

So leadership is both an intensely personal and a relational process of constructing meaning and purpose. To describe it as a journey is a cliché, yet the way we proceed down a path is as important in leadership as arriving at the destination—indeed, I believe it is more so.

LEADERSHIP THAT LIBERATES

In subtitling this book *Moving beyond myths and heroes to leading that liberates*, I want to convey two main ideas. The first is that leadership as a practice and a body of thinking needs to be liberated from *itself*. The discussion in Part I of the book shows how leadership has become a stifling and often predictable way of thinking—one that largely fails to step back from itself and ask basic questions or challenge shibboleths. At a deep level, societies, leaders and followers have become trapped by this ideology into punishing and ultimately unsustainable ways of working and living.

The second idea is that the purpose of leadership should be to liberate. Good leadership aims to support people (including leaders themselves) to make thoughtful choices about what to do and how to influence. Leadership can liberate us from confining or oppressive conditions—imposed by structures, others and ourselves. Rather than being used as a means to compel compliance and conformity, to dominate or prescribe, leadership can invite us to imagine, initiate and contest. Proceeding with a liberating intent requires leaders to be acutely conscious of power relations, to commit to using power and authority ethically, not in competitive self-interest or to control others. Parts II and III of this book are addressed to those interested in broadening their leadership to make it more freeing in its intent and effects.

While I explore the idea of liberation in detail in Chapter 3, it is worth fore-shadowing some important questions here. If leaders are being encouraged to act in the interests of liberation, whom are they seeking to free, and from what? From the imperatives of survival in an implacable global market? From the 'iron cage' of employers, bureaucratic routines or work–life pressures? From the explicit and implicit power relations that configure our lives, conditioning us to regimes of work and consumption, or to relentless surveillance and evaluation? From our desires and needs for security, belonging, meaning? From apathy? From ourselves?

One person's freedom is another's prison. Followers, for assorted and often sound reasons, don't always want to be emancipated by a person presenting as their liberator. Further, in acting upon this intent, we may become captive to a wider ideology that puts the pursuit of individual freedom above other values.[8]

Such concerns are central to the discussion that follows and, in my view, to any searching analysis of leadership.

A DIFFERENT WAY OF WRITING

Anyone who knows the leadership literature knows how pompous and self-important some of it has become. This is as much a problem of the way it has been constructed and written about as it is of leadership itself. Most leadership books promise clarity and resolution: that problems will be solved, and material success achieved, with the sweeping heroic flourish that is our contemporary understanding of leadership. Instead of fixing things, however, such promises are usually complicit in perpetuating the status quo.[9]

Partially in response to my own disaffection with the leadership literature, I now want to write in a different way—more personally, relying on both research and experience, and with an explicit intention of engaging a wider range of readers who are doing leadership work, but would not normally consider reading a leadership book.[10]

The conventional vehicles for academic work—journal articles, books and research studies—typically pretend that the author's personal perspective and interests are incidental to the written content. I believe most books about leadership emerge from personal experience, and in this one I choose to make a point of that. I have written it in a more personal, narrative way than is customary for academics for several reasons. I don't want to position myself as detached expert: we can rarely be entirely detached in the study of human activity. But writing personally is risky because it is not considered to be what 'serious' books do. Almost all scholarship on management and organisation is written as if the author is absent, as if objective truths were being recorded.

At another extreme, popular writing about leadership in business publications and newspapers is larded with managerial jargon, and usually breathless in its claims.[11] The result is a 'McDonaldized' leadership, offering quick gratification but little lasting substance.

The book arises out of my own journey of learning about leadership—from teaching leadership to executives, MBA students and others, and from observing and researching leadership in a variety of settings. I use cases, stories and personal experience. While I also draw on extensive leadership research to support what I say (and the bibliography is a guide), this research is not the main story.

Foregrounding my personal experience in this way carries possibilities as well as risks. The stories will, I hope, illustrate my points more vividly, and make insights arising out of experiences shared with the reader more striking. The risks are many, but the one I am particularly mindful to avoid is joining the legion of leadership books in which 'Do it my way' is the tone, and moments of modest personal insight are all too often proffered as epiphanies.

So this is a book about leadership which is not like most other leadership books. It is about the way we are in our work, our organisations and our lives— and how we might be. How do we bring presence, compassion and insight to how we are and how we influence others? This is what I am interested in as leadership. All of us are involved in this work, whether we are doing paid work inside—or at the upper levels of—traditional organisations, or simply doing the crucial, but no less significant, work of shaping the daily lives of others in families and communities.

OVERVIEW

The first part of the book explores what is wrong with leadership, including the practice (Chapter 1), theory and ideas (Chapter 2) and teaching of leadership (Chapter 3). In the first chapter, I suggest that many parts of public life have increasingly become captive to a particular model of leadership that emerges from business. Business leaders have come to represent the standard for leadership. These people—often CEOs magnified by media profile—have come to represent leadership, to speak for it, to be held up as experts in it. Audiences have come to expect, and demand, a certain kind of performance from these, and consequently other, leaders. In this chapter I show how and why contemporary notions of leadership have seduced and constrained both leaders and followers.

The second chapter shows how the path taken by leadership studies in recent times has contributed to narrow understandings of what leaders should do. How and why has knowledge about leadership come to privilege some voices and marginalise others? Why is it that leadership research and discourse are so dominated by masculine voices and preoccupied with size and status as markers of success? Why are great deeds of leadership so rarely, it would seem, detected among women or among people in the community and not-for-profit sectors? How has the way that leadership has been studied and conceptualised changed the way it is done? Values of growth and conquest, materialism and individualism have come to permeate leadership training and development. Leadership as an idea has been too narrowly aligned with the interests of corporatism and global capitalism. Further, the ways in which we have studied leadership, including the framing and resourcing of analyses, have contributed to the capture and conversion of leadership ideology as a tool of particular political or business interests.

In Chapter 3 I explore ideas of liberation in the context of leadership education. Drawing on experiences gained through teaching leadership to MBA students and other groups of managers, I describe three processes that help to unlock thinking about leadership, and open people to new ways of doing it: being reflective; working experientially; and thinking critically.

Part II of the book, 'Practices of liberating leadership', explores some ideas that are not usually discussed in leadership, but that I believe create possibilities for doing leadership in a more liberating way.

Chapter 4 puts the case that reflective leadership starts with going back, into our childhoods and backgrounds. Our first experience of leadership is in the family, and the way we adopted a position in the early years is likely to affect the template for the appetites and desires that play out in adult life, including the way we do leadership. To allow ourselves more options in going forward in leadership, we need to start by going back. This challenging process allows us to map what is termed in the literature our 'implicit leadership theories'—largely unconscious assumptions, often built early in life about leadership, following and our place in these scripts. By articulating these less conscious templates, we begin to free ourselves from them. We begin to spot when we are simply reacting to events in ways that are no longer necessary or productive. This allows space to exercise our own leadership in new ways, as well as to see leadership in new places.

Power is central to leadership yet neglected in much leadership writing. Paradoxically, leaders often consider themselves to be powerless because, for example, they feel wedged into a hierarchy of command. In Chapter 5, I introduce research which helps us recognise the dynamics of power, and enables us to see how to locate ourselves within institutions in ways that are more mindful of our own power. I explore ways of being effective in leadership that do not necessitate lining up with a hierarchy or perpetuating all its conventions. These include naming what is going on and various forms of whistleblowing, re-examining taken-for-granted ideas, and resisting or subverting autocratic authority.

Paying attention to bodies also invites new insights for leadership. Chapter 6 suggests that a significant but unexplored area for innovation in leading differently is awareness of bodies, and how physicality is deployed in leading and being led. Drawing on two case studies, I show the power of thinking through and with the body to initiate and support change in rigid or moribund environments.

Chapter 7 further develops ideas of how leadership practice might be anchored in the here and now, with a focus on the breath. It may seem unusual to suggest conscious breathing can help leaders, but such techniques are proving themselves in innovative development programs. For example, meditative techniques involving mindfulness and breath-consciousness are used to help improve focus and clarity in decision-making, negotiation, conflict resolution and mediation work. Typically, the energies of leaders are focused on plans and achieving material outcomes such as economic returns in the short, medium and longer term. One result of this relentless focus on meeting future targets is a neglect of what is happening in the present. Indeed, sometimes autocratic behaviour is tolerated as required leadership performance in meeting financial objectives. There is evidence that this exacts a high price on leaders, as well as the people who work and live around them. Many people in organisations are seeking ways to avoid being sucked into activities that undeservedly drain energy—ways to make the moment matter more, to value relationships (work and home) in the here and now, to stop putting off significant life experiences, to find more happiness and balance in the present. Breath work acts as a reminder of mortality and the gift of life, liberating leaders and followers from compulsion, encouraging them to slow down long enough to make considered choices about where their efforts go.

Working with new ideas and practices of personal history, power, bodies and breath goes to the heart of who we are—our identity. Part III turns to the deeper implications of seeking to lead differently in identity work, spirituality and leading with less ego. In Chapter 8, I explore several contemporary 'solutions' to the problem of crafting or inhabiting a viable leadership identity, such as working towards 'work–life balance' and finding our 'authentic' identity. I suggest that postmodern ideas about identity work can help leaders to situate themselves more powerfully at the changing intersection of competing constructions of self.

Spirituality in leadership is the subject of Chapter 9. While not rejecting efforts to find spiritual meaning in leadership work, I suggest that leaders should be wary of invoking spiritual ideas when the purposes and beneficiaries of that effort are not made explicit, or where they are used for organisationally or personally aggrandising ends. The push for spirituality and authenticity being urged upon leaders risks becoming a narcissistic preoccupation, a vehicle for self-improvement or materialism that is fundamentally at odds with spiritual values. Rather, in Chapter 10, I propose the idea of 'less-ego leadership' as a way of drawing together the themes of the book. Here the intent is to explore ways of leading with less, not more, ego. The Epilogue returns to a more personal expression of why liberating leadership matters to me.

To summarise, then, this book offers no comprehensive models or checklists for leadership. Instead, it advocates that leadership is a process of critical and compassionate engagement with the world. Further, it argues that leadership is a commitment to challenging accepted wisdom, to reflecting deeply on our motives so as to avoid co-option, to being mindful of relations between our bodies and psyches, to being in the moment, and to leading with the intent of freeing—both the self and others.

PART I

What's wrong
with leadership?

1

The seduction
of leadership

⚸

Leadership is a serious sign of social pathology . . . that induces massive learned
helplessness among members of a social system

Gary Gemmill and Judith Oakley (1992)

In early 2006, Jeff Skilling and the late Ken Lay, the leaders of the giant corporation Enron, stood trial in what promised to be one of the most keenly watched
cases of corporate leadership failure. In a few years, they had gone from being
hailed in *Fortune* magazine as 'one of the deepest and most innovative management teams in the world'[1] to being disgraced as corporate leaders. Both found
guilty of fraud and deception, they were facing combined jail terms in the
hundreds of years. A few months later, Lay died suddenly of a heart attack.

In the late 1990s, Enron was regarded as the model company of the future.
It was an energy company that was supremely profitable, despite not owning
much in the way of power stations or gas plants. How it actually made profits
was a bit of a mystery, but few felt confident to question its financial practices
or novel accounting techniques. Investors loved it, and the largest and most
powerful American financial institutions—including regulators and accounting
firms—were gullible to its charms, fawning in their admiration.

The Enron leaders were treated like prophets. Ken Lay, the chairman, and
Jeff Skilling, the CEO, featured on the front covers of business magazines,
attracting widespread admiration for their audacity in refusing to be bound by

old ways of thinking in the energy industry. They were portrayed as crashing through to change the rules of the energy game forever, as the young Elvis in his gold lamé suit had done in the music industry.[2]

Lay and Skilling held court at prestigious American business schools, honing leadership performances that seduced their audiences and themselves. They gathered around them groups of followers, including politicians, analysts, bankers and regulators—all dazzled by the conjuring up of massive profits without the nuisance of maintaining much in the way of energy infrastructure. Videos of meetings addressed by the two leaders show captivated audiences. Articles in the business press praised them as 'audacious' and 'brilliant', while esteemed academics such as Christopher Bartlett at Harvard wrote case studies about what could be learned from Enron's leadership and the way the firm went about its business.

The more the press salivated, the more Skilling and Lay basked and colluded in this spiral of adulation: they were 'the smartest guys in the room', leading the sleepy energy industry into the future. Their accountants, Arthur Andersen, lawyers and regulators were all collusive in approving practices that

Jeff Skilling, CEO, at the height of Enron's success
Getty Images

4

were subsequently shown to be highly deceptive, if not fraudulent. Alan Greenspan, then Chairman of the Federal Reserve, received an Enron award at a gala ceremony. With a few exceptions, brokers and analysts did not probe the lack of transparent balance sheets, and those who did promptly found themselves out of a job. Critics were scorned, dismissed as having 'Enron envy'.

It was not until several years of Enron's spectacular success had passed that a couple of individuals started asking questions. A relatively new employee of Enron, Sherron Watkins, began expressing concerns about methods of accounting. Bethany McLean, a young journalist with *Fortune* magazine, undertook some basic analysis of Enron's balance sheets and simply could not make sense of them. When she and her editor met with Skilling and other Enron executives, their concerns were not appeased. McLean went ahead and wrote her article, suggesting that Enron stock might be overpriced.[3] It was not incidental that these two early whistleblowers were women and newcomers, outside the cult of adoration that had developed around Enron. While others feared to ask questions that challenged powerful opinion-shapers, neither of these women had quite as much to lose. Meanwhile, many of the smartest, most senior and most influential members of America's political, corporate and financial elites had been seduced.

I argue throughout this book that leadership is often accomplished through this sort of collusive seduction, which can become so powerful as to forestall any criticism. This chapter explores how and why seduction happens, drawing on further examples to show the aesthetic, political and psychodynamic reasons why we surrender to leaders and how they come to believe their own mystique. Recognition of these mechanisms and dynamics is the first step in understanding how it is that bad leadership can prevail—how leaders self-inflate as followers surrender. We need to address these dynamics squarely in order to begin to release ourselves from them. As Peter Gronn has warned, 'the exploitation of heroic leader prototypes impedes meaningful public engagement with the complexities of political and social reality'.[4]

HOW LEADERSHIP SEDUCES

The Enron story, along with many others that I could have selected as examples, shows a common pattern in leadership. This pattern has been likened to falling in love.[5] Here, I describe it as seduction.

What do I mean by seduction? To seduce is to *lead* astray. The words 'seduction' and 'leadership' have common origins.[6] The Latin root of seduction is *se ducere*, and *ducere* means leadership. Mussolini was known as *Il Duce*.

In the fifteenth century, 'to seduce' meant to divert from allegiance or service. By the sixteenth century, the usage was more specifically gendered, meaning to induce a woman to surrender her chastity. While seduction was initially a word denoting a process whereby men seduced other men from their earlier loyalty, later women became the objects of seduction, persuaded to yield their chastity. In modern usage, it is women who are more likely to be described as seductive—as alluring and enticing—and, in contemporary use, men are rarely portrayed as seducible by other men.

When I have talked about the seduction of leadership with audiences— particularly male-dominated ones—there is an uneasy moving in seats. The idea of men being seduced, and moreover men being seduced by other men, is confronting at a number of levels: it can offend a prized sense of autonomy and judgment, among other things. However, the same audiences recognise the features of seductive leadership described above. A common response is to protest: 'Yes, but seduction isn't necessarily a bad thing.' Seduction can, of course, be an enjoyable process. But I suggest here that, just as we now recognise the 'groupthink' mentality[7] which can create illusions of invincibility and under- mine good decision-making, by looking in more depth at the seductive potential in leadership, we are able to make finer judgments about when seduction is harmless and when it is dangerous. At what point and under what circumstances, for example, do followers suspend critical faculties or abdicate responsibility?

The seductive process commences when leadership is located in one person, who is seen by audiences and followers as 'above other men'.[8] It is not surpris- ing that this happens in Western societies, which tend to be individualistic, and where CEOs are encouraged by big pay packets to think that they are respon- sible for an organisation's fortunes. Despite little empirical evidence to support the formula that leaders determine organisational success, the cult of the CEO is rarely questioned.

That leader then starts to enjoy the benefits of being seen as superhuman. An inflated persona is constructed, with legends and myths developing around it. These leaders are celebrated in the business press, and their views and presence are sought to grace all sorts of occasions. Some are asked to sit on government and advisory panels, and thus accumulate significant political power. Myths of physical virility and invincibility develop around some leaders, and have been shamelessly cultivated by the likes of Mussolini and more recently former Italian Prime Minister Berlusconi.

Under these circumstances, such leaders start to believe themselves to be so great that they are outside the constraints applicable to 'ordinary' people.

This leader starts to believe that his 'visions' are unquestionably deserving, and therefore can legitimately come to serve for others as well as himself. A range of narcissistic, ego-inflated, sometimes neurotic and psychopathic behaviours can develop.[9] LaBier, for example, notes how irrationality and psychopathology can be highly adaptive in the workplace—for example, in financial institutions where reputations depend on big financial deals, there are in-built incentives to inflate and deceive when stating amounts transacted. Similarly, in the United States, corporate leader 'Chainsaw' Al Dunlap was celebrated in the 1990s for his sadistic capacities to 'execute' (the word is important) radical downsizing in the corporations he headed. His management style was welcomed as bringing a necessary discipline; meanwhile, he adopted humiliating tactics of escorting people from workplaces without notice. Dunlap met an ignominious demise when it was found that he added little to the value of companies, but not before he had been feted for his toughness—including by the late Australian media boss Kerry Packer.

In understanding how such leaders are swept along on a tide of narcissism and self-aggrandisement, personal backgrounds are often significant.[10] Look carefully into the early years of some and you find difficult childhoods, producing a consuming determination to remake themselves, to rewrite their own history, and so forge a new and more successful identity. Many political leaders, including Tony Blair and John Howard, endured difficult early years—often characterised by rejection. As I explore in Chapter 4 on the importance of personal biography, the earlier self is often being denied as the leader reconstructs a more potent and irresistible self-identity.

For male leaders, the remaking of identity often becomes bound up with the establishment of a heroic, death-defying masculinity. Enron's Jeff Skilling, for example, organised adventurous treks of dirt-bike riding for himself and his senior colleagues. These feats are recorded on video, and the mythology around them permeated Enron, installing these leaders as physical heroes as well as intellectual ones. Themes of conquest and manly appetites are often implicated in the reconstructed persona of the leader.

For their part, followers often fall prey to the conviction, charisma or promise that the leader holds out. Under the spell of this mystique, followers—including managers, employees and even senior stakeholders such as directors and regulators—suspend their critical faculties and become compliant to the leader's wishes and the dictates of the culture.[11] This pattern of behaviour has been widely documented in cases of ethical contravention and moral failure in companies. Examples range from the indictment for obstructing justice of giant accounting and consulting firm Arthur Andersen, for shredding evidence about its advice to Enron, to the case of Shell in Nigeria, where the assurances of leaders and organisational reputation silenced—at least for a time—evidence of environmental damage and political corruption. It is not uncommon to find otherwise smart and well-educated people surrendering their doubts to the certainty of leaders. Highly regarded individuals sat on the Enron board. Caught up in leadership's aura of success, perhaps they felt like they too could do no wrong.

When people set off looking for more leadership—individuals, groups, organisations and nations—what is going on? History and public policy research suggest that calls for leadership are heard most often when anxiety and appre-hensiveness about the future are pervasive, and when the problems facing a group require a radical shift in approach. People in such situations are seeking a leader who can relieve a group from its stresses. At some level, they may be looking for a 'father figure', a god or saviour to lift them out of their suffering or insecurity.[12] This yearning for leadership is all the more powerful because it is usually unconscious or repressed. Leaders and followers collude in the imagin-ing of leadership as heroic feats that will fix problems and usher in a new era. These practices are seductive because they release individuals from the work of leading themselves, from taking responsibility for thinking through diffi-cult problems and for critical decision-making. Heifetz and Laurie describe the dilemma in the following terms:

> We call for someone with answers, decision, strength, and a map of the future: someone who knows where we ought to be going—in short someone who can make hard problems simple. Instead of looking for saviours we should be looking for leadership that summons us to face the problems for which there are no simple, painless solutions—the challenges that require us to work in new ways.[13]

STEVE VIZARD AND DOUBLE SEDUCTION

In 2005, on the other side of the world from Enron, another story of leadership seduction was being played out.[14] Steve Vizard, a young Australian lawyer turned media entrepreneur, was fashioning an identity for himself as a new breed of corporate entrepreneur. He was funny, winning, and quickly earning public roles as diverse as a director of Telstra (the largest Australian phone company) and chairman of the Art Gallery of Victoria. Vizard was adored by ordinary Australians because, as a highly successful television comedian, he had himself poked fun at establishment figures. He was the perfect leader for an Australian culture wary of 'tall poppies'. Tall, extroverted and widely regarded as charismatic, he was a lovable larrikin of a man who had also managed to become a multi-millionaire through his media and entertainment interests.

He accrued prodigious personal wealth, but was also seen as a philanthropist, committed to giving something back to local Melbourne and Australian communities. With his interests in diverse business activities, including creating and selling his own television and film productions, he was also a devoted family man, winning the award for Australian Father of the Year in 2002.

Vizard rapidly accumulated a lot of political, business and public support. Politicians begged him to lend his profile to good causes, major events and fundraising initiatives. This spiral of social and professional influence was supplemented by family connections, especially in judicial and media circles. Vizard was described by David Elias in an article in *The Age* as 'the man who knew everyone'.[15] A former associate told Australian Securities and Investments Commission (ASIC) regulators that Vizard seemed a born leader: 'his sheer physical appearance . . . you can't help but see him . . . he stands out . . . has a terrific ability as a comedian, a commanding presence and an endearing personality'.

Yet, during 2005, Vizard became embroiled in a scandal that saw him publicly humiliated, provoking his resignation from many of his board and leadership positions, and an absence from Australia of several months. Some thought his crimes deserved jail. This inglorious unravelling of Vizard's leadership began in December 2000 when he had a dispute with his former bookkeeper, Roy Hilliard, and pursued a search warrant to freeze Hilliard's assets. Hilliard had charged that his former employer, Vizard, had asked him to do 'unlawful things', and had engaged in tax evasion and insider trading. What began as a trial against Hilliard became a searching examination of Vizard, his business and his character.

Among many things that emerged from the case was that Vizard had been given leeway and the benefit of the doubt by his bankers, Westpac, and by Victoria Police. Authorisations had not been checked. On allegations of tax evasion and insider trading, investigating police officers had said they accepted the celebrity's version of events as a 'reasonable assertion'.[16] Vizard was in danger of having criminal proceedings brought against him, but his accountant refused to sign a witness statement and that case collapsed. Vizard had denied under oath that he was involved in insider trading and tax evasion, opening the possibility of perjury charges.

In the end, Steve Vizard escaped major proceedings. He apologised for one case of insider trading, was fined $390 000 and banned for ten years from acting as a director. Subsequent proceedings against Hilliard in which Vizard was called to testify redeemed none of the players in this corporate drama: Hilliard briefly went missing and Vizard stonewalled, claiming poor recollection. But the lessons, for our purposes, are less about the extent of Vizard's culpability and more about how this story of a fallen hero shows seduction at a number of levels—how members of the establishment, the media and even the police were so beguiled by his image and charisma that they failed to notice flaws or follow up on normal checks. His networks 'protected' Vizard from the normal surveillance and inspection that would apply to less-applauded individuals, processes that perhaps would have been in his own interests as a check to his tendency to grandiosity.[17] The case proved to some that, as one commentator put it, 'having money, mates and power puts you above justice and decency'.[18]

In a move that I describe as a double seduction, Vizard himself was seduced. When all sorts of senior and important people believed that Vizard could do no wrong, he was also persuaded that he would be protected by the charmed circle that had formed around him. Throughout these events, Vizard continued to smile and wink at TV cameras, giving the appearance of a man who felt himself untouchable.

Why was there such public outrage when Vizard's flaws were exposed? People in all walks of life had invested in the icon that was Vizard. They believed that he was a different sort of leader, in some way more decent and trustworthy because he was 'an ordinary bloke' who'd managed to do very well for himself. The public felt betrayed when this lovable larrikin, with his ostensibly refreshing leadership style, was revealed to be deeply flawed.[19]

AESTHETICS AND PERFORMANCE

Both Jeff Skilling and Steve Vizard were persuasive performers. To understand more about how seduction works, we need to pay attention to what's called the 'performative' dimensions of leadership, including the aesthetics, or 'look' and visual appeal, of leaders.

In much of the business writing about leadership, it is assumed that the leader–follower relationship is rational and cerebral, that audiences assess a leader's vision and track record and thereby decide whether to be persuaded and led by it. In fact, history is studded with examples of leaders who have achieved power through exploiting the visceral, less rational appetites of their followers.

Research into leaders such as Hitler, Mussolini and Stalin shows how dramatically stage-managed leader performances captivated audiences and rendered many pliable agents of the leader's vision. Leadership scholar Peter Gronn, in his analysis of the cults that grow up around such leaders, shows that aesthetic appetites—among both leader and led—play a pre-eminent but neglected role in the accomplishment of leadership.[20] He also maintains that these historical examples can tell us much about the contemporary achievement of 'heroic leadership'. Each of these political leaders cultivated impressions of omniscience and infallibility, and in the case of Mussolini, age-defying virility. Hitler was observed using rouge to improve his complexion. Stalin was never to be photographed in a way that captured his short stature. Mussolini was the subject of as many as 30 million pictures in 2500 poses (according to one estimate), including sportsman, aviator and lion tamer. Where the reality of a leader fell short of the desired impression, devices were used to maximise the physical distance between leader and follower—for example, by tightly controlling photographic images, stage-managing and rationing public performances, and hiding the leader in reclusive retreats. These strategies ensured that the myths remained untested against reality.[21]

These historical examples of leader presentation appear amateurish alongside the image-crafting or 'spin' that is now routine, not just for political leaders but for corporate leaders as well. For reasons I discuss in Chapter 6, the aesthetic and performance dimensions of leadership have been crucial, yet neglected, in much scholarly work on leadership.

Like seduction, performance is not something that can—or should—be banished from leadership. What is needed is to understand how these processes work and what their consequences are—for example, the extent to which they feed a leader's sense of grandiosity or encourage followers to relinquish responsibility for decisions that affect them.

GRATIFICATION IN LEADERSHIP DEVELOPMENT

The seductive processes that often accompany leadership are observable in many organisational settings. One context in which I have undertaken considerable research is leadership development programs—where managers and executives learn how to be leaders.

As I document in Chapter 3, the field of leadership development and teaching is an enormous industry, with those delivering it ranging from prestigious universities and business schools, global consulting companies and professional services firms through to small and single-person operators such as executive coaches. There is also great diversity in the approaches taken to teaching leadership, including intensive or immersion group experiences and approaches based on survey and feedback data, through to something close to one-on-one psychotherapy.

Here I want to focus on the seductive strands that are interwoven through some of these approaches to leadership development. Particular templates of leadership development seduce audiences—that is, they collude with and sometimes re-enact the notion of the great heroic leader who will deliver a vision and relieve followers from the challenges of advancing in uncertainty. My argument is that we need to identify and understand the ways in which this seduction happens and explore the consequences for leadership development.

In the field of leadership development, extraordinarily high fees are paid to some teachers, who are treated like gurus.[22] Managers travel the world to glimpse these 'great ones'; companies compete for an association with them and exclusive access to their secrets. For example, a doctoral student who had worked in the Singaporean army described to me the processes by which Peter Senge, author of the acclaimed *The Fifth Discipline* and an architect of 'learning organisations', was brought in to train Singapore's military elite. Senge's methods are distinctly Californian, and include lying on the floor and visualising images, yet his reputation was such that the officers dutifully accepted the need to not only submit to them, but to re-enact them with their own troops.

'Spiritual leadership' is emerging as a significant component of senior-level leadership development. I discuss this phenomenon in detail in Part III, but it is worth noting here that this introduces different elements to the seductive process. Participants are initiated into a brotherhood of confidential insights, with jargon, acronyms, retreats and rituals that are exclusive to the group. There is clandestine appeal in these leadership development methods, and the lure of being seen as 'chosen'. Such secrecy can, as we know, repel critical scrutiny and challenge.

A story about teaching leadership[23]

As part of my research, I participate in and observe many examples of leadership development. In the example that follows, I was observing a program for senior Australian managers which took place over several weeks. The content of the program included many subjects of interest, but the session I describe here was specifically about leadership.

Around the room were 43 rapt faces, captivated and enthralled. The person holding their attention was a master leadership teacher, from a prestigious business school. He was immersing them in stories of heroic leadership—cases of great men doing great deeds against enormous odds. You couldn't help but get involved in the unfolding story—the extraordinary stakes, the moments when all was almost lost, the flaws revealed when the chips were down (not fatal, thank goodness!).

I sat watching—dazzled and, I have to admit, envious of the ease with which this teacher held his audience. You could have heard the proverbial pin drop; there was no shifting in the seats or other signs of distraction as there had been for an earlier female presenter. The theoretical and 'learning' points were powerfully delivered and felt, although when I later looked at my notes, not all that profound. The leadership teaching was going on at two levels here—in both the content being taught and in the way it was being taught. And both were utterly seductive.

Yet I was puzzled. A good third of the participants were women—senior, articulate executives. I'd been observing them for a couple of weeks by then. They were smart and street-wise—earning the respect of colleagues for their leadership in their organisations and in their contributions to this program. Yet, in all the sessions, I couldn't recall a single woman leader being offered as an example in the discussions. The model of leadership with which the group was presented was both masculine and firmly heroic. Nobody seemed to notice this, let alone draw attention to it. In a break, I approached the urbane and charismatic presenter to comment on the lack of women represented in cases. He concurred, lamenting the absence of good cases of women leaders. But I wasn't disturbed only by the absence of women in these heroic stories; it was also the way leadership had been constructed and then modelled by the teacher.

This was a group of senior executives. Initially they were somewhat competitive with each other, and some with the presenter. There was a ritual played out in which some participants asserted their knowledge and experience, and then the presenter, acknowledging their expertise, would draw on his charm, knowledge and reputation to demonstrably and unequivocally re-establish his 'command' of the group. In this room where leadership was being analysed, the dynamics being played out in the room were neither identified nor processed in any way. Leadership, we were being asked to accept, equalled the lessons learned from the case studies, without once acknowledging the model of leadership and followership that was being reinforced in the class.

The performance of the presenter mirrored implicitly the understanding of leadership being offered: it was about triumphal individual mastery, despite setbacks and difficulties. The performance also repelled serious challenge, being so powerful and convincing that the audience obligingly stayed within the questions and limits set. Participants were seduced into an enthralled compliance, and could be heard in the breaks declaring: 'I could sit and listen to M (the presenter) all day.' This example of leadership development was very well-rated by participants, judged as a great success.

The teacher's performance, with its mastery and power, *seduces*. It enacts, in the classroom moment, a form of leadership that is idealised in the content of teaching: the capacity to deliver powerful 'visions' or insights, to respond to challenges, to win over and convert the disaffected, to be the person who pulls it all together, the hero of the moment.

Classroom participants collude in this; the seduction is not one way. Some identify with the heroic presenter. They see—in that presenter or leader—a way for themselves to be, an idealised version of themselves. Others are drawn by the idea that someone powerful will take charge and know what to do, that all that needs to be done is to surrender and be guided. These responses are not unique to this audience, but observable in almost all groups. They apply to people of both genders and all levels of power and authority.

There is also 'a kind of love' feeding leadership dynamics in these situations.[24] Leaders—of certain kinds and in certain situations—sweep people off their feet, bringing romance and a spring in the step to those around them. They transform the follower's sense of self. Participants feel themselves touched and transformed by the experience; there is a sense of mystical connection and release from feelings of fear, chaos, anxiety and painful normality.

14

The seduction of leadership

This kind of experience of leadership and leadership development can therefore feel enormously satisfying and transformative. But dangers arise when leaders or teachers render audiences pliable and passive. It may become difficult for followers to challenge the leader's wisdom: to do so risks the condemnation of the leader or group. Followers or audiences often can't see what's going on because they are part of the system. Besides, they don't want to. They do not want to witness challenges to a project in which they have now invested deeply—emotionally and materially, with their time, effort and money.

Other preoccupations and fears are often re-enacted, in some form, in the leadership development classroom, as participants jockey for visibility and opportunities to build their reputation. There is competition to gain the presenter's attention, to bask in the glow of presenter approval and amass kudos or 'street cred' with class members. Such desires feed the potential for leaders to seduce and for participants to collude in their seduction.

The arguments and observations I make about these seductive dynamics in leadership and leadership development are substantiated in research in political psychology, group dynamics, psychoanalysis and elsewhere—but not, in general, in leadership studies. In these other disciplines, there is exploration of the 'search for the father' that can preoccupy individuals and societies in particular contexts. For example, Freud was among early theorisers of group behaviour who showed that many groups are alike in their capacity to idealise leaders and escape responsibility through conformity or obedience.

While it is not the task of this book to restate this evidence, I am suggesting that, in both leadership and leadership development, these deeper dynamics are sometimes ignored. Behind the leadership 'veil' of objective knowledge-building and information transfer, there is a lot going on emotionally, psychologically, psychodynamically and politically.

By probing the psychodynamics of seduction and collusion that often underpin leadership relations, we make an important move in understanding and so releasing ourselves from bad leadership.[25] It is these, less visible, dynamics that provide the subject-matter for much of this book. Exploring them will, I believe, enable us to move from being alternately alienated and seduced by leadership to a freer space where we are able to challenge conventional habits of leadership and position ourselves—as leaders or followers—in more thoughtful and less collusive ways.

2

What's wrong with ideas about leadership?

⅋

Leadership has been the subject of an extraordinary amount of dogmatically stated rubbish.

Chester Barnard (1938)

Over the last 50 years, leadership has become an iconic idea. In many contexts, leadership is treated as if it has inherent moral value, in and of itself. More thinking has gone into *how to do leadership* than into *what leadership is for*: the instrument has become the purpose. In this chapter, I explore the problems with how we have been thinking and theorising about leadership, and suggest some more liberating ways to understand it.

I begin with a brief history of leadership writing, showing how the idea of 'the need for leadership' has come to permeate every corner of contemporary Western society. Anyone who wants to succeed in, or even survive, institutional life is now expected to aspire to leadership.

How has this imperative for leadership come about? And what kind of leadership is being offered as a solution? Business and management thinking has played a key role in shaping the importance of leadership and the ways in which good leadership has been defined. I suggest further that continual claims to offer 'new' ideas and evidence about leadership should be read as political and ideological manoeuvres, designed to perpetuate the status of the field of leadership, and leadership itself, as evidently valuable and important goods.

Drawing on critical perspectives, I show how the study of leadership has colluded to perpetuate what has been characterised as its 'canonisation'.[1] Leaders and leader-watchers alike are implicated. Everybody who declares an interest in leadership—myself included—benefits from the status and reverence that has come to be attached to it. This is why people re-title courses and programs (which may be about managing people, or communicating effectively, or ethics and corporate responsibility, or even community development) as 'leadership'.

To begin to be more open in our thinking, we need to step back and gain perspective on our persistent invocation and infatuation with leadership. We need to identify how leadership has been produced as a concept in order to begin freeing ourselves from its powerful hold. It is only by going outside this conception of leadership and studying its production, as well as what it leaves out,[2] that we will develop a more challenging, complex and meaningful account.

A SHORT HISTORY OF RECENT LEADERSHIP THINKING[3]

What has given rise to the leadership industry we have today? From the late nineteenth to the early twentieth centuries, leadership was an idea that was mainly and desultorily discussed by the odd military historian and philosopher. In the first half of the twentieth century, a few political scientists—such as Harold Lasswell—influenced by Freudian ideas, wrote about psychopathology, and how political leaders might seek out power and the platform of public life to discharge their neurotic needs.[4]

But it was with the work of early American management theorists, such as Mary Parker Follet and Chester Barnard, in the 1920s and 1930s that leadership started to make its way into the business context and business people began to be presented as doing leadership. Follet was a pioneering organisational and leadership thinker whose innovative research contribution was largely overlooked by management experts until recently.[5] In *The Functions of the Executive*, first published in the 1930s, Barnard made a strong case for thinking about business leadership as a moral activity: 'the quality of leadership, the persistence of its influence, the durability of its related organisations, the power of the co-ordination it incites, all express the height of moral aspiration, the breadth of moral foundations'.[6]

Interest in leadership gathered momentum after this, especially among American scholars and those interested in its application to business. The picture of leadership that had emerged in the early part of the century was that

18

certain people were 'born' to lead.[7] What became known as the 'trait approach' emphasised the fact that leaders possessed a distinctive temperament and appetite which arose from personalities and backgrounds that equipped them to lead. Leaders had high levels of drive and ambition, focus and conviction, and the emotional and physical robustness to withstand setbacks and doubts.

However, two world wars and experience of dictators and megalomaniacs dampened enthusiasm for leadership. Both Hitler and Mussolini, in adopting the titles *'der Führer'* and *'Il Duce'*, styled themselves as leaders. The dark side of leadership, and the almost as dark side of followership, were devastatingly revealed and extensively studied.[8] Not only could the force of leadership be applied for evil purposes, but populations might willingly follow. Events in the 1950s, such as American McCarthyism, showed the potential for audiences to be whipped up into a frenzy of righteous venom by powerful ideas invoked by charismatic individuals.

Leadership—especially as the study of natural dispositions and character traits—fell out of favour in the optimistic and entrepreneurial spirit of postwar capitalism. Though the history of leadership sometimes writes this manoeuvre as simply a matter of empirical evidence[9]—that few large studies 'validated' the presence of identifiable traits required for leadership—it was more than this. Research did confirm a lack of evidence for such traits, with new arguments suggesting that it was the group context which determined who emerged as a leader, and how that leadership was shaped.

But the change in thinking also reflected the political, economic and cultural forces of the time. Ideas about leadership traits became unpalatable in the immediate postwar period because of recent experience with uncontrollable political leadership and with Hitler's alarmingly deterministic ideas of inborn superiority. Besides, if leadership capacity was determined innately, or was instilled by early adulthood, what scope was there to develop leadership? If leadership could not be developed or trained for, where did that leave the military, large companies or the many educational institutions teaching leadership? Confronted with evidence of the dark side of leadership, many scholars turned to management: leadership was out and management was in.

By the 1950s and 1960s, management was being elevated into a science.[10] Sociologist Loren Baritz made an observation in 1960—which might equally be made today—that 'the men who manage and direct industry find themselves incapable of controlling their organisations'.[11] Faced with an imperative to find new ways to manage ever-expanding organisations, business turned to the social sciences to enhance this control, as Baritz demonstrated. In these efforts to assist business, the skills of management lent themselves to more scientific analysis than leadership had. The rise of management education and business schools, in the United States particularly, can be read as part of this ideological effort to tame and transform the desire for, and exercise of, power into 'management science'—an activity that was respectable, replicable, teachable and accordingly commodifiable—able to be bought and sold.

Managers busy worrying about how best to manage no longer thought much about what or who all this management was for. The management practices which had been developed tended to subordinate and redirect individual ambition into vast organisational bureaucracies which, through performance management systems, could ensure that only those most compliant to the overall purposes of the organisation rose to the top—to formal leadership positions.

Exemplifying these principles were organisations like IBM and its founder, Thomas J. Watson. Watson established IBM in 1924, and over the next few decades the company became enormously influential, as his business leadership extended into the political and public realms. Watson established training programs and rituals at IBM that added a dose of Freemasonry to strong American Protestant values, which saw hard work as God's work.[12] These rituals ensured a high degree of predictability and conformity throughout the company, despite the motto displayed in every IBM office—'THINK'. As shown from the example below, taken from the *Songs from the IBM Songbook*,[13] Watson was adulated as a very particular kind of leader: tightly self-controlled and the ultimate organisation man. He commanded an army of clones, required to emulate his teetotal habits and even his preference for no facial hair.[14]

To: THOMAS J. WATSON
(to the tune of *Auld Lang Syne*)

T.J. Watson—you're our leader fine,
the greatest in the land,
We sing your praises from our hearts
we're here to shake your hand.
You're IBM's guiding star
throughout the hemispheres,
No matter what the future brings,
we all will persevere.

You've made our IBM so great
in every land supreme,

Our service meets all needs of men
and works just like a team.
You've brought us through to victory,
with leadership that's prime,
We'll always love and honor you
for the sake of Auld Lang Syne.

Throughout the mid-twentieth century, interest grew in harnessing scientific psychological methods to business and management.[15] The rise of empirical psychology has profoundly influenced how we came to understand leadership. Large-scale surveys, psychological instruments and hypothesis-testing began to be used to test the quality of leadership and to advise on how to monitor and improve it. By the 1980s, such methods for measuring and developing leadership were being used not just in laboratories and classrooms, but also extensively in organisational recruitment, training and 'performance management'.

What effect have scientifically and quantitatively oriented research methods had on our understanding of leadership? Building on some of the earlier critiques, British sociologist Nikolas Rose argues that psychology contributed, through its various disciplines, to the notion that 'the invention of the self' is the primary ethical value guiding modern and postmodern life.[16] Psychology has also produced the technologies by which societies measure what is a 'normal' and desirable self. Rose shows the ways in which such technologies have per-meated the world of work, allowing employers to exercise enhanced control in the designation and shaping of what, in management parlance, is called 'hi potential (leadership)' or 'talent'. Rose, among other critics, has warned that, rather than accepting such instruments as objectively measuring leadership, we should step back and examine the ways in which the process of leadership assessment has been produced, particularly the ways it puts value on some individual qualities while obscuring the systemic forces and power relations by which these qualities are defined and reproduce themselves. Further, the focus on self-development has reinforced an emphasis on the individual, rather than the group, as the natural site in which to locate and study leadership.

By the late 1970s and early 1980s, organisations were viewed as being 'over-managed' and 'under-led'.[17] There was too much control and not enough vision. An increasing disaffection with bureaucratised management practices set the stage for the re-emergence of leadership. Into the vacuum stepped 'trans-formational leadership', in what became known as 'the new leadership era'.

The new appetite for leadership that surfaced was to be supported by the sophisticated armoury of psychological testing that had been developing, particularly in the United States, and fuelled by the expansion of that country's global business and military ambitions.

To summarise, then, over the course of the twentieth century 'leadership' and 'business' came to be integrally connected. As early as 1950, sociologist Alvin Gouldner observed that the businessman was being elevated as 'the natural leader' of American society, as 'a man [sic] whose *unusual endowments* justified his leadership' (Gouldner's emphasis).[18] Gouldner and other critics, such as Baritz (writing in 1960), warned that some of these developments handed too much power to overlapping business, expert and political elites.

Yet the trend for business leaders to be held up as personifying leadership has continued. Because business has invested in the development of leaders and managers, research on leadership has increasingly been undertaken in the corporate sector. Methods of exploring and analysing leadership have also changed, and are now less likely to be anchored in understandings of history, power and social forces. The purposes to which all this leadership is being put are rarely explicitly considered, though in practice leadership has increasingly been harnessed to the internationally expanding ambitions of industry.

A few scholars and observers continue to express concern about the love affair business has had with leadership, and the patchy evidence about the long-term impact of particular corporate leaders on organisational success.[19] Yet the popularity of this conception of leadership shows little sign of abating. Further, recent leadership writing has demonstrated a nostalgia for and subtle return to the idea of leaders possessing identifiable dispositions (even if these are no longer labelled 'traits'). For example, in 2005 an article by Jim Collins in the *Harvard Business Review* proposed that leaders combine 'fierce resolve' with 'humility', with CEOs of large American companies given as exemplars.

As I go on to argue, it is not enough for leadership teachers, students and advocates to be carried along by their enthusiasm for leadership, or for finer and finer tests of the dimensions of leadership. To understand where leadership's power as an idea has come from, in order to be freed to ask important questions about leadership, we need to take a more systemic, historical perspective.

TRANSFORMATIONAL LEADERSHIP

Since the early 1980s, transformational leadership has become perhaps *the* key idea in leadership theory.[20] Transformational leaders work by tapping into and inspiring the higher motivations of followers while 'transactional' leaders rely on influencing followers via material rewards and sanctions. James MacGregor Burns, a political scientist, first delineated the notion of *transforming* leadership in 1978. Burns argued that such leadership was effective because of its explicit ethical component, and accordingly 'may convert leaders into moral agents'.[21] Subsequent formulations of *transformational* leadership have focused less on ethical outcomes and more on the process of inspirational influence.

A large body of research has been devoted to transformational leadership, and its popularity has been enhanced by an array of instruments, most notably the Multifactor Leadership Questionnaire (or MLQ) developed by Bernard Bass and Bruce Avolio.[22] Bass and subsequent advocates have given transformational leadership legitimacy by arguing that such leadership raises followers to higher levels of moral consciousness—independently of its context, task or purpose.

The engine-room of leadership research for the last three or four decades has been the United States, and most research and writing on transformational leadership has also come from American scholars. American culture reflects strong values of individualism and universalism, and these values have percolated into work on leadership.[23] Its scholars have preferred individual-centric explanations for success, and have often acted as if there are universal rules for leadership that can be distilled and applied regardless of context. The idea that leadership can be created with the right template has been animated by a research methodology which I describe as 'track down the truth about leadership and train in it'.

Matching the dichotomy between transformational and transactional leadership is a similar one distinguishing leadership from its lowly counter-part, management.[24] In this account, while managers are necessary to control resources, it is leaders and especially transformational leaders who create visions and inspire followers towards new meanings and reinvigorated purpose. Bennis and Nanus's 1985 bestseller, *Leaders*, offered the triumphal view that trans-formational leaders 'can invent and create institutions . . . can choose purposes and visions . . . can create the social architecture that supports them . . . can move followers to higher degrees of consciousness, such as liberty, freedom, justice and self-actualisation'.[25] In this quote, one sees how readily business researchers may position corporate leaders as society's modern saviours, and how enthusiastically they may invoke and annex discourses of freedom and self-development to the capitalist project. In a further example, scholars Quinn and Snyder describe how the leader as change agent seeks 'first to increase his or her moral power so as to model courage and "attract" the change target into a relationship of self-exploration, commitment and growth'.[26] Few advocates for this inspiring leadership probe examples of its misuse. They rarely touch on the larger societal consequences of this kind of leadership in the hands of a narrow corporate elite claiming the moral high ground.

As I discuss in more detail in Chapter 9, transformational leadership often draws on a discourse and language of spirituality that naturalises its claim to be an intrinsically moral activity. A sizeable genre of leadership writing, from the 1980s through to the present, pines after leadership that is fused with goodness, caring and a 'servant' mentality. This ardent literature preaches morally responsible forms of leadership without seriously asking why such forms of leading might be difficult to realise in business, or why they might elicit scepticism from those at the bottom of organisations.[27] The point for us is not to deride these often well-meaning ideas, but to dig deeper and ask what or whose interests are really being served when transformational leadership is exhorted.

In the rush to promote visionary transformational leadership, all sorts of claims have been made for it—that it reflects 'new' knowledge and offers 'a new paradigm'. As part of the appeal of transformational leadership, *charisma* has also made a comeback; indeed, the two are often regarded as closely related. Max Weber, who first identified the power of charisma, wrote about it with some caution. But recent leadership research often assumes charisma is a good thing and there should be more of it. Conger and Kanungo, for example, argue that charismatic leaders:

> transform the nature of work by making it appear more heroic, morally correct, and meaningful . . . work becomes an opportunity for self and collective expression . . . The idea is that eventually followers will come to see their organisational tasks as inseparable from their own self-concepts.[28]

Should corporate leaders be doing this kind of transforming? Should employees be so powerfully persuaded to surrender their self-concept to their organisation's tasks? Is this good for the individual? The organisation? Indeed, is it good for charismatic leaders themselves to be the object of such adulation? My suggestion here is that these high-sounding aspirations for leadership risk delivering greater enslavement to narrow corporate goals.

THE MILITARY VIEW

The military establishment provides a good case study through which to explore the way in which a set of understandings about leadership develops.

What's wrong with ideas about leadership?

Early researchers of organisations often worked in military organisations, and some of the first executive development institutes grew out of military 'staff' colleges. Military organisations typically pride themselves on developing leadership, and a good deal of leadership research continues to be undertaken in or is supported by military organisations.[29]

Some years ago, I was at an Australian conference on gender and work where a session was devoted to issues of leadership in the military. We were addressed by an array of women in mid and senior roles in various parts of the military—the navy, army and air force. I had taught MBA students with military experience, and had been disconcerted by the confidence exhibited by some that they 'knew' leadership. It wasn't until I listened to these conference speakers that I realised just how much economic investment went into sustaining the military's ideal that it is the natural home and training ground for leadership.

The military hires the best experts and consultants, and conducts the most extensive training in leadership. Some of it must be valuable, yet I was struck by the conformity, by the willingness to 'toe a line' of leadership with parade-ground precision. Pictures presented—of adventuring personnel parachuting out of planes, navigating battleships and steering tanks through tricky terrain—did little to allay these concerns. The spokespeople for this view of leadership were women—dutiful in their delivery of the military line. There was no allowance here for doubts about military purposes, for debate about warfare or its methods, or for the darker side of leadership that we know comes into play in life-threatening and high-pressure situations.[30] Nor was there much room to question how applicable these military models were to other workplaces.

The military picture of leadership which is usually offered is mined with assumptions—that extreme situations like warfare demand impeccable discipline and leaders who can command it, no questions asked. Such assumptions create the need for steeply hierarchical structures, with rigidly enforced, unquestioning obedience. Yet rapid changes in technology, communications and political tensions demand constant adjustments in the techniques of leadership in warfare. At certain times, spontaneous courage, responsiveness and initiative are required from individuals at all levels. Military cultures where there are intense pressures to obey or conform, risk the abandonment of individual moral responsibility and a dehumanised response (as shown, for example, in the treatment by some soldiers of Iraqi prisoners in the Abu Ghraib prison).

DISCOURSES

The discourse on leadership—that is, the ways in which leadership has come to be discussed and written about—often frames and limits understanding of what leadership can be. Post-structuralism is a form of contemporary theorising that, among many other insights, shows that how we write and speak —discourse—changes the way we can think. Hence, discourses of leadership may conceal as well as illuminate, directing attention to certain parts of the phenomenon while encouraging us to not notice other parts. If a particular discourse becomes habitually inculcated, it tends to become canonised; and over time, what were hypotheses about a phenomenon become orthodoxy: a 'regime of truth'. It becomes increasingly difficult to stand outside that regime and question it.

Books about leadership provide a telling example—and an enormous number of them exist. Large tomes on leadership with self-important titles in heavy black writing regularly emanate from the heavyweight US university presses. The format says 'I am a serious book'. On the back cover are accolades by academics and business leaders who are pillars of their fields. Some appeal by tapping into fears: 'Only if you read this book will you truly make it in the ranks of leadership.'

Yet open and read these books, and many seem designed for dummies. The print is large with lots of space. They are written to a formula, and by a team of writers who know the formula. Each purports to offer innovation and challenge, but few question the assumption that leadership per se is good. These books are liberally sprinkled with examples from large multinationals, which meets the need for topicality and 'relevance',[31] but also shores up the reputation of the writer, as the implicit assumption is that he (and it is usually a he) must know what he's talking about if he's worked for such notable firms.

What are the effects of these ways of writing about leadership? They construct a discourse that has the implacable weight of authority—big organisations cited, endorsements by high-profile people. These authors, the reader assumes, must therefore know 'the truth' about leadership. The discourse encourages readers not to notice the assumptions and values slipped in from prevailing economic or managerial orthodoxy: that individuals, not groups, deliver leadership; that they achieve by competitive edge; that 'winning' is always good and an appropriate aspiration; that success is measured by the size and scale of material achievement or international conquest, and so on. Further, although discourse of this kind often takes a high moral tone, it is generally silent on some of the deepest drivers of the impulse to lead, such as desires for power, dominance and booty. Compare the sanitised story these books tell with a much older work on leadership, Machiavelli's *The Prince*, written in the sixteenth century. In this book, the raw stuff of leadership is told as it is—how to rule, how to crush opposition, how to hold on to power.

Readers who don't connect with the contemporary discourses of leadership described above often discount their reservations about it and, faced with this template, disqualify themselves as leaders. I encounter people who are strongly influencing direction, defending standards, supporting and innovating in their workplaces and communities, yet who don't see such aspects of their own work as leadership. They might be 'a change agent' or mobilising a community organisation, but they exclude themselves and their work from the leadership category. Many MBA students I teach begin by thinking that the version of leadership they need to know, if they are to succeed, is the kind typified in the tomes by high-profile corporate stars. When we encourage students to step back and inspect the ways in which ideas of leadership are constructed, they begin to allow that there might be other meanings of leadership that are valuable but discounted. By looking more carefully at these processes of truth-creation about leadership, we may all begin to release ourselves from performing against the standards set by the discourse.

Writing on leadership has been extended beyond organisational studies, to be popularised and marketed to a wide general audience.[32] In the Introduction I borrowed George Ritzer's now-famous adjectival phrase, to refer to the result of this popularisation as 'McDonaldized'[33] leadership. Apparently loaded with visions and values, this kind of leadership is curiously bland and predictable. Soon we find ourselves hungry again: looking for answers and programs that promise to deliver more lasting leadership.

If we turn to the leadership development industry, we find that this too sits within a regime of truths supported by interlocking systems of expert and economic power. Appraisals, performance-management systems and '360-degree feedback' reproduce and reify a particular production of leadership. The leadership self is tested and evaluated until it is a mirror image of the tools. New recruits into organisations face a battery of tests to gauge their potential and 'fit', and then are measured and reassessed to see whether they deserve the label 'hi-potential'. Organisations become deeply dependent on these technologies in their appointments systems and succession planning. Through these mechanisms, the aspiring leader becomes compliant, earnestly performing within a regime of leadership while structural power remains masked and the bigger question remains unasked: *What is all this leadership for?*

CONVENTIONAL WISDOMS AND CRITICAL ALTERNATIVES

How have these forces and historical threads limited the way we understand, practise and develop leadership today?

The business and corporate worlds have taken leadership to their hearts and made it their own. While leadership languished as an idea during two world wars, it burgeoned in the late twentieth-century boom of international capitalism, when it became tied to corporate objectives of growth, profit and material advancement as measures of societal advancement and well-being. Thus capitalism and the managerial agenda have installed many assumptions into leadership, focusing it especially on the heroic performance of the individual.

Business and management scholars have often acted as if they invented leadership. For example, the editors of a textbook about leadership and change published in 1999 declare: 'After two decades of research on leadership and organisational change, there exists no universal set of prescriptions or step-by-step formulae that leaders can use in all situations to guide change.'[34] There are several things that are breathtaking about this declaration: first, it does not see any worthwhile analysis or research about leadership that predates 1980; second, it assumes that a 'universal set of prescriptions' is the one outcome we are all looking for; and third, it sets itself up as delivering this. In a further example, the popularity of transformational leadership, and its newer claims to be 'post-heroic', have entrenched in the discourse the assumption that leaders should *transform*—rather than, say, *preserve* or *disrupt*.

We have been so surrounded by this view of leadership that it has become difficult to think of leadership outside this framework of meanings. In this view, leadership is:

○ a weighty responsibility that is usually borne by men in high places;
○ an individual performance (despite claims that followers are part of leadership);
○ an activity developed and played out in interlocking elites of the military, business and politics, centred around the interests of large-scale global capital;
○ generally concerned with expanding an organisation's growth, 'reach' or material success through normative influence, and without mention of power;
○ of such importance as to generate a leadership development industry, involving many people in teaching and training others to be leaders;

o   of such importance that it is among the most researched of all subjects, demanding large-scale surveys and a proliferation of instruments to measure leadership or its potential;

o   a task requiring disembodied, cerebral command and tending to assume physical manifestations of leading and following to be irrelevant; and

o   assumed to be of inherent moral value, neglecting frailties, vulnerabilities or the dark side of the leader psyche. When such ignoble dimensions are revealed in particular cases, the individuals concerned are dismissed as not leaders after all, but just a few 'bad apples'.

This dominant account of leadership tends to leave out:

o   the hunger for power that is commonly a central driver of leadership;

o   the power structures within the wider society that enable some individuals to rise more 'naturally' and easily to leadership positions;

o   the emotional and often unconscious dynamics that explain why leaders are afforded legitimacy, even adulated, encouraging followers and entire societies to abdicate their responsibilities—sometimes to disastrous ends;

o   the proving grounds for leadership, including childhood and adolescence, during which young people develop appetites and desires such as the drive to transform themselves, or the view that their own agenda deserves to serve for others;[35]

o   the physical and embodied side of leadership;

o   the sexual performance and sexual identities that are often played out in leadership roles;

o   the role of class, ethnic origin and history in habits of leadership; and

o   long-term outcomes of leadership.

In the above account leadership research and writing is described as if it were one coherent body of thinking. Of course, it is not. In Table 2.1, I list some of the conventional wisdoms and then draw on critical writing to contrast some different ways of thinking about leadership.[36] In the rest of this book, I explore some of these critical perspectives in greater depth.

There are a number of scholars voicing concerns about the narrowness of leadership thinking, and I have drawn on some in Table 2.1 and throughout this chapter. For example, Peter Gronn's careful studies of 'distributed' leadership

Table 2.1 Leadership: Conventional wisdoms and critical alternatives

Conventional wisdoms	Critical alternatives
Leadership is a good thing.	Leadership can be a bad thing.
Purposes such as growth, efficiency, global expansion and dominance are assumed, not questioned, as goals of leadership.	Purposes are questioned, asking who or what leadership is for.
Leadership as a single-handed, heroic performance that is: – the property of the individual – ahistorical – decontextualised e.g. military leadership generalised to business organisations.	Leadership is socially constructed with followers in a context: – followers attribute leadership – ILTs (implicit leadership theories) determine where we see leadership and who personifies—societies and organisations find leadership where they expect to find it.
Ascension into leadership is a matter of experience, training, mentoring.	Leadership arises from backgrounds and how we respond to appetites and hungers: it requires identity work.
Focus on positive qualities that leaders need, e.g. humility and resolve.	Exploration of dark sides, e.g. narcissism and grandiosity.
Focus on bold deeds, acts of courage and sacrifice.	Relational leadership includes interactional and emotional work of leadership from beneath and within.
Leadership is a rational activity: – requires cerebral/cognitive mastery – physical dimensions ignored.	Leadership includes meaning/symbolic management—emotional and physical work are important.
Gender and sexuality of leaders are invisible except women's gender which is included as a variable to be studied.	Leadership assumes able-bodied male. Need to reveal gendered, culture-centric assumptions.
Leaders create visions and inspire followers to new levels of moral elevation.	Leaders create meaning to reinforce legitimacy, arousing passion but may also be a device for manipulation.

What's wrong with ideas about leadership?

Conventional wisdoms	Critical alternatives
Power is treated as a tool of leaders which is necessary to get things done.	Leadership is supported and mediated through structural power relations. Power precedes leadership, in turn reinforcing power relations.
Leadership produces change.	Leadership is often invoked to avoid radical change, supports status quo.
Learn about leadership through: – scientific study, large samples – reliable measures/instruments – replicability, validation, modelling – 'track down the truth (which is empirically knowable) and train in it'.	Learn about leadership through: – rich, deep observation and reflection – case studies, ethnographies – histories, participant observation. Immerse and expose subtleties and complexities of authority and power relations within a context.

show how leadership is collectively created. Keith Grint has also drawn on detailed historical (rather than business) examples to develop a model of leadership as socially constituted. Among the most extensive critiques are those from feminist and gender researchers, who show how leadership has always been studied and performed around gendered assumptions. In their provocative 1991 paper, Marta Calas and Linda Smircich provide a dissection of works on leadership to show how even the writing of leadership has been imbued with themes of seduction and masculine conquest.[37] David Collinson has also made a strong case to push out the boundaries of leadership thinking to include cross-disciplinary work on gender and power and to break down dualisms such as leader/follower and control/resistance.

Joyce Fletcher, among others, has pointed to the importance of 'post-heroic' leadership, a 'less individualistic, more relational concept of leadership'.[38] It recognises leadership as a shared or distributed practice; a dynamic and multi-directional social process (not necessarily hierarchical); and an activity aimed at collective outcomes such as learning. A growing body of writing documents the ordinary and extraordinary situations where people lead not as heroic individuals but as part of a cooperative group.

Despite these more careful and critical accounts of leadership, the conceptual templates, expectations and interests in leadership I characterised earlier remain remarkably durable. The alternative insights influence corners of scholarship rather than mainstream theorising and practices of leadership. We seem unable to unshackle ourselves from conventional and seductive accounts of leadership. Why is this? And how can we understand the tenacity of these leadership views?

Feminist scholars have shown how critiques can often be incorporated by dominant discourses with the effect that those dominant views endure because they appear to be more enlightened. Well-intentioned critiques—such as the call for leaders to be collaborative or relational—can be given lip-service while actually having the effect of more deeply entrenching the status quo, and leaving the power and privilege of leadership untouched. This is a sobering prospect for anyone offering a critique of leadership, myself included.

Fletcher's account of the persistence of heroic individualism suggests that, despite some change in the rhetoric at the broad societal level, the infatuation with this model of leadership remains pervasive in popular narrative. She lays some of the blame at the feet of researchers, saying 'it is not enough for organisational theorists to call for new types of leadership or write books about the need for change'.[39] Leadership researchers, she says, need to start confronting and working with taboos in leadership: 'deeply embedded, emotional issues' which are activated when we start to talk about 'gender and power-linked aspects of self identity'.

Critical and feminist theorists show that most leadership research, including studies of transformational leadership, continue to present prescriptions—heroic or post-heroic—as if they were gender neutral. The critics argue that, although there is a search for a different kind of leader—a 'post-heroic hero' who displays characteristics different from the traditional model—even this leader continues 'to enjoy the same godlike reverence for individualism associated with traditional models'.[40] Further, despite efforts to replace heroism, individualism insidiously inserts itself in the post-heroic remedies. According to Gronn, concerns with individualism have been met with reassertions of individualism.

None of these difficulties is a reason to avoid critique. However, we should remain alert to the cannibalising canon of leadership studies, which has shown itself to be adept at reinvention while not seriously available for overhaul. An example is the movement aimed at developing 'emotionally intelligent' leaders. As Steve Fineman and others show, insights about the importance of emotion in leadership get translated into an emotional toolkit by which leaders increase their control over employees. Leaders who are highly emotionally literate become able and authorised to demand new levels of emotional labour from employees.

Only by challenging the assumptions on which leadership is based will we be equipped to seriously anticipate the 'transformation' so often promised by leadership. We need to bring into the study of leadership more insights about power, gender and the systemic forces that prefigure power relations. There needs to be more reflection about the history and values on which particular perspectives have been built. Drawing on the work of social theorists like Michel Foucault,[41] we should be interested in revealing the way powerful interests (such as business and expert elites) have produced certain sorts of knowledge, which have been in turn reinforced as the 'reality' or 'truth' of leadership. Leadership studies would then include, for example, more of the historical analyses of the kind that I have touched on above, and perspectives from positions other than the top levels of business, the military and other large, hierarchical institutions. We need also to look at how leadership and the study of leadership are processes of construction of identity and reputation. Whether our work is in training leaders or whether we tilt towards leadership ourselves, my intent in this chapter has been to show that our task is not just to learn how to be a leader. It is to grapple with the complex conceptual structural and political roots of leadership aspiration and to ask ourselves what leadership is for.

3

Teaching and learning about leadership

৪৪

Education is the practice of freedom.

Paulo Freire (1972)

*There are no known keys to success or irrefutable laws [in teaching leadership],
despite the ever-growing mountain of pulp and pointless training activity that is
built on the misconception and misrepresentation that there are.*

Graham Mole (2004)

How can people learn about leadership? Can leadership be taught and, if so,
how might such teaching invite questioning about purposes and support transformative efforts among aspiring leaders?

What follows in this chapter is a series of personal experiences and experi-
ments in teaching and learning about leadership, drawing on examples of my
own and others' experiences of teaching managers and executives. I show how
insights from the classroom and from educational research have considerable
relevance for leadership, particularly in thinking about purpose, and in working
with power and authority—an issue I take up in more detail in Chapter 5.
I provide an account of my evolving approach to teaching about leadership,
including the three values I have come to believe are central: being reflective;
working experientially (or with the leadership and group dynamics of the
class); and thinking critically. Drawing on insights about classroom dynamics

and learning, I suggest that leaders should always be asking themselves about their purposes, their assumptions, and the power relations of which they are a part and potentially reinforcing. Effective leadership, in my argument, shares some characteristics with effective teaching. They both require leaders to encourage followers to take a broader view, to question and challenge oppressive relations in order to free themselves and others.

But I start back in my early days as a teacher, when I was introduced to ideas of liberation and first began thinking about what teaching was for.

LEARNING HOW TO TEACH

When I first started teaching postgraduate students in the mid-1980s, I thought my job was to summarise and convey the content of designated textbooks—to be a dutiful sales agent for the truths of 'managing change' or 'business ethics'. My students were adults and experienced public-sector professionals. They sat, often exhausted (it was evening and they had already done a day's work), as I relayed textbook homilies on, for example, 'organisation development'.

I was simultaneously working on my PhD at the time, and when we came to the topic of teams, one of my supervisors suggested that I introduce some of my own research findings to my teaching. These findings contradicted the dogma of the textbook about the all-purpose value of teams. I was also encouraged to try a different technique of teaching. I circulated a transcript from one of the management team meetings I had studied, and class members took on roles, speaking the parts of management team members. We then had a discussion about what was going on at a deeper level at that meeting. My students could readily identify with this discussion, as they had all been trapped in interminable meetings where little real work occurred. In class, we were able to start to peel back the official ways teams were seen, and begin to identify what was really going on in groups at work, including the rich veins of fantasy, resistance and work-avoidance that lies not far from the surface of most meetings and their ritualised habits and discourses.

When I moved to the Melbourne Business School in 1988, I was propelled further into thinking about what my job as an educator was. In this environment, where teaching mattered a great deal, my teaching was evaluated unevenly—sometimes poorly—by my largely male MBA audiences. I struggled to assert my credibility and my authority. I'd be challenged by students asking questions like: 'Have you done consulting in this area? With which organisation?' Whichever way I responded, it seemed I was dismissed as doing 'the soft stuff'.

Teaching and learning about leadership

(I don't think the word 'soft' is coincidental here, as phallic imagery and metaphors appeared frequently in the routine challenges to my authority and power.)[1]

These experiences, which I have written about elsewhere,[2] took me into research on teaching, the work of educationalists such as Paulo Freire and feminist writers. I realised that I had been, often quite unsuccessfully, seeking to emulate what is described as 'the banking model' of teaching.[3] The banking model assumes the student to be an empty vessel into which the teacher deposits 'knowledge'—knowledge of which the teacher retains control. In choosing which information to deposit, the teacher reinforces his or her power as the one who knows, while the student is further entrenched as powerless. While the banking model seemed sustainable for some of my male colleagues, I knew it wasn't working—in any sense—for me.

As is so often the case, it was these experiences of failure that began to teach me about teaching. I started paying attention to power in the classroom and asking how I wanted to situate myself in the historically and structurally determined power relations of education. What was my job as a teacher and how might I explore options outside conventional educational and business school models?

I set off in search of other ideas about how to be the person with some knowledge and authority, but without a power that necessarily subordinates others. Freire, the famous Brazilian educator, was an early advocate of thinking about education as 'the practice of freedom'. He argued that too often educational authority and the teacher's power were used to oppress, to harness learners to the teacher's regime, and to perpetuate a status quo of distinction between those who know and those deemed ignorant. This process was hidden behind the benign and uncontested mask of education.

From Freire and others, I saw a new possibility: that education could—perhaps even should—unsettle and invite questioning of the power regime that assumed teachers were knowledgeable and students weren't.[4] Good teachers and leaders in this alternative model support the learner or follower to empower themselves. It is the teacher's job to build students' capacities for learning, not to convey knowledge about the objective world, but to support people's efforts to understand and act in their world differently. This requires teachers to act more like 'midwives' than 'bankers': drawing out ideas and capacities that are already stored in the student, but not yet converted to learning or available for reflection and application.[5] The teacher's role is 'pulling out knowledge not putting it in'—or, in William Yeats's metaphor, 'not filling a bucket but lighting a fire'.

Power is more complicated in this classroom. Neither teacher nor student is seen as owning knowledge. Patti Lather describes what this means for teachers:

> the need to take responsibility for transforming our own practices so that our empirical and pedagogical work can be less toward positioning ourselves as masters of truth and justice and more toward creating a space where those directly involved can act and speak on their own behalf.[6]

However, adopting such a position is far from straightforward, particularly for female teachers. These are issues which I explore later in this chapter, but for a moment I want to return to my story.

These new insights about the purposes of education were powerfully attractive. They offered a different view of my role, not just in the classroom but in my institution and in my wider leadership work. It was attractive for many reasons, including—I should confess—the fact I felt I could more easily comply, even succeed. It also, perhaps dangerously, offered a way of 'differentiating' what I offered to students. It seemed to fit my role, as a still relatively rare female professor, to be more of a midwife than a banker. But I also agreed with its intents—and still do in most important respects.

But there were and are problems with gaily sailing down this path of seeing myself as an educator intent on liberation, and I'll return to these shortly.

CAN LEADERSHIP BE TAUGHT?

This is a question that has provoked extensive debate among leadership practitioners and scholars.[7] However, it is perhaps unsurprising that the question has not been put to rigorous, long-term evaluation. Leadership is more than a demonstration of skills. It is hard enough to settle on some definition or evidence of leadership, but harder still to hold constant all the other factors that go into its formation in order to isolate the impact of the classroom experience.

In addition to the empirical and operational challenges involved in testing whether leadership can be taught in the classroom and then demonstrated outside, vested interests might discourage such an investigation. There has been a very large and sustained investment in the teaching of leadership that few have an interest in undermining. All sorts of institutions, including universities, corporations (and corporate universities), business schools and not least military organisations, dedicate serious effort to 'leadership development'. A lot of people at varying stages of their careers are required to do things as part of these courses that are supposed to improve their leadership or, more pragmatically, deliver 'value' for their organisation.

Overviews of leadership development provide a sense of the scale and diversity of this industry. Writing in the early 1990s, Jay Conger identified four approaches:

o *Conceptual*: focusing on transferring content, teaching concepts and leadership theories;
o *Skill-building*: identifying and providing practice in leadership competencies or capabilities;
o *Personal growth*: based on the assumption that self-awareness is at the heart of good leadership, and can include outdoor and out-of-comfort-zone experiences which teach the leader about themselves;
o *Feedback programs*: which rely on instruments such as '360-degree feedback' or scales of emotional intelligence.

Many leadership development experiences blend elements of these approaches. Some add coaching and opportunities for leaders to undertake action research in their workplaces—that is, to try different leadership techniques, then reflect and identify further learning from these experiences.[8] Other programs include opportunities for leaders to undertake placements—intensive or recurring over a period—such as working with not-for-profit organisations and in the front line of service delivery. These 'immersion' experiences are often aimed at helping leaders to reinvigorate their underlying values and sense of purpose.

In my early years of business school teaching, I looked at leadership from a distance. But by the mid-1990s, I had worked my way up to professor, written and taught a lot, and begun seriously researching leadership. I had also studied and observed how leadership was being taught by academics and business gurus. I was interested in the kinds of advice offered in the leadership category and how they did it—how they talked, postured and positioned themselves as being leaders in a learning environment. As discussed in Chapter 1, I watched audiences (including myself) be seduced by the performance on offer and, less often, the content.

Though much of this leadership teaching was popular and well evaluated by participants, from my vantage point some seemed to be neither good teaching nor good leadership. There are strong cultural norms about what leadership teaching should look like, and who should teach it. There is some-times collusion with the heroic ideal of the leader that means that audiences expect heroic leadership teachers. In leadership development, the size of the presenter's reputation and standing, what companies they work for, and other markers of power, are often emphasised in marketing and by presenters themselves in their introductory remarks. Presenters sometimes begin with a version of the following: 'I am a big and important person, make no mistake, and the world recognises me as someone who has important things to tell you', although often tinged with humorous self-deprecation. The marketing and conduct of leadership programs is often underpinned by a premeditated strategy of inflation: inflating the presenter's reputation and inflating the worth of what they have to say by the prices that are charged, the scale, exclusiveness or rarity of the event.

In a recent book, *Leadership Can Be Taught*,[9] the 'class-as-case' or 'case-in-point' methods developed by Ron Heifetz and his colleagues at the Kennedy School, Harvard University, are documented. Such methods aim to give people the experience of leadership in the classroom, with all its risks, obstacles, temp-tations and opportunities. The 'class-as-case' technique, and my experiences of experiential methods as participant and teacher, have informed the teaching approach I now adopt.[10]

One of the risks in leadership teaching is that successful teachers can develop godlike reputations. Some leadership teachers, such as Heifetz, are skilled at working with such dynamics. Indeed, he argues that it is the job of a leader to resist audience reactions such as dependency and 'give the work back to the group'.[11] It is a central challenge of leadership to not allow yourself to be positioned as though, or believe that, you can do the work of leadership alone. Leaders need to resist the fantasy that they can single-handedly move a group to a new way of doing things.

Yet there is a paradox here: the more skilfully the teacher resists pressures to be God, the more godlike they can become, at least with some audiences. For example, though Heifetz makes explicit efforts not to feed an audience's dependency, and despite the efforts of commentators such as Daloz Parks to not perpetuate adoration of the leader (Heifetz in this case), these dynamics are very hard to avoid. What may matter more, then, is how the leader or teacher is attuned to, and committed to working with, both dependent group dynamics, and their own needs and hungers.

However skilful and experienced the teacher, it is important to acknowledge that teachers of leadership are never outside the power relations of the classroom.

Their power and authority—or lack of it—precede them and are then actively being negotiated and reproduced in class. The gender, race and cultural backgrounds of teachers and students are inextricably woven into these power relations. As I explore in Chapter 5, when a leadership figure is from a non-dominant group— say, female or Asian in a Western business context—the authority that audiences are willing to bestow is often initially more compromised or tenuous. These people have to *earn* leadership against stereotypes that are usually unconscious. Victorian Police Commissioner Christine Nixon observed that most radio-show hosts simply felt more reassured and comfortable to be interviewing a burly 2-metre tall man on police matters than herself, a middle-aged woman.

Leadership is also usually seen to be men's knowledge: taught by men, to men, using the examples of great men. Having a woman teach leadership is counter-intuitive. It puts power in the wrong hands. Tensions are exacerbated further when, as in so much leadership development, the participants are senior and powerful—already accustomed to thinking of themselves as leaders. Even coming into a classroom situation, for these sorts of participants, often involves a moment of humiliation. In being there, they are (in principle) acknowledging they have something to learn. They are surrendering to the power and author-ity of another (something they don't do often), and the person to whom they surrender needs to be someone demonstrably potent themselves.

Participants and audiences in leadership programs are often looking for answers and can collude with these dynamics. Sometimes they demand con-tent: lists of tips, steps or cases of 'what's worked' in well-known organisations. Even if presenters know that the usefulness of such approaches is limited—for example, information-transfer rather than active learning may occur—it remains tempting for teachers to simply provide what audiences say they want. Leaders and teachers seeking a more liberating practice need to be observant of power relations in the context in which they are working, and reflective about what is happening for them. They need to provide enough structure and authority to 'contain' deeper anxieties, without fostering unreflective dependency or abdi-cation of the responsibility for learning.

A LIBERATING INTENT

In 2004, after a year's leave, I started teaching a new Master of Business Adminis-tration (MBA) subject called 'Leadership and Change' in what I hoped was a different and more liberating way. I had taken leave from the business school in 2003, immersing myself in Eastern philosophies and qualifying as a yoga teacher. These experiences changed the way I approached my business school teaching in profound ways—some deliberate and some emergent. For example, in yoga I had been exposed to different 'ways of being' a teacher, seeing the potential of voice, breath and bodies in mediating openness and learning.[12]

When I returned to teaching, I wanted to build on these experiences and develop a new and different curriculum. I wanted to teach differently—including more collaboratively—and a colleague, Richard Searle, joined me in a co-facilitative role. I also wanted to extend my use of experiential methods, and attended the Kennedy School's 'Master Class' for teachers of leadership, led by Ron Heifetz and Marty Linsky. I drew on long-standing interests and these more recent experiences to guide the new Leadership and Change subject.

Three values were central: reflection, experiential learning and taking a critical perspective on leadership. The following appeared in the subject guide:

- ○ Reflection is the basis for learning and development as a leader. Students are encouraged to dig into their own history investigating their own path as leader and follower, reflecting on major life experiences and values, assessing how they have learned about leadership and where they can develop further.
- ○ Learning comes from experience. *Leadership and Change* has an emphasis on experiential learning: we observe, analyse and learn about leadership from the 'here and now' group dynamics of the class. The class also takes ownership for learning.
- ○ Leadership theory provides a body of ideas and concepts to be examined critically. Leadership is not a technical activity or bundle of skill sets. The subject aims to identify the values and intents of those advocating leadership and argues for leadership that questions premises and initiates new directions.

The three 'legs' of my subject—reflection, experiential methods and a critical perspective—have all, in their own right, been extensively discussed in research, and efforts to incorporate them into education have been widely documented. The argument for leaders to be reflective and for teachers to promote reflective practice has been developed particularly by Donald Schön in his path-breaking books *The Reflective Practitioner* (published in 1983) and *Educating the Reflective Practitioner* (1987). Postmodern theorists have also added their own interest in the structural conditions of 'reflexivity', which basically means a commitment to seeing the connection between what one thinks and the structural circumstances of one's situation (power, resources, and so on) that enable and constrain which ideas can be taken up. With their interest in reflexivity, post-modern theorists are concerned beyond the individual to map how societal and cultural conditions shape and limit reflexivity. For example, they ask how historical truths are constructed so that they are no longer available for challenge or modification. Reflection, reflectiveness and the more theoretical notion of 'reflexivity' share a commitment to not taking action or statements at face value. The reflective leader seeks to step back from their words and actions and understand where they come from and what impacts they have.

In terms of experiential learning methods and working with the 'here and now' of the group dynamic, I draw on the work of the British Tavistock Institute and the Australian Institute of Socio-Analysis, my training in 'psycho-social' ways of thinking and my experiences of being a participant in various experiential programs. As described above, the way in which Heifetz and his Kennedy School colleagues adapted experiential methods for use in the leadership classroom continues to guide me.

The third leg of my subject draws on the burgeoning body of thinking called Critical Management Studies (CMS), itself part of a wider tradition of critical ideas including postmodernism and poststructuralism which have permeated disciplines as diverse as accounting, anthropology, literary studies and education. CMS challenges the production of management knowledge itself, and interrogates the purposes to which it is put. Further, teachers who draw on critical perspectives argue for the educational value of encouraging management students to think critically about what is going on in their organisational lives and under the banner of management.[13]

Critical theorists are far from having one voice. However, for our purposes there are some important themes. In general, critical thinking pursues freedom through revealing conditions of suppression which are not ordinarily visible. Psychologist and philosopher Michel Foucault has, perhaps more than any other theorist, shaped our understanding of the ways power and knowledge work in society, and how to unmask these relations in the interests of greater freedom.[14] Foucault is interested in the ways in which a sense of oneself is constructed and experienced. Also termed 'subjectivity', this sense of self is shaped by social institutions, such as schools or churches, and can appear to be complete and taken for granted. Our ways of knowing about ourselves can thus seem to be simply 'reality' or 'truth' until they are interrupted or 'refused'. Some of Foucault's writings are directed towards encouraging us to notice and linger at these moments of interruption, because of what they reveal and their potential to disturb otherwise uniform, complete and windowless subjectivities. It is not until we stop and step back that we allow or see different ways of seeing ourselves. While these insights are explored in detail in Chapter 8, Foucault's ideas show that the knowledge we accept as the truth or reality is always produced out of power relations. Because such relations are embedded in societies, through socialisation and institutional habits, we don't see them until we cultivate a critical consciousness. Once we are able to do so, we begin to free ourselves and others towards new 'practices of the self'.

Social theorist Pierre Bourdieu is also interested in how to make visible what he calls 'habitus', or taken-for-granted assumptions and practices. Bourdieu advocates various ways to redress the lack of transparency in these assumptions. One for researchers (although it also applies to managers and leaders) is to maintain great respect for the people they are observing or working with— being 'attentive to the almost infinitely subtle strategies that social agents deploy in the simple conduct of their lives'.[15]

At the time of writing this book, there is no substantial body of critical thinking about leadership, although there are articles and books.[16] One of my intentions here is to begin to map out and draw together what might be called Critical Leadership Studies. I believe this is badly needed. Critical perspectives give us reasons to ask, and ways of asking, about the power and deeper effects of our actions. They thus provide a welcome antidote to much of the leadership literature which positions the leader as architect and orchestrator of change, above scrutiny rather than inside it.

The three values of reflection, experiential methods and critical thinking are each derived from well-established bodies of thinking, but to my knowledge there are no other curricula which use them collectively as the basis for learning about leadership. My overall intent was to have students critically identify, reflect on and challenge leadership orthodoxy: to expose themselves to and experiment with different versions of leadership. The curriculum was built around questions such as: Is leadership a good thing? Who benefits from investment in leadership? What are the purposes to which leadership is put? What is going on when there are calls for leadership? We explored the contradictions within leadership literature, claiming to be about change but rarely questioning the power relations that sustain leaders and their investment in the status quo.

Participants in my leadership classes usually start the subject with expectations of learning how to be better leaders. Many expect me to tell them how. Over the subsequent weeks, they begin questioning prior understandings of what is regarded as 'natural' and 'good' leadership, as well as how they should learn about it. Encouraged to critique popular prescriptions for leaders, they start to see that these may be built on gendered or racialised assumptions. Drawing on critical ideas about identity, we look at how the identity of 'leader' justifies and is supported by cultural narratives such as omnipotent heroism. Students are also encouraged—indeed, sometimes jolted—into different ways of learning. The word 'teaching' is a very unsatisfactory one to capture what occurs in our classroom.[17] I see my role as one of creating a space where students see that they can learn from each other and themselves, through reflection, in addition to authoritative sources such as readings.

By the end, I want students to be appraising critically what is being offered as leadership in their workplaces. I want them to be thinking about their own experience at the hands of 'leadership', and about options for how they might participate with deeper insight in organisationally sponsored leadership initiatives. In some instances, this translates into becoming more personally 'empowered', seeing possibilities of exit or being courageous in naming oppressive institutional practices. Towards the end of the subject, we review a widely cited article on leadership. Students recognise that, though this might have been the sort of article most would have hungered for initially, its oversimplified template falls far short of the kind of learning we have experienced in class.

Drawing on a mixture of methods that are experientially and psychodynamically informed, I aim to raise consciousness and equip students with ways of 'reading' power relations, including those in the classroom: between myself as teacher and them, but also between privileged and other student subgroups in class. We explore anxieties with a less structured classroom process and a collaboratively constructed body of learning. Students are asked: What forms does leadership take in the class? What effects does it have? Are there different spaces available for some members of the class to exercise particular forms of leadership? How do individuals, and we as a group, disentangle and loosen ourselves from deeply entrenched leadership orthodoxies, and what does this allow?

The MBA experience[18]

In this section, I describe two experiences teaching the 'Leadership and Change' subject, one with an MBA and one with an Executive MBA (EMBA) group. The MBA students are postgraduates with a minimum of three years' work experience and an average age of 29, while EMBAs are typically older and more senior, though some are without an undergraduate degree. The EMBA is delivered intensively during four-week residential modules, while the MBA consists of three-hour sessions over twelve weeks. Both groups comprised around 40 participants, and I was coming to the completion of the MBA subject as I was starting with the EMBA group.

The MBA class contained a mixture of part- and full-time students, about half arriving straight from work in business suits. Often there is not much contact between these two cohorts, and each holds stereotypes about the other—for example, that the full-timers are more serious about their study and competitive about marks, while the part-timers are more relaxed and just want to pass. Over the duration of the subject, stereotypes were named and worked through, and relationships across the two groups became stronger. Similarly, in relations between men and women there seemed to be a great deal of what felt like good work. In our early classes, men dominated discussion. However, and with support from theoretical content, the gendered experiences and expectations of men and women became more discussable. This provided a platform for a more meaningful and critical discussion of gender issues in leadership in class and in individual writing projects.

It became clear from the students' comments in class and to me, through their written work, and through my own sense of what was happening, that this subject became a powerful catalyst for learning. The students started to 'see' themselves, their histories and their habits with new eyes. They visibly experimented with different ways of behaving in the group: shutting up, talking honestly, asking others for help, seeing and committing to collective goals of group learning, and supporting risk-taking by their peers.

This subject was a highlight of my teaching career, and I was deeply moved by what the class accomplished. I believe the experience enabled most students to step back from their assumptions about themselves and leadership. They applied new insights about power and gender to understand better how societies and organisations constrain the way women and men perform in leadership, but also deliver possibilities for action. In students' work, in their class contributions and in their discussions with me, there was evidence of liberation—of seeing things afresh and this insight in turn generating new possibilities for their own leadership work.

I started teaching the EMBAs as the MBA subject was concluding, and this timing was significant. I carried over to the new and different group assumptions that were, with hindsight, misplaced and I embarked upon the subject with less careful attention to their different circumstances than I should. The EMBA participants were more seasoned executives, with only a couple of women in the group. Despite their seniority, there was more anxiety buried in this group about academic standards. For many, it was a long time since they had studied, if at all. There was also more pressure created by the intensive format where participants take four weeks away from workplaces and families.

Preparing for the first session, I felt great—open, warm, ready to give. I was dressed informally and wanted to connect. I moved the group from their tiered lecture theatre to a flat room with no desks. I smiled and welcomed them. I introduced myself and spent a few moments outlining the features of how I wanted us to work together: reflexively, experientially and critically. I started to feel hostility in the room. Then I got them up and breathing for about three or four minutes. I talked a little more, writing some concepts on the whiteboard. I asked them to draw a picture of themselves. A couple groaned and a few just sat. I asked them to form into pairs to discuss not their pictures but how they had reacted to the task. My intention was to encourage some reflection and discussion about participants' reactions to a very different kind of activity. Again there were a number who just sat, practising passive resistance.

I asked the question 'How did you experience our start?' First, stony silence. The hostility was palpable. Then I was attacked for just about everything: for moving them to another room, for asking them how they experienced the start, for not introducing myself properly. I was attacked for requiring them to do work between modules, and thus 'breaching the contract' they had negotiated, by which their EMBA work would start and finish with the intensives. One participant stood at the back of the room for the whole session. A number were visibly furious during the session, and stormed out at the end.

I, and my next three sessions with the group, became a focal point of anxiety and anger. There were jokes about why no one would sit in the inner circle of the horseshoe, closer to me. Each time I stopped talking and asked participants to do things, such as work in pairs, there were long, chilly silences. A few isolated voices supported these initiatives, but it became obvious that such votes of support were viewed by the rest of the group as a political act. Unforgivably, on a couple of occasions I got locked into slanging matches with participants who attacked my credentials, the research base for what I was arguing and the legitimacy of the tasks I was proposing. Each time I attempted to encourage the group to take note of its own dynamics as a way of learning about groups and leadership, there was widespread resistance and I came under pressure to offer more 'content'.

There are a number of ways that these two contrasting experiences of teaching leadership, ostensibly drawing on the same material, can be understood. While I have teased these analyses out elsewhere,[19] the thing I want to focus on here is power and a liberating intent. Everything in my consulting work and research on leadership was suggesting to me that senior executives needed a different kind of space to explore ideas without the relentless pressure of day-to-day work environments. I wanted them to have the freedom to learn, to explore the bigger picture of what was going on in society, in organisations and in their own lives. I wanted them to discover critical thinking, to have a trans-formative experience, to see the world and their part in it in new ways. I now see that there was a lot of naivety in this dream, and a lot of projection too. But at this stage I thought I could single-handedly and genially persuade these aspiring leaders to relinquish the competitive, individualistic instincts so well honed in their careers and lives, and to embrace a new way of being.

What I intended as a transformational and liberating experience became arbitrarily coercive for most of the EMBAs. The EMBA group was paradoxically both more powerful, and more subject, than the MBA cohort. Partly because the EMBA was a recently relaunched program, the participants and their employ-ers were powerful. Intense marketing and recruitment efforts made the school keen to placate participants and corporate sponsors, who had invested them-selves, money and time in a conventional educational product. They weren't about to join with me in challenging methods of management learning. The risks of a high level of client power had not been anticipated or discussed in advance. When members of the group started to feel anxious (which, some would argue, is a prerequisite of learning), the immediate institutional response was to shut down the source of anxiety rather than commit to working through it, or to learning about leadership from this experience.

The EMBAs were also, in other ways, powerless. All subjects were compul-sory in the program. They were under pressure in an academic environment in which some had little confidence or experience. There was also anxiety about how participation in the course overall would be evaluated by employers: some were worried that their very absence might jeopardise, not support, career prospects. Finally, there were ever-present worries about the fall-out on family and relationships.

Turning to my own power, in my resolve to facilitate 'transformation', I paid insufficient attention to where EMBA participants were at, and how I should adapt my ambitions accordingly. Coming from the culmination of a successful MBA class, I extrapolated their receptiveness (that I had carefully built up) to the EMBA group. I failed to see that I was exercising power and that that power was perceived as particularly arbitrary in an already overly disciplined environment. I was so focused on challenging the pedagogical assumptions of the program that I failed to recognise the coercion that may have been experienced in my invitation to breathe (explored further in Chapter 7).

Teaching the theory of power relations is one thing; working with our own power relations is quite another. Part of me imagined I could facilitate a more transformative and liberating classroom simply by 'being' different. A critical perspective requires that we look beyond individual actors and identify the structural ways that pedagogical practice is disciplined. These include: student expectations and anxieties; institutional responses; one's own fears of losing expertise; status; and self. Markers of identity such as gender are never outside these forces. So the fact that I was a woman teacher in a faculty of mostly men, teaching a predominantly male group, was significant.

With hindsight, I monumentally underestimated the impact of structural factors (the structure, reputation and marketing of the EMBA program, characteristics of the client group, etc.) and overestimated my capacity and agency to overcome these factors. This meant that, paradoxically, I reproduced a key fantasy of leadership: thinking that I could stand outside the power relations in which I was embedded and single-handedly orchestrate transformation.

RISKS AND CHALLENGES IN TEACHING

Teachers who are interested in teaching in a liberating way are encouraged by the literature to:

- question and challenge categories of knowledge and stereotypes about who has knowledge;
- increase opportunities for individual learners to connect their own experience with intellectual constructs and theory; and
- work with authority and structures in nuanced, not predictable or pre-emptive, ways.

A colleague who does a lot of experiential advisory work with senior European executives advised that one of the things he has learned is never to do what participants are expecting you to do. This resonates for me with a Zen Buddhist approach, which is to teach through puzzles, rather than by giving the answers a group craves (as described in Chapter 1). Showing how to be a teacher who is an 'expert-in-not-knowing' is an important part of modelling the openness that one is after.[20]

These ways of working contradict many of the assumptions and values that permeate our thinking about leadership. For the teacher or leader to admit that they don't have the answer or are not completely in control is to fly in the face of cherished leadership wisdom on two levels at once—the intellectual and the experiential. The challenge, as described by Heifetz, is that audiences or followers are being disappointed *enough* to learn, but at a rate that they can tolerate.

Teaching in ways that challenge and disturb power relations has particular pitfalls for women. Women have often been at the vanguard of teaching innovation, because they usually face more obstacles in the construction of their authority.[21] It is important not to assume that women have access to the same tools and methods of authority-building as men. A finding that is explored in more depth in Chapter 5 is that women with power are judged differently. Similarly, women leaders are often forced by circumstance—by an unusual level of visibility and scrutiny, for example—to bring heightened levels of reflection and innovation to how they do their jobs.[22]

These systemically created conditions create a common challenge for women—to teach and lead in ways that do not abdicate the need for authority and structure, but that simultaneously do not foster dependency in students. A fantasy that is sometimes expected of women is that power will be dissolved in their classrooms, that their (expected) commitment to community and collaboration will somehow dissipate ego and hubris.[23] Of course, this never happens, nor should women teachers be automatically held to higher benchmarks of care or selfless dedication.

The view that women bring a different teaching or leadership style is also risky because it plays into stereotypes of women as nurturers, better suited to the subordination of their own power. As Walkerdine describes: 'Women teachers became caught, trapped inside a concept of nurturance which held them responsible for the freeing of each little individual, and therefore for the management of an idealist dream, an impossible fiction.'[24] Similarly, the stereotypical expectation that women will favour devolution and self-direction over coercion has sometimes in practice led to the disappearance of essential structure, which can be disempowering for students. Most audiences need 'good enough' structure as a platform for them to then allow that structure to release its grip.

At the same time, teaching processes mediated through rigid power relationships and centralised authority and knowledge are more like conditioning than education. This is particularly the case in management and leadership education, where students are adults bringing significant work and life experience to the process. One's aim as a teacher or leader should be to provide enough structure and authority for students to feel some trust that they will be supported to develop, take risks and responsibility for their own learning.

Some leadership education reinforces the worst habits of corporate life. It encourages learners to reproduce in education the individualistic, competitive, driving and sometimes dependent (discussed in Chapter 4) values of corporate life. Yet surely, if we are interested in promoting leadership, we should be encouraging people to question these values and habits.

In this chapter, I have drawn on research and examples from my experiences teaching leadership to show why and how we might proceed differently: reflectively, experientially, critically and with a liberating intent. I have also drawn on a substantial body of educational thinking not generally applied in the leadership field. Though teaching is not the same as leadership, educational research and experience provide valuable insights for people learning to do leadership in new ways. These include:

○ exploring valuable and sustaining purposes such as liberation and learning;
○ illuminating ways to identify and keep group energy focused on the meaningful purpose or important challenge in a situation. This might be as simple as helping a group to see and learn from unfolding dynamics, such as working with diversity or managing conflict;
○ being alert to the complex and seductive power and gender relations in educational and institutional settings that are pervasive but generally unexamined and can undermine underlying purposes;
○ paying attention to and naming what is happening in the present, including noting defensive habits and rituals, such as 'busy' activity and ticking off tasks on an agenda, which might look like work, change or learning but are not really;
○ giving priority to relationships, the importance of the emotional work of leadership and promoting individual dignity;
○ listening and watching with a critical consciousness so that what's deemed 'normal' or 'necessary' to get the job done isn't simply accepted;
○ avoiding collusion with stereotypes such as 'leaders have to have all the answers' or 'leaders must be seen to be in control';
○ learning how to identify and work with power relations and power dynamics that can get in the way of, or support, the group's purpose;
○ being reflective about one's own power;

○ illuminating the risks of trying to teach, lead and foster learning in more challenging ways, including (as my EMBA example showed) that a transformative intent can be experienced as coercive.

There is no point seeking to be liberating and not paying close attention to our own motivations and susceptibilities, or to the power relations in which we're embedded. In Part II, I turn to explore ways of thinking about and working with these more tacit dynamics of leadership.

PART II

Practices of liberating leadership

4
Going back

٭

They fuck you up, your mum and dad . . .

Philip Larkin (1974)

The nuclear family is a tiny political system and a primitive leadership system

James MacGregor Burns (1978)

Famous men are usually the product of an unhappy childhood.

Winston Churchill (quoted in Gardner 1995)

*Executives arguing in the boardroom over issues of corporate strategy are
unconsciously still dealing with parental figures and siblings over issues of power.*

Manfred Kets de Vries (2006)

Families and childhoods provide our first encounter with leadership, and the
roots of our leadership aspirations and styles. In this chapter, I argue that
renewed attention to backgrounds will build leadership understanding in two
ways. First, effective leadership requires at least some self-knowledge, some
awareness of one's hungers and appetites and some determination to not use
a leadership position simply to play out or gratify those urges. Second, backgrounds provide valuable clues for explaining why and how leadership goes
wrong. To go forward in developing and deepening leadership, we therefore
first need to go back.

Leadership and the accounts of leadership offered in business contexts generally ignore childhoods and backgrounds. Because there are interests invested in training people for leadership, the evidence that early formative experiences shape appetites for leadership and followership has been neglected. But in the rush to learn how to develop leadership, we have thrown out the baby with the bathwater. By attending to early life from birth to early adulthood, including to families, parental and sibling relations, we learn a lot about our basic predisposition towards leadership. Whether individuals aspire to leadership themselves or feel deeply distrustful of people in authority, whether they withdraw, rebel, challenge, attack or defer, often replays an earlier history. It is not that our orientation to leadership is set and unable to be changed by an early age, but by going back and paying attention to the experiences that have shaped our early life, we can begin to unshackle ourselves from them. They cease to become the unconscious drivers of our relation to leadership, and become more available for us to modify and adapt to contemporary circumstances.

A second reason why backgrounds should be put back into leadership is to provide a much fuller understanding about why and how particular instances of leadership go wrong. Let's return to the pair of leaders running the Enron corporation (see Chapter 1), chairman Ken Lay and CEO Jeff Skilling.[1] Lay was a Baptist preacher's son who was brought up in straitened circumstances in the American Midwest. Skilling was a 'nerdy' kid who, although smart, struggled in high school. In his twenties, he wore thick glasses and began balding prematurely. Both individuals were powerfully motivated to 'become' someone, to put humble origins and embarrassing histories behind them[2] and remake themselves as charismatic leaders who would win the adulation of those around them. Although they went about this in different ways, in both cases it was their responses to early experiences that fuelled intense hunger to gain power and assert themselves over those who had doubted them. Their backgrounds also provide more clues as to how they went about this. Skilling's leadership style was macho while Lay pursued profile and connections with America's business and political elites.

Leaders who are disconnected from their early identity, and intent on crafting a grander one for themselves, often become more vulnerable to corruption. They start believing the myth that they have created about themselves—that they are smarter than the average person and can therefore put themselves above the rules and norms by which others live. Leaders, in these cases, develop identities that are built on deception. They get locked into performances that are inflated and purport to have 'the answers'. These performances are seductive and convincing for the leaders themselves and for followers, who want to align themselves with the 'chosen' ones.

Without looking into backgrounds, it is harder to comprehend why some leaders and followers are successful in 'managing their hungers',[3] while others abuse their power and position. When leaders become corrupted by hubris or greed, or operate from an assumption about a 'natural' right to lead, often at least part of the explanation lies in early experiences. These experiences are rarely examined or reflected on by leaders themselves, and few analyses of corporate failures encompass the frailties and vulnerabilities put in place in the leader's childhood. More often, the limited conclusion is that these apparent leaders turned out to be 'bad apples'.

In this chapter, I show how leaders can become more reflective about their backgrounds in order to foster better and more liberating practices of leadership. I draw on my work with managers to argue that, by paying attention to and becoming more reflective about the experiences that have shaped our early lives, we find more freedom to grow and lead differently. These experiences cease to become the unconscious drivers of our relationship to authority, and become more available for us to modify and adapt to present realities. The kind of biographical work I describe here is challenging, and needs to be undertaken with appropriate support. It is a deeply personal—and potentially lifelong—journey of self-learning, part of what I explore later in this book as the identity work of leadership (see Chapter 8).

THE NEGLECT OF BACKGROUNDS[4]

Recent studies of leadership, for reasons discussed in Chapter 2, have generally rejected exploration of childhoods and early experiences as both too deterministic and too idiosyncratic. The idea that certain people are 'born to lead' is not only inconsistent with democratic and meritocratic ideals, but also with economic ambitions to designate and educate leaders.[5] While there are signs that it is now more acceptable to bring childhoods back into our discussion of leadership, this tends to occur as a footnote rather than as the major focus.[6]

A disregard of the influence of childhood in thinking about leadership has been part of a more general rejection of psychoanalysis and Freudian thinking which has gathered force over much of the second part of the twentieth century. Freud's insights have been cast as unscientific and not visibly therapeutic. In-depth psychoanalysis, so the argument went, encouraged people to dwell on their past rather than 'moving on'. The subsequent work of people like Adler, who also connected adult orientations to early experiences, was relegated to corners of an ambitious, empirical psychology.

There is not sufficient space here to comb over this debate in any detail. Yet it is important to recognise that, while Freud and his successors have provided handy scapegoats, no one working in 'the people professions' (psychotherapy, counselling, medicine, health care, etc.) doubts that some self-knowledge is important to psychological health and development. Although Freud's ideas are almost absent from leadership writing,[7] many of the insights he pioneered are mainstream—not just about childhoods, but about group dynamics and the role of the unconscious in daily life. Practitioners vary in the emphases they put on doing biographical work, but most acknowledge that emotional robustness is built from a platform of self-awareness.

This self-knowledge involves, at a base level, an understanding of what has shaped one in the past and a capacity to differentiate the childhood self from the contemporary self. Many therapeutic interventions are aimed at helping individuals to recognise the past and come to terms with its effects, then using this understanding as a platform to free people to envisage new ways of responding and behaving. Through this process, people who have developed responses to cope with a difficult childhood, such as cutting off emotionally or being unable to trust caregivers, are able to consign such responses to a childhood self and give themselves permission to adopt new responses more appropriate to an adult. Our pasts thus influence—though need not circumscribe—us. They are an important part of our identity, but not the whole self. In my experience, it is not until one's biography is at least made conscious through articulation—even if it is not yet understood—that some new ways of being can be imagined.

In much of the recent work on authentic and spiritual leadership, a great deal of emphasis is placed on self-awareness and acting from self-knowledge.[8] Examples are given of leaders who 'know themselves', who understand their talents, strengths, values and desires, and who demonstrate a consistency of behaviour and action around this authentic self. In Chapters 8 and 9, I explore these ideas further, but the point to be made here is that many of the efforts to build authenticity in executives are curiously neglectful of childhood. Leader self-awareness is often treated as an ahistorical 'variable' that can be cultivated without recourse to the idiosyncratic and episodic terrain of childhoods.

HOW CHILDHOODS ARE IMPORTANT IN LEADERSHIP

How might childhoods be brought back into our thinking and work on leadership? In this section, I introduce some ideas and research about how backgrounds shape motivations and approaches to leadership which I have found effective in my work.

My point is not that certain childhoods create leaders, but that all childhoods shape people's appetites for and vulnerabilities in leadership. Leadership has a childhood,[9] and having a grasp of our own leadership background offers a powerful means to:

O highlight hidden or less conscious assumptions we make about leadership;
O tune into the desires, hungers and vulnerabilities that may play out in our leadership roles;
O identify psychic obstacles to changing our approaches; and
O explore potential areas of personal growth and innovation in the way we do both leadership and followership.

The family is our first experience of leadership—as followers to our parents, carers or older siblings. And it is also our first experience of trying out leadership or tactics of influencing others. Children see and learn how to get essential attention and how to win scarce resources of time, favour and love. We learn in families how to get our way—by imposing our will or our physical superiority; by negotiating with, listening and attending to other family members; by entertaining and being amusing; by forming alliances; by eliciting pity or guilt. We learn how to compete, how to distinguish ourselves from others (especially siblings) and how to claim our special place in the world.

The ways in which we learn how to do these critical leadership activities become powerful, yet often unconscious, drivers of our behaviour as adults in organisations. Experiences in organisations can provoke an unconcious re-enactment of versions of these early patterns: we might identify with authority, firmly enforcing the right way to do things; or we may engage in approval-seeking; or we could stamp our feet and set off on our own direction.

In *New Faces of Leadership* (2002), Valerie Wilson and I conducted some research of 'diversity leaders'. We were seeking to know more about senior executives who were demonstrably comfortable and adept, for example, when leading global or virtual teams whose members came from different cultures.

We isolated several features of personal histories that seemed to play a part in how leaders related to the world, particularly in the extent to which they were trusting and open to others and flexible in their approach to leading. These factors, which are elaborated below, included:

○ parents, and whether fathers were present or absent;
○ birth order, size of family and relationship to siblings; and
○ disruptions such as experiences of 'border crossing' and feelings of being an 'outsider' while growing up.

Parents

Research of leaders has found that a significant proportion of political leaders—men in particular—have had a period in childhood where the father has been absent.[10] This may have occurred due to parental separation, father's serious illness or premature death or simply the father being emotionally unavailable. As historical and psychoanalytic studies of leadership show, an absent father can influence the motivation for, and style of, leadership in several possible ways. One interpretation is that the child, without a strong paternal figure, sets about being the 'big father' themselves. This process is intensified particularly for sons if there is a deep attachment to the mother. Bill Clinton is a classic example of these influences.[11] The mother may (perhaps unconsciously) convey an expectation that the child will be the father: 'the man of the family'. These conditions feed the child's emerging sense of themselves and what they need to do. In the narcissistic extreme, the adult quest for leadership is an endlessly repeated search for (the lost father's or mother's) admiration.[12]

A father's absence can also allow space for—especially male—leaders to develop their own, less conventional or traditional, style of leadership. Without the strong shadow of an authority figure, these leaders often develop temperaments that include traditionally feminine strengths such as highly valuing relationships. In Clinton's case, a household characterised by conflict between his mother and stepfather appears to have prompted premature sensitivity and strength in negotiation and mediation.

Howard Gardner, a distinguished educationalist and leadership scholar, notes that the backgrounds of leaders—including absent fathers—often require of the child a 'precocious dependence on themselves'.[13] In the case of leaders like Churchill, adversity and loneliness forge such self-reliance. Great leaders are also, according to Gardner, able to shape and tell a story that ignites a group's or nation's imagination. Fertile ground for such leadership qualities occurs where the child is forced to stand apart, and is experienced at initiating and surviving risk.

From our research, Valerie and I suggest that, in situations where fathers are present, the child (and especially the first-born) is exposed to, and more likely to identify with, a clear paternal model of leadership—strong, dominant and typically unemotional. Young people who grow up with fathers present are more likely to turn into leaders with a directive style of leadership—the child internalises the male parent as the model for leadership, then later reproduces this model in their own expectations and style of leading.

In contrast, children with a missing parent are required to formulate their own models of leadership. They take longer and go via a more circuitous route, sometimes a close maternal relationship, to find their leadership identity. The greater ambiguity about what is required may actually represent a benefit and opportunity for aspiring leaders, especially young men. It often translates itself into a leadership model that is more attuned to and comfortable with expressing emotion.

These same background circumstances are discussed by leadership analyst Alistair Mant. He makes a distinction between 'ternary' leaders who focus on a higher purpose and 'binary' leaders who remain locked in a pattern of dominance and seeing leadership as a triumph of stronger will. Mant argues that nurturing style, or style of mothering and birth order, 'provide the bedrock upon which personality is built . . . The foundation . . . characterises the quality of leading and following that an individual will be capable of and impelled towards.'[14]

Birth order and siblings

A large body of research looks at the effect of birth order on family climates and experiences of childhood and adulthood.[15] Here I draw together research findings about how birth order might affect leadership, acknowledging that other contextual factors may mitigate these effects in individual cases.

The first-born children in families are typically the focus of a lot of parental attention.[16] They can experience high expectations, substantial parental interest and intervention in their lives, and close monitoring. Such conditions can be good or bad for these individuals. Research indicates that first-borns are generally high achievers. They benefit from parental input, and often reach the high academic and achievement goals that are set for them.

However, parents of first-borns also set out to create their child in their own, sometimes idealised, image. First-borns can suffer from parental high standards that fail to recognise or respect their individuality. Typically, first-borns identify strongly with parents, internalising parental voices and taking on a role as parental agent if there are younger siblings. As leaders, this can translate into an over-developed sense of responsibility and rigidity. A sense of being 'born to rule', or entitlement to lead, can undermine their capacity to work with and trust others. The high standards they set for everybody, including themselves, can also prevent them from seeing the bigger picture. First-borns frequently carry the weight of the world on their shoulders and find it hard to allow others to share the load, particularly if those others go about it differently. Some first-borns, particularly first-born girls, also have an over-developed hunger for approval. Unless faced, this need for approval can dog them into adulthood and stop them from standing up effectively to authority figures.

While there is a preponderance of first-borns in the ranks of leaders and high achievers, they don't necessarily make great leaders. As Michael Grose notes: 'Many first-borns confuse assertiveness with aggression and gain co-operation through coercion.'[17] The challenge for first-born leaders is to let go a little and accept that there is more than one way to get things done.

Second-born children in the family routinely find a place for themselves by doing the opposite of their older sibling. Differentiation is the name of this familial position, and often this takes the form of being the rebel, the radical or the taunting extrovert, who disregards parental conventions.[18]

Later-born children are, in general, likely to experience much less attention from parents and a more relaxed style of parenting. This family climate can take both positive and negative forms. At one extreme, it can be neglecting for the child as they struggle to get enough attention and love to feel all right about themselves. More positively, they often benefit from fewer expectations, and a more spacious and open childhood where they are left to their own devices to find a more idiosyncratic path into adulthood and possible leadership.

Our research on diversity leaders supports the idea that those who grow up in large families, and particularly those later in the birth order, have a natural interest in, and an instinct for, democracy. With parental resources becoming scarce as more children appear, the later-borns in large families often have to fend for themselves, and learn how to 'read' and negotiate with older and powerful siblings in order to get what they need. Later-borns thus find a path to leadership and influence despite little claim to hierarchical or formal authority, and this can be a very valuable lesson to learn.

Disruptions

Leaders who are comfortable working with diversity often had childhoods characterised by crossing borders—geographic, cultural, linguistic, socio-economic and emotional. Family factors, such as fleeing difficult conditions in home countries and migration, or father's occupations (for example diplomats or entrepreneurs) meant that, as children, the 'diversity leaders' in our research had been exposed to multiple cultures, language groups and socioeconomic classes. As children, they often had experiences of being a newcomer or outsider to an environment. This meant that they developed skills of observing new or alien cultural norms, becoming what novelist Saul Bellow terms 'first class noticers'.[19] While they also developed the capacity to adapt to these new norms, many found that, knowing there were other approaches, they could fall back on their own resources and not necessarily 'go with the crowd'. These leaders found out, often at quite a young age, that they could survive without others' approval or the benefits of belonging.

These ingredients and experiences mean a number of things for the adult leader. For some whom we researched, it meant a ready identification with the underdog. Having known an experience of being on the outer, they were likely to challenge traditions, power structures and other bases by which outsiders are excluded. Another legacy of this kind of background can be finely honed skills of observation and a repertoire of non-conventional influencing skills. An example was a leader who, in rather rough and ready Australian business contexts, was extraordinarily charming and skilled at making others feel comfortable. These capacities had been developed as the requisites for survival in a new country with a different language. Other researchers have also found that path-breaking novelists, artists and other original thinkers have often felt like outsiders in their youth or early adulthood. Such experiences can forge a freshness and originality of vision, as well as a stance that is not readily awed by authority, status or threats of rejection.

When Valerie and I conducted further research and came across leaders who achieved a great deal by defying or circumventing convention rather than adopting more conventional leadership means, we often discover that 'border crossing' has been part of childhood. For example, the founder of Hotmail, Sabir Bhatia, told the story of his first 'audience' with the Microsoft CEO, Bill Gates. Gates was keen to purchase Hotmail, and most observers saw this as a David and Goliath meeting at which the much smaller player would simply be grateful for Microsoft's attention. Yet, sitting across the table from the Microsoft lineup of senior negotiators, including Gates, Bhatia had remained unintimidated, holding out for a higher price for the business he had built. Bhatia's composure and refusal to be awed were more comprehensible when he revealed that his father had been a diplomat and he had travelled extensively as a child.

The learning about leadership from this example and others in our research is that early experiences of being an outsider teach the leader that they can survive without necessarily belonging, and they can achieve without conforming. They are often less in awe of high-status individuals because they have less to lose by being rejected.

The evidence here and in *New Faces of Leadership* encourages us to look further into backgrounds, growing up and early adulthood, in order to understand leadership. How people navigate early experiences and what they take from them are central—though often unconscious—planks in the way they approach the task of leading and influencing. Work on backgrounds also provides important clues for leaders and researchers about areas of emotional vulnerability and frailty that might be denied or repressed, but can actively undermine adult leadership, as I elaborate in the next sections of this chapter.

WORKING WITH LEADERS ON BACKGROUNDS

Each of us brings our own history with us to leadership. By digging into and understanding this history, we can open new ways of doing leadership and followership.

In my leadership teaching and coaching with MBA students and executives, I often find that the work we do on backgrounds has powerful, and for some lasting, impact. When people are encouraged to look back, take their past seriously and ask themselves questions about identity, several things happen. They begin to see themes in their histories which they continue to act out, such as needing approval or high levels of control. They see patterns in their ways of participating in organisational life, their expectations of leaders and their own habits of leadership. This allows them to see that there are choices about how they might lead.

I use the concept of implicit leadership theories (ILTs) to assist in making the connection between one's personal history and beliefs about leadership.[20] These are pictures or templates in our minds of what leadership looks like and who can do it. Attending to this picture helps people to unpack and explore their implicit or unconscious assumptions about how they must or must not be as a leader, as well as their often ambivalent feelings around this.

Going back

Working with MBA students, I introduce the idea of ILTs and research about childhoods and leadership. Students begin a process of writing regularly in a journal, learning to reflect in a deeper way not only about what happens in their lives, but about their responses to these occurrences. They read a biography of a leader which includes their formative years, and they are encouraged to choose leaders from fields beyond business, such as achievers in the arts or sciences.

Although everybody's history is different, and plays out in adulthood in different ways, there are experiences which are commonly volunteered. One is that men have often inherited the view that leaders must be clear and certain about directions, and tough and single-minded in the execution of those directions. Uncertainty and shows of emotion or weakness are seen as inadmissible in leaders. The origins of this view usually lie with parental, school or sporting role models, and reflect espoused norms of masculine leadership as much as what is actually observed or experienced. Many younger men struggle to put on this mask of leadership: they may privately feel 'not up to it', but persevere nevertheless because they believe that this is the performance they must deliver.

Similarly, personal biography work is powerful for women. Over the course of adolescence and the early career years, many come to think of themselves as 'hard-working', 'conscientious', 'committed' and 'being good with people', but these are simultaneously designated as something other than leadership.[21] Often these categories and definitions of appropriate behaviour are reinforced in family dynamics and the gendered segregation of family-centred leadership work: mothers doing the relational and emotional family work, behind the scenes, and fathers assuming more public leadership roles.

In their early careers, women have often succeeded in male-dominated business environments by being hard-working, clever, conscientious and dutiful. Their assumptions and observations are that leadership requires a single-minded, driven and tough performance—one from which many women disqualify themselves. As careers progress, they reach a point where performing faithfully against norms starts to be stressful, as well as less successful. This happens in several ways. First, the path of establishing their value by committing everything to work starts to be perceived by women as unsustainable, particularly if they have a family or are thinking about starting one. Second, the strategy of dutiful emulation becomes palpably less effective as women move from junior roles, where they can be mentored and 'coached' by older men, to more senior roles where they are competing with those very men for leadership opportunities.

In the research I undertook investigating the absence of women in senior executive ranks, and reported in *Trials at the Top*, women judged as 'trying to be too like one of the boys' were perceived by senior men as inappropriate leadership material. This perception has been documented in research, and was also famously demonstrated in the *Price Waterhouse v Hopkins* case in the United States in the late 1990s. Ann Hopkins was found to have been discriminated against and denied promotion to the position of partner precisely for acting and conveying the same values and norms as male partners.[22] Women, once they ascend close to leadership positions, thus get contradictory messages about what they need to do to succeed. The strategies that guaranteed success in schooling, university and junior to middle careers cease to work so effectively.[23] Their assumptions about themselves and what is required in leadership start to become deeply, personally untenable.

To enable such women to move forward, it is necessary to support them to unpack the origins of their dutifulness and their historic patterns of succeeding. Deconstructing their own socialisation in this supported and contained way allows them to question assumptions and stereotypes about leadership, and helps them to find new ways to validate their own strengths and capacities for leadership. It is also necessary to assist them to see gendered workplace norms where women's success is often attributed to hard work, while men's is attributed to ability. These undertakings are often emotionally painful, and involve confronting a discriminatory reality that women may have built their early careers by denying or discounting. Though initially confronting, such insights are ultimately freeing because they help explain that individual experience can only be explained fully when it is seen as part of a social and cultural context.

This work on family and childhood experiences enables both men and women to identify how gendered social norms have shaped their own beliefs and expectations. Such beliefs are normally regarded as 'personal'—private or idiosyncratic—but the process of revisiting from the vantage point of adulthood reveals structural and social influences. Helping people to tap into and validate their experiences, as well as equipping them with theoretical concepts to do this, is an important part of freeing them to rethink what leadership means and might mean for them. These processes—the biographical with the conceptual work—are empowering because they move students away from a position of seeing categories like leadership as somehow fixed, and their challenge as being to 'measure up' to this standard. They are freed to take a more active role in how their leadership contribution might be defined, constructed and taken up. It then becomes possible to imagine resisting or subverting conventional leadership scripts, and to be able to see that this activity—of contestation or challenge—might itself constitute leadership.

DEPENDENCY AND OBEDIENCE

Another benefit from biography work is assisting in what Heifetz and Linsky call 'managing your hungers'.[24] They argue that leadership depends on having the capacity to step back from one's appetites, knowing what is driving the need to be heard or included, the impulse to dominate or to shock. Doing biographical work helps to map habitual relations to authority—whether individuals typically attack or challenge authority, whether they exit the situation, exhibit dependency or look to be saved by leaders. Having at least passing familiarity with the topography of our individual needs and anxieties, we can then begin to 'read' our rising heartbeat, the prickle of emotion and the heat of adrenalin. Until leaders do the work of understanding how they have been shaped, they will be hostage to old patterns. I would like to provide an example of how leaders I have observed do this.

In my research with senior teams and organisations, obedient or compliant behaviour is often widespread. Paradoxically, sometimes the more overtly successful and senior the group, the more deeply dependent the behaviour that is often exhibited. So, for example, boards and senior management teams are frequently environments where dictatorial patterns of leadership and compliant followership go unchallenged beneath thinly maintained fronts of teamwork.

Research on groups has widely documented the phenomenon of 'groupthink', where excessive concurrence-seeking behaviours in the name of loyalty and not breaking ranks induce teams to make catastrophically bad decisions. Subsequent studies have introduced additional insights to explain these mechanisms of conformity, such as norms of masculinity, which disallow expressions of doubt.[25]

Here I'd like to suggest that attending to personal histories might assist in understanding obedience in groups and the way individuals in a group can occasionally rise above the pressures to toe the group line. I am not suggesting that we do analyses of the birth order of board directors—though that may indeed be revealing; rather, I am proposing that we recognise that personal histories play out in even the most elevated organisational settings. One which is prevalent is the hunger people at all levels can feel to align oneself with the powerful parent figure, taking forms such as the desire for daddy's or God's approval. For example, organisational and leadership scholar Yiannis Gabriel documents employees' feelings of being in awe of, touched or blessed by the attention of a chief executive or leader.[26]

In our rush to elevate leadership, we have neglected to see the tendencies towards dependency and obedience that are almost always part and parcel of it. Dependency is one of the biggest problems for leaders and leadership. When followers exhibit dependency, they look to the leader to solve things; they abdicate responsibility for the problem facing a group. They imagine that the leader will deliver a solution—clarity, an end to suffering, a dazzling resurgence in the share price or feeling of camaraderie. They project a confidence and certainty on to a leader as a way of managing their own anxieties.

Importantly for our purposes, it is not only lowly followers who exhibit dependency—it is also leaders themselves. When I describe the pervasiveness of obedience and dependency in leadership situations, audiences are often dismissive: 'But we're not like that. We're leaders'—as if the two are mutually exclusive. But dependency can take many forms. At a pathological extreme, it is sycophantic and grovelling. But it can also be the root of loyalty, commitment to the team and the need to speak 'with one voice' (of course, in the service of institutional causes, this is usually invoked as 'solidarity', 'stability', preserving confidence or the share price). Sometimes, and in my experience, the more senior the group and the more they dismiss the possibility, the higher the risk of dependent behaviour.

Though pervasive in organisations and teams, dependency is rarely admitted. Because of managerial emphasis on values such as 'initiative' and being a 'self-starter', dependency is a taboo. This is a good reason to focus on it. Further, taking a biographical, as well as a group dynamic, perspective can help to both explain and see ways out of these patterns.

Wilfred Bion, in his classic group research undertaken during and immediately after the Second World War, identified the main ways that people in groups avoid work: fight/flight (attack the leader or exit); dependency (waiting to be told what to do); and 'pairing' (pinning hopes on a pair of people who will lead the group to a new world). Bion's work has informed much thinking about group behaviour—though not, with some exceptions, leadership thinking.[27] One such exception is Ron Heifetz, who brings a background in psychiatry to his leadership work and who argues that, mostly, followers are desperate for leaders to tell them what to do.[28] Particularly in situations of what he calls 'adaptive leadership'—where groups need to work out new ways to do organisational work rather than just apply the usual rules—leaders need to find ways of not colluding with this dependency. Acts of leadership involve helping focus the group on overriding purposes or values, rather than telling them what the solution is.

Keith Grint (2000), in his close analysis, makes a similar point about Martin Luther King's leadership. As a leader, King courageously and consistently identified the problems and the symptoms of racist America, but he did not instruct people in how to fix them. On the contrary, in the famous 'I have a dream' speech given in 1963, King puts the responsibility firmly back on the people to fix the problem, saying:

> Go back to Mississippi, go back to Alabama, go back to South Carolina, go back to Georgia, go back to Louisiana, go back to the slums and ghettos of our northern cities, knowing that somehow this situation can and will be changed. Let us not wallow in the valley of despair.

King gave advice—though it was sparse—on how to conduct oneself, for example 'by not drinking from the cup of bitterness and hatred', but was notably silent on actual programs for change. Grint shows the value, in this kind of leadership process, of calling people's attention to, and having them identify with, a common set of problems then demonstrating faith that they will be solved. King galvanises people, but tells them that *they* must do the work. This example suggests the powerful tensions with which leadership often works: energising and mobilising followers while not colluding with their continual readiness to be dependent, devoted or dutiful.

TAKING A STAND: CATHY WALTER'S STORY

Cathy Walter is one of the few women to have established a reputation as a respected and senior company director in the Australian corporate landscape of the 1990s. I first met her when she was a member of the first group of MBA students I taught, in 1988. She is a lawyer by first training, and at that stage was running a law firm along with completing her MBA studies and looking after two young sons.

Walter is smart and assertive. This was evident from our first contact: she was no wallflower in class. Her composure and confidence would certainly have been nourished in childhood. As the much-loved daughter of a judge and from a family of lawyers, Cathy enjoyed being the bright and determined daughter in an illustrious family. A confidence in being around older men and an appetite for those kinds of interactions may have been laid in these early years. However, she didn't stay in the law. Quite early in her career, she made the first of a series of transitions: to managing partner of a law firm and, equipped with her MBA, she soon began accruing board positions as a non-executive director (NED). Just into her forties at this point, her career as a full-time NED was ramping up and her appetite for work, power and influence was building rather than abating. Throughout the years from late 1990 to early 2000, Cathy had a comparatively low profile as a director—acquiring a 'portfolio' of positions on the boards of blue-chip companies, as well as on those of less high-profile and not-for-profit organisations.

I found it hard to understand why she pursued this course. I wondered whether Walter's intelligence would be muffled by the closed and tightly prescribed protocols of board deliberations. If she was motivated by the power, the sacrifices that needed to be made looked awfully high to me. From my research of boards, I knew something of their norms and ways of conducting themselves, and wondered at her preparedness to commit her energies to such traditional environments.

Nevertheless, events in 2004 at the National Australia Bank (NAB) catapulted Cathy into a dramatically different performance of leadership. The NAB is Australia's second largest bank, and at the time of these events was widely regarded as the most successful and profitable. Competing major banks in Australia, such as ANZ and Westpac, were still rebuilding after crises of different kinds. The CEO of the NAB, Frank Cicutto, was a long-term employee anointed by his predecessor, and while not charismatic, was seen as financially very solid. It was hard to imagine him ever being displaced, or the bank's position of pre-eminence ever being challenged. Cathy was the only female director on the NAB board, but she was among the longer-serving ones.

In early 2004, serious shortcomings emerged in the investment side of the bank where around A$180 million (later found to be more like A$360 million) was revealed to have been lost by foreign currency traders over the previous weeks.[29] The events became public and the matter escalated as the bank's risk-management procedures were scrutinised and revealed to be flawed—though they were arguably not so very different to those in place in other large banks.

Going back

The NAB's board went into 'crisis management' mode, and various investigations were launched, including by PriceWaterhouse Cooper (PWC), with whom the NAB had a close relationship. These events followed an earlier, expensive A$4 billion write-off of an American acquisition, Homeside. They were enough to see the CEO resign, followed not long afterwards by the board's chairman.

A range of events added to Walter's earlier disquiet that the independence of the PWC investigation into the NAB's foreign exchange losses was compromised. One of the problems was that PWC had already undertaken between A$11 million and A$17 million of consulting work for the bank in the previous year. It also appeared to Walter that board directors, and particularly members of the relatively new Risk Committee, were getting prior access to the PWC findings. Walter thought there was a conflict of interest and, after several efforts to raise these concerns verbally with fellow directors, delivered a thirteen-page memorandum to the NAB board. A legal firm and another accounting firm were brought in to verify the probity of the PWC investigation. On 12 March 2004, the PWC investigation was released, criticising the NAB's culture and its board's performance, with passing reference to its Audit Committee (of which Walter was chair). The board Audit Committee was re-formed with a new chair, and Walter was stripped of her membership. Pressure was mounting on Walter, and at a board meeting in late March the board asked for her resignation.

Walter refused and publicly released her initial memorandum. She set about a methodically researched and strategically executed plan of action whereby she publicly forced the board to accept accountability. She argued that there should be a planned replacement of the entire board, including the chair, Graham Kraehe (who was chair of the Risk Committee when the critical losses were incurred), and herself. A special shareholders' meeting was scheduled to put Walter's proposal to a vote of all shareholders. But the meeting was cancelled at the last moment. It eventually transpired that the board would be substantially replaced. Some members left immediately and others (including the chair) were to be phased out. Walter then resigned.

During this period, Walter was branded by one journalist as a 'terrorist', and frequently portrayed in the business press and by fellow board members as irresponsibly threatening the stability of the NAB. She came under intense pressure to cave in and shut up, to observe board 'solidarity' in the interests of the bank. She moved from being a respected board director with a sound reputation to being seen, at least for the time of the controversy, as a pariah. Although she enjoyed a great deal of support from the wider community and among some shareholders, there was speculation that she would not be welcomed on to other boards. It was widely felt that she had sabotaged her NED career. But she continued because she felt there was an overriding issue at stake—perhaps the most important issue of corporate governance that a board ever faces. The NAB board, she felt, was refusing to accept this responsibility. If it didn't, then many governance protocols would be revealed as a sham—CEOs could be removed but board members would endure, whatever mistakes they made.

Events at the NAB elucidate tensions that are widespread in leadership—between lining up behind the powerful in the interests of 'stability' on the one hand and, on the other, provoking change. Very often, in leadership, loyalty and obedience triumph. In the early days of the crisis, it was clear that most parties expected the board to endure: the 'experience' of board members was needed, and it was unimaginable that there might be a spill or complete turnover in membership. In Australia, board decision-making had rarely been challenged, and directors had almost never been publicly asked to leave for performance reasons. Occasionally directors have departed 'to pursue other interests', but in general entrance to and departures from boards are shrouded in confidentiality and code. Individual board members and whole boards have rarely been held publicly accountable for company, let alone their own, performance. Board relations had been a place where almost all stakeholders, with the exception of the odd eccentric shareholder, had more or less accepted the idea of board members being, sometimes regrettably, beyond scrutiny. Walter had been part of this unchallenged governance template.

The question that is foremost in this case is what propelled Walter to move from being an able and well-respected NED, but one with no history of rocking the boat, to one who took this courageous and most personally difficult stand. She would undoubtedly argue that it was the importance of the issues at stake. While that is part of what is going on here, it doesn't complete the explanation. Other board members maintained their solidarity, and to varying extents seem to have been happy to have Walter scapegoated rather than publicly take responsibility. In the annals of corporate governance, such stands are very rare. If boards are replaced, typically this occurs through some combination of intense shareholder scrutiny, regulatory or governmental intervention.

Once Walter had satisfied her lawyer's mind that this was serious wrongdoing, she was relentless and fearless in her pursuit. While she arguably may have made tactical errors during the campaign to force the board to accept its responsibilities, she practised what could be characterised as sustained and successful subversion of compromised leadership. In so doing, she practised leadership herself.

The fact that Walter was the lone woman on the board was not irrelevant, a subject explored in the next chapter. She had never enjoyed quite the same cosy glow of inclusion that led her male peers to stand 'shoulder to shoulder' when adversity struck and, in this sense, she had less to lose. My sense is that an inner integrity and confidence, which did not rest on group acceptance and belonging but which was nurtured in childhood and within her family, enabled her to put aside a dutiful or loyal performance and instead embark on a leadership one.

Walter's leadership has subsequently been widely recognised in the Australian community and in sectors of the business community. In standing up to board colleagues in the interests of governance, she is seen to have made a landmark contribution to the way boards operate in future. She did this without the NAB imploding (as many predicted), but in a way that has contributed (along with the new CEO, John Stewart, and the NAB management team) to a rethinking and restrengthening of the 'brand'. Contrary to predictions of her corporate demise, Walter remains a director on a range of listed and not-for-profit boards and government 'think tanks'. Since 2004 she has taken on new board commitments including the chairmanship of a superannuation fund and is sought after as a mentor and commentator on governance and the role of directors.

This story provides insights into the pressures on senior people to conform, rather than to show leadership. It also shows why taking a leadership path is risky and requires courage. I have argued in this chapter that to do this diffi- cult leadership work requires some self-knowledge and an understanding of how even—or perhaps particularly—senior people can find their leadership undermined by appetites and vulnerabilities stemming from their personal history. By making more conscious our understanding of personal background, how we connect with others in groups and operate as leaders, we avoid acting out inappropriate impulses in leadership roles. Attending to early patterns can help to explain cases of both leadership failure and those where leadership liberates.

5
Working with power

∞

leadership became a fetish . . .
power was left out of the story

Loren Baritz (1960), on the history of management thinking

relations of power are not something bad in themselves, from which one
must free one's self . . . The problem is not of trying to dissolve them in the
utopia of perfectly transparent communication, but to give one's self the rules
of law, the techniques of management, and also the ethics, the ethos, the
practice of the self, which would allow these games of power to be played
with a minimum of domination.

Michel Foucault in Bernauer and Rasmussen (1988)

In most business analyses of leadership, power is barely discussed. Why has power been left out of the story of leadership? How might new ways of thinking about, and working with, power open the way for more liberating leadership?

One reason for the neglect of power is that it has been seen as a distasteful, corrupting influence in leadership. Leaders are often simply assumed to have enough legitimate power or authority to do what they need to do. Conversely, power-hungry leaders are usually dismissed as the few rotten apples in the otherwise unblemished crate.

The question of how one finds enough power to act and do leadership differently seems to me to be at the core of leadership. Most leaders find that the formal authority that may come with a role cannot be relied upon.

Additional sources of power and influence must be drawn upon, including personal charisma and strengths in communication, networks or contacts, professional credibility, and so on.

When I talk with senior people, they often admit they feel powerless to act, or lead, differently without unreasonable risk to their professional status. Leaders, paradoxically perhaps, often feel powerless. On the face of it, they may have access to all sorts of sources of power. At a deeper level, many admit to feeling quite powerless to direct important matters in their lives, or to spend enough time on things that matter most to them and their organisation. This chapter introduces ideas about power that help to explain such paradoxes: of being in a position of authority, yet feeling unable to empower oneself and others to act differently.

By neglecting power, scholars of leadership ignore a rich source of understanding of what the drive to leadership is all about, how it can also go wrong, and how to lead with a different consciousness of power. Any leader's power is a product of broader social and political relations—constantly under construction, being reinforced or undermined even as that person remains in an official leadership role. A sense of powerfulness is produced in relationships. It is rarely reliably permanent or able to be completely controlled by an individual. Such contradictory and shifting experiences of powerfulness and powerlessness can only be explained with a more sophisticated understanding of power than current leadership accounts offer. Opening our eyes to these more complex understandings of power has the capacity to free leaders towards new possibilities of positioning themselves.

While I could follow the textbook template and begin by defining power, then providing an overview of theories of power, I would rather start differently, with an account of my own relationship to power and some experiences that have changed the way I think about power in leadership. I then draw on research and theories about power to show how thinking differently about power and change can support a more liberating kind of leadership work.

THREE PERSONAL EXPERIENCES WITH POWER

Powerlessness

In my work with students and people in organisations, I have often come across the problem of perceived 'disempowerment'—of people who feel they are not listened to and are unable to act to change conditions in their workplaces. When I start talking about leadership and how individuals might act differently, they say they feel paralysed or impotent to change an implacable system. This sense of powerless passivity is also evident in many cases of ethical failure, where people in organisations can see bad things happening but feel unable to act or blow the whistle. When things get really bad, the most common response is 'exit'[1]—an action which often ensures that nothing changes.

Feeling disempowered is how I would characterise much of my own early career, particularly my experience as a junior female faculty member trying to teach and research differently in the business school of an eminent university.[2] I routinely felt marginalised and sidelined, if not occasionally ridiculed and threatened. This was not necessarily at the hand of individuals, but by the whole institutional edifice which seemed perpetually disconcerted by everything about me—from the ideas that emerged from my brain to the way my body approached pedagogy. That interface included the university and the business school, its staff and students, and the stakeholders and constituencies which supported these bastions of the establishment. In such situations, one rapidly learns that silence and compliance to norms and traditions is a safer, if more deadening, place to be.

I could well have continued in a condition of feeling perpetually marginalised. Among the things that prompted me to start thinking differently about my own situation was my research, particularly tapping into feminist research and reacquainting myself with political and social theory. What this research showed was that marginalisation and domination arise not so much through individual personal relations, but through often-invisible processes inherent in structural conditions. The research helped me to see that what I was experiencing was not just a matter of my own failure or tardiness in learning how to play the academic game; there was more going on here.

Further, I began to see that one of the ways in which the status quo of power relations is preserved is the treating of these experiences as an individual matter, and encouraging the individual to accept the responsibility for adjusting themselves to 'fit' or get out. A common example of these processes at work is when women leaving senior roles in organisations cite 'personal reasons' or 'work–life balance' and wanting more family time. If the same women name difficult or discriminatory working conditions as part of the reason they are leaving, they fear that they will be branded as 'whingers', not 'team players' and will have difficulty finding other jobs. Though there may be some elements of truth in their volunteered reasons for leaving, because the cultural conditions surrounding their exit remain undiscussed, keeping the discourse focused on individuals ensures that nothing changes.

In short, I began to theorise my experience. As I started to do this and talk about these insights, I could see that this was valuable for others. Even the naming of experiences became a powerful act. It sounds simple, but there was nothing easy about this. I felt, in a very direct way, a tension that continues to ricochet around my career and life—that is, simultaneously seeing and acting on the possibilities of my own power and recognising the profound and deep structural obstacles that constrain me and bring me back into line. We almost always have some power to act, but we are always also imprisoned: the two experiences coexist. Part of working with power is to be able to identify and name these tensions.

Finding power

The second episode came quite a bit later, when I was more established in my career, having worked up the academic ladder and established some small reputation in the area of gender and diversity. A group of academic colleagues were in a forum discussing the difficulties of environments where there are deeply gendered (and masculinised) assumptions about how the work is to be done. I was intent on revealing these to a mixed gender audience, some of whom seemed sceptical that women teachers faced particular obstacles. I related my experience of teaching a class of male managers, and I also replicated in this forum the act of removing my suit jacket. I described and re-enacted my shock at realising that the act of jacket removal was interpreted differently when a woman teacher did it. A man removing his jacket may be seen as, for example 'getting down to business' and may have his credibility enhanced. In my case jacket removal seemed to detract from and dramatically reduce my credibility. A friend and organisational scholar with a particular interest in power, David Knights, was in the audience. He said something simple to me like 'But you have power, you've just shown that'. This comment may not sound significant, and it didn't have an immediate effect. But I began to see that being preoccupied with my own marginalisation had prevented me from 'seeing' the possibilities of my own power and how I could, and do, work with it.

Again I went back to theory and this time, drawing on David's work among that of others, I began to understand the nature of power in new ways. Specifically, I began to see—following the work of Foucault—that power could be much more usefully understood as constantly being constructed and reinforced through discourse and discursive relations (themselves to some extent a product of structural relations). In *Discipline and Punish*, Foucault began to elaborate a view of power that upended previous ideas. Instead of power necessarily being negative, coercive (even violent), or simply imposed, it can incite, seduce or enlarge. Instead of looking at power as a one-sided imposition of the boss or the guard on the subordinate or prisoner, we might look at power from the other perspective. Namely, power can be exercised in all sorts of more tacit ways such as in resistance or non-cooperation by those with less formal power.[3]

Over the next few years, I became more and more interested in the topography of power, resistance and subversion. With reading and research, I started to see that institutional power wasn't a monolith, and that I wasn't powerless. I may not have had access to the intricate networks of male or insider power that many of my colleagues seemed to invoke so readily, but I had other things— I could be different in the way that I did my job. In resistance and subversion, I often exercised power. Further, this very resistance clearly came across to some people as acts of leadership. Declaring that I couldn't attend an 8 a.m. meeting because of child-care responsibilities stopped being an instance of me feeling oppressed by structural assumptions and started to be a way of exercising power and acting to change things.

At the same time, I continued to have experiences where I drastically miscalculated the depth and force of the structural power ranged against me and my attempts to do things differently. I slipped from believing that I had no power to being seduced by the myth of agency—that by sheer force of will or intention, I could override structural power. Foucault is again helpful here when he makes it clear that:

> Power is not something that is acquired, seized, or shared, something that one holds on to or allows to slip away; power is exercised from innumerable points, in the interplay of non-egalitarian and mobile relations.[4]

These situations induce a healthy respect for institutional power and the many ways that individuals are coerced and disciplined into silence and obedience. Yet the learning for me was not to wallow in powerlessness, but rather to work with the tension built into these more complex understandings of power: to not expect unfettered agency and to resist illusions of grandiosity while also seeing that one can be powerful towards meaningful and liberating ends, often in surprising ways.

Owning power

In a more recent example, I had a further opportunity to think about how women, including myself, position themselves around power.[5] I was attending a conference and the female keynote speaker provided a fascinating account of the first women professors in Europe, showing that they needed to become 'outsiders' in order to be recognised and employed by universities. In the nineteenth and early twentieth centuries, women were frequently banned from university positions, or there were prejudices about women's research which meant that only by taking their work to the universities of other countries were they able to get less-biased recognition. The speaker described neglected details of these women's families, relationships and private lives, emphasising that they were 'ordinary' women who had been subject to a process of legend-building with which they themselves were uncomfortable.

For members of the female-dominated audience, these historical accounts were resonant: coping with institutional discrimination and struggling to gain recognition; juggling one's own sense of identity as an 'ordinary' woman, with a family and partner, alongside a reputation as an outstanding pioneer in one's field.

The presentation themes also had connections to the keynote speaker's own biography and reputation. Regarded as an original and prolific researcher, she had also moved around in order to gain appropriate recognition. In question time, several audience members picked up on these connections between the speaker's research and her own experience. One asked how she felt about being made into a legend. The speaker didn't seem to hear the question. The question remained unanswered, at least by the speaker, in the following discussion. Over lunch, I was sitting with a group of young women academics who knew my work and they asked: 'Amanda, how do you feel about being the subject of some legend building?' I admitted that I didn't know how to respond to the question. I didn't know whether to try to define 'legend' or simply dispute the implication that I have acquired some power due to having a reputation of sorts. My response was awkward and felt not at all helpful to the women with whom I was sitting.

My observations and discomfort got me thinking about power and ordinariness, and how I sit in and with power. It feels odd being allocated the power of being a 'legend' when one doesn't feel particularly influential or powerful. Women often don't feel themselves to be powerful, and that is not just a matter of individual perception—it is a systemic property. Over generations and across cultures, political and social systems have been constructed that ensure women don't get access to power. Feelings of powerlessness are historically substantiated and objectively real for women of most races and nationalities.

In a further exchange over lunch, another woman said to me something like: 'Well it's all right for you to say those things about the need for change.' She meant that I do have institutional power because of my seniority, which does allow me to 'say things' that people with more tenuous positions would not. Similarly, when I talk about these ideas and what I do, people will often say to me: 'That's all right for you. I couldn't do that in my institution.' It would be inappropriate for me to deny the relative power that I have—as an English-speaking, white woman living in a relatively democratic society—and the freedom that comes from that. I also have power due to my education, socioeconomic status and professional position. Part of working with power, it seems to me, is owning up to the power that accrues to those in dominant groups.[6]

Sometimes it is hard for those who have felt oppressed in many contexts, such as women, to also recognise their relative power. In my own case, I have been assisted by Aboriginal leaders, particularly Lillian Holt, the former Director of the Centre of Indigenous Education at Melbourne University, who is featured in Chapter 9 of this book. In a collaborative research project with Lillian, I started out thinking we were researching Aboriginal leadership. It gradually became clear to me that the first topic I needed to understand, before professing to investigate Aboriginality, was my own whiteness, with the relative racial invisibility, and therefore power, that this afforded me.[7]

Drawing on these experiences, I hope to show that stepping back from one's own situation, to theorise about rather than just react to power relations, offers new possibilities for thinking and positioning oneself. While I am not saying that one can ever stand outside of the power relations or structures in which we exist, I am arguing that making these more visible is an empowering thing to do—for oneself and others. In my case, it has enabled me to be more mindful about the power I have, and the subtle ways I can challenge norms and exercise power toward ends I believe are valuable. Instead of feeling caught like a pawn in a game with fixed rules, by exposing myself to different ideas and theories of power, I have been able to see new and different possibilities in how I do the work I want to do. It has also helped me confront the relative power I have and how I exercise this around others. People in positions of leadership are better equipped to maintain their integrity if they are aware of their position in, and maintenance of, the webs of power around their role, rather than in denial about it.

UNDERSTANDINGS OF POWER

Views of power in the social sciences and in leadership reflect changing paradigms or dominant understandings about the way the world works. The discussion here indicates how these shifting ideas about power have been taken up in managerial and leadership accounts.[8]

Among early organisational theorists, Max Weber offered an analysis of power that acknowledged the less rational dynamics that often underpin relations between leaders and followers. He identified charismatic power as something neither rationally based nor attached to a formal role. Meanwhile, in much of the business literature, power was regarded as something to be eradicated from rational management. By the late 1970s and 1980s, power was recognised as inevitable in organisational life, with articles like Kotter and Schlesinger's in the *Harvard Business Review* treating power as a managerial 'contingency'.[9] Leaders needed to calculate how much power they had and how much they needed to execute change, then adapt their strategies accordingly. A flurry of managerial advice followed, advising managers how to 'use' different approaches to power in various circumstances to minimise resistance. This contingency view, which converted power into a tool for leaders to enhance their control, was—not surprisingly—enormously appealing.

In other parts of the social sciences, more robust theories of power were emerging. In 1974 Stephen Lukes published *Power: A Radical View*, arguing that power was produced in structural relationships, often invisibly and without the conscious initiation or compliance of power-holder or subordinate. In this 'radical structural' view, the exercise of power could occur without a perpetrator, victim or overt evidence of conflict. Power was exposed as a deeply structural property that predetermines how people see the world, without them necessarily being aware of it. Power became something that was recognised as present in the most apparently benign situations. For example, someone sitting down watching television at the end of the working day is subject to a web of power perpetrated and populated by agents including media organisations, advertisers and regulatory bodies. All of these exercise power over the TV viewer, creating an appetite to be entertained or distracted in certain ways, programming the sorts of images and information available, and so on.

The application of Lukes's insights across the social sciences eventually led to a great deal more interest in the subtle, systemic but also context-specific ways that power relations are sustained. More oppressive power relations are those where surveillance is internalised: here it is the individual and informal group that disciplines through their own norms. Research confirms that individuals police themselves and their peers more vigorously than a manager with a stopwatch can ever hope to (Chapter 8 on identity contains examples).

Subsequently, Foucault's ideas about power described earlier in this chapter have become very influential. In particular, the work of David Knights, Hugh Willmott, Cynthia Hardy and others in the field of organisation studies has weaned us from a simplistic model where power is held totally by the powerful and exercised over the powerless in visible situations to induce compliance and conformity. Power is present in almost all situations, and it does not necessarily feel negative or coercive. For example, many organisational 'culture change' initiatives, aimed at creating a 'family' atmosphere or making people keen to come to work, are experienced as positive, even though at a tacit level power is exercised to ensure everyone behaves like a 'team player'.[10] Even in highly disciplined situations, power can be exercised by people at the bottom of hierarchies through acts of resistance, humour and subtle sabotage, as well as on the picket line.[11] Further though, even practices of resistance are circumscribed by power relations. For example, the ways women resist are likely to be different to those of men; the possibilities for a child-care worker employed by a wealthy Saudi family would be very different to those for men on an assembly line.

A key issue debated in theorising about power concerns the degree to which power is predetermined by structural relations or available to individuals to assert their agency with personal action. This is known as the 'structure versus agency' debate, elaborated most powerfully by social theorist Anthony Giddens (1991). Contemporary economic ideology informs this debate. For example, free-market liberalism has disdained arguments that social structures or historical disadvantage render people powerless. Instead, policies are based on the assumption of individual power and the 'self-made' narrative, where people can pull themselves up out of disadvantage through their own initiative ('by their own bootstraps').

The neglect of power in contemporary discussions of leadership is no accident. I argued in Chapter 2 that the way leadership has been constructed as a set of ideas and practices serves the purpose of elevating leadership to a necessary and often noble activity. In this view, power in leadership has often been ignored, or simplified as an overlapping category with leadership alongside authority and influence. Yet the theories summarised above can inform a better understanding of leadership and guide leaders who have an intention to liberate. The theoretical ideas alert us to the more subtle and tacit ways power can oppress in practice, and encourage us to develop a more nuanced understanding of our own power—as in my example of 'owning power' described above. These theories also help explain how a leader's power is constructed: never complete, always being negotiated, and with the possibility of leaders occupying different positions around power, such as resistance. It is to these ideas that I now turn.

NEW WAYS TO LEAD WITH POWER

Because, historically, we have often assumed that leadership and power overlap, leaders have been assumed to have little interest in resistance. Power and resistance have been constructed as a mutually exclusive dichotomy in which leaders are on the side of power, not resistance. Yet, as I have indicated, more recent work on power suggests a much more complex picture.

In this section, I draw on some research that has informed my thinking about how power may be exercised in resistance, interruption and subversion. I suggest that, rather than these activities being the antithesis of leadership, they might instead be considered as constituting new forms of leadership.[12]

In rethinking the relationship of power and leadership, the work of women scholars has been prominent in offering a critique and reconceptualisation of leadership. Researchers such as Judi Marshall, Patricia Yancey Martin, Judith Pringle, Jill Blackmore and others show that women are constrained by contexts in which leadership is defined as a male performance: assertive, decisive and action-orientated. Accordingly, in the leadership literature there are often gendered assumptions about what power is, how it should be employed by leaders and to what ends. Blackmore, for example, argues that leadership and the power that accompanies it should be redefined as the ability to act with others and to support them to do things.[13] Traditionally such behaviour, when accomplished by women, is not recognised as valuable leadership work.

The work of Deborah Meyerson, Maureen Scully, Joanne Martin, Joyce Fletcher and colleagues has been aimed at revealing that much valuable leadership and change work in organisations done by women leaders is routinely undervalued.[14] Joyce Fletcher uses the verb 'to disappear' to convey the active way in which organisations de-legitimise the relational work of leading, such as talking and consulting.[15] She has been particularly interested in such emotional or 'relational' leadership, which gives emphasis to mutually empowering work, to creating conditions that allow groups to flourish, and to promoting learning and innovation through connection as well as individually autonomous action.

Working with power

Deborah Meyerson has developed the concept of 'tempered radicals' to chart and affirm the neglected practices of leaders who are intent on working towards the success of their organisations while also being true to themselves and their values. Many of these radicals are already marked as 'different' by their organisations—for example, in being a woman in an otherwise male-dominated senior management group, or an African-American in an otherwise predominantly white environment. Meyerson shows how people who might otherwise be in a marginalised position nevertheless work as leaders to influence and foster change. Among the strategies identified are 'quiet resistance', 'leveraging small wins', organising collective action, and broadening impact through negotiation. Meyerson's finding is that stating one's views clearly and in forums where they might not otherwise be heard is a powerful thing to do, even if there seems to be no overt 'action'.

In deciding how we want to lead, another powerful action is to leave an organisational situation and clearly state why to the hierarchy. Sometimes workplaces become intolerably toxic.[16] Leadership in this situation might be a considered decision to remove oneself from associating and perhaps colluding with a damaging work culture. The act of exiting is not necessarily a refusal to take power; conversely, it may have powerful impacts. When explicit and visible, it can provoke scrutiny from shareholders or the media; it can change the leadership team dynamics; and it may indeed open the way to other configurations of relations.

In *Doing Leadership Differently*, I argue that one route to subversion is to challenge prevalent organisational norms that allow—indeed applaud—a strong sexual identity among male leaders, while bringing intense pressure on women to camouflage their sexual identity as women. Sexual identity here means, in the broadest sense, one's identity as a woman. I use the term in preference to 'femininity', because the latter is often a pejorative term in business.

Decisions about how one 'does' gender and sexual identity in leadership have the potential to become powerful acts. Staying in a position of camouflage of sexual identity—such as wearing androgynous clothing, never mentioning one's children or colluding with a dominant view denying the impact of gender in a workplace—has an effect by accepting the status quo of leadership. An act of leadership is to challenge assumptions by saying, for example: 'Yes, my gender is relevant to my leadership. My gender is relevant to how I do my job. It is relevant to my values, my style and my identity as a leader.' Other ways women can and do position themselves as women include lobbying for training standards or professional development which do not require intensive residential periods, as these assume a support person at home for children.

There are many ways in which gender identity can be brought powerfully into one's leadership, and these are not just available to women. For example, both genders can name workplace norms that require men and women to conform to a stereotyped view of toughness or single-minded commitment to the organisation. As I have described elsewhere, men in the Australian context often experience pressure to feign an interest in sport, or to conceal doubts about corporate directions and expectations that have intolerable consequences for personal lives, such as relentless demands for travel. Being prepared to raise such concerns carefully and selectively can be, I argue, powerful things for any leader, male or female, to do. Such concerns are usually shared by at least some others and, by creating a space for them to be recognised and discussed, this leadership act gives permission and encouragement to others to work for change also.

Building on the work of Meyerson and Scully, and of Bradshaw and Wicks,[17] I have developed a framework that introduces a different way of thinking about power and options for action, specifically for women doing leadership work. The framework aims to recognise that leaders can undertake powerful acts beyond the usual understanding of directing from the top.

The framework has two dimensions: the 'voicing' or articulating of concerns; and whether one works for change from inside or outside the organisation. The 'voice' dimension is derived from the work of Albert Hirschman and his book *Exit, Voice and Loyalty*, first published in 1970. He conceptualised 'exit, voice and loyalty' as the three options available to employees in organisations. Voice is the verbal expression of concern to someone in a position of influence or authority. One version of voice is complaining or whistleblowing—staying within the organisation but using various channels and mechanisms to register protest and argue for change. 'High voice' includes activities like formal complaints, taking matters high up the hierarchy or going to the media. 'Low voice' includes more discrete, tempered actions, like ensuring important matters appear on agendas or are given explicit consideration in meetings. 'Exit' is quiet departure, and loyalty is conformity to organisational norms. I represent this framework in Figure 5.1, showing how each of the four positions provide options for leaders to exercise power in potentially liberating and transformative ways.

Figure 5.1: A framework of options for working towards change in leadership

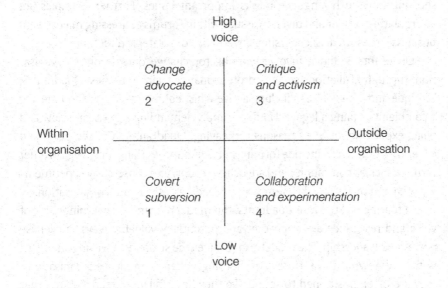

Quadrant 1 is 'covert subversion' and includes lower-level protest strategies, such as not conforming to dress or discussion codes, undermining public/ private dichotomies by, for example, bringing children to work or breastfeeding at work, challenging jokes and complaining about other discriminatory conventions. It involves resolving in one's own day-to-day work not to stay silent or allow instances of discriminatory communication to pass unnoticed.[18] It includes actions that are integrated into one's personal practice in what Meyerson and Scully characterise as 'spontaneous, sometimes unremarkable expressions of authenticity that implicitly drive or even constitute change'.[19] Other examples are resisting pressure to work extended hours continually or to forego maternity leave. Quadrant 1 activities also include what Collinson describes as 'resistance by persistence', where employees 'demand greater involvement in the organisation and render management more accountable by extracting information, monitoring practices and challenging decision-making processes'.[20]

Quadrant 2, 'change advocate', involves high voice strategies—the use of one's formal authority and informal influence to name oppressive practices and lobby for change. Volunteering for high-profile roles and using those roles to voice the need for gender-inclusiveness are examples, as are writing papers or submissions, calling meetings and forming networks to focus attention on the need for change. Meyerson and Scully's tools of 'tempered radicalism' include discursive courage, deconstructing the customary language of 'insiders' and showing how such language masks important issues. Further examples are interpolating gender and diversity issues within forums addressing mainstream business issues such as leadership, governance or strategic direction.

Quadrants 3 and 4 involve working for change outside one's organisation, through affiliations such as professional or training bodies. Quadrant 3, 'Critique and activism', can include active whistleblowing—leaving and making a complaint or filing a legal action—or simply demanding an exit interview and being explicit about one's reasons for leaving. Quadrant 4, 'Collaboration and experimentation', can include forming networks and working for change in other forums, such as community and advocacy groups, and consciously experimenting with and modelling different ways of leading outside one's organisation.

In teasing out the four quadrants, the model recognises that minor acts of voice and resistance are important and potentially valuable ways to exercise power and leadership. The model also revalues the strategy of leaving an organisation by viewing it as a strategy of choosing. When people leave organisations, they are often positioned to sound like they have failed. Research shows that the large number of women 'leaving' is actually a large number initiating new roles and careers—which have radical outcomes on the women, their families and other women who witness this choice.

Psychoanalytically informed research on power argues further that leadership may not just require resistance, but also at times demand betrayal. Organisational scholar James Krantz argues that, in cases such as Worldcom and Parmalat where corporations have become corrupted by hubris, senior executives may be required to make decisions and act in ways 'that breach existing social, psychological and intrapsychic configurations—transgressions often experienced as betrayal'.[21] Krantz makes clear that he is not concerned here with betrayal for personal aggrandisement or for wicked ends; rather, he advances the idea of 'virtuous betrayal', which is leadership that says the unsayable in the service of a higher purpose. This purpose may even be the survival of the organisation. While such an act is never popular, it is sometimes the task of leadership to destabilise 'both the status quo and whatever emotional equilibrium has developed around it'.[22]

Power is always present in leadership work and it can operate in oppressive or more freeing ways. Leaders have available ways of working with power which may either support the status quo and its possibilities of coercion, or seek to reduce oppression.

However, 'empowering' others, or even empowering oneself in this leadership work, is rarely simple and straightforward.[23] The first requirement is to cultivate a deeper understanding of how power plays out in groups, organisations and society. Leaders need to recognise and own the power they do have because of structurally determined power relations. Many of us have privilege—for example, I have the privilege of whiteness in a predominantly white society and the privilege of working in my native language. I have had access to education and relative economic security. These structural endowments have equipped me with the capacity to be articulate and assertive. In working with power, it is important not to assume that the power which flows from privilege is available to everyone. Few enjoy the benefit of being treated on the basis of ability or merit alone.

Leaders also need to explore their own feelings of powerlessness and what stops them being courageous. In my work, I am often asked—and sometimes expected to demonstrate—the ways that women will do leadership differently and more humanely. My experience is that any practice of leading differently needs to be prefaced with a structural and more nuanced understanding of power. We are not helping any leaders—men or women—by expecting that doing leadership differently is simply a matter of choosing to act and exercise power differently. People's power to act, even as leaders, is always constrained by forces that are visible to them and those that are hidden, structured into circumstances of birth, race, class—or those that are banished from consciousness. Developing a deeper understanding of power—its structural and personal determinants—is crucial to leaders. It is not until we 'see' the power relations around us and including us that we are, even temporarily, released to work more empathically with others, imagining better ways to lead and live together.

Liberating leadership requires acting differently with power. It does not mean pretending that power doesn't exist. Rather, this chapter has explored ways of leaders working with power in more freeing ways. To summarise, such ways may be consciously aimed at de-disrupting and reorienting the status quo rather than lining up behind it. They may include more attention to the emotional and relational work of leadership; finding ways to challenge oppressive conditions by naming and resistance; acts of transgression, subversion and conversion; as well as noisy exits or exercising different kinds of leadership outside work organisations to support change.

Such ways of leading differently with power often involve identity work, an idea I explore further in Chapter 8. Leaders may be required to relinquish some certainty or some deeply held ways of understanding themselves and their roles. New ways of empowering others may, perhaps surprisingly, include doing leadership in new and different physical ways. It is to this—the body work of leadership—to which I turn in the next chapter.

6
Bringing bodies into leadership[1]

&

What might we sense and know if we listen to the body? . . .
We may sense knowledges of experiences long forgotten by the mind
but always known by the body . . .
And we may sense present experience and bodily knowledge
that refuses and surpasses language.

Catherine Casey (2000)

How might paying attention to bodies tell us new things about leading? In this chapter, I explore bodies—why they have been ignored in leadership thinking and how body work might be part of delivering more freeing, enlivening kinds of leadership.

Bodies and body performances are a central part of leadership, yet they are rarely given much attention. This taboo is not accidental. Theories of leadership have often sought to elevate leaders above the physical frailty of bodies. This chapter turns the focus onto physical bodies, their attributes and the movements they make, including stature, voice, gestures and physical characteristics designating gender or suggesting ethnic origin. I say 'physical' though bodies are not objective facts. For example, it is hard to view or imagine a body without first designating its gender. Bodies and bodily performances are never experienced or appraised as pure physiology.

In this chapter, I draw on profiles[2] of two Australian leaders who have paid attention to bodies—their own and those of others—with initiatives that have stimulated change and openness in moribund organisational contexts. They are

Chris Sarra, an Indigenous Australian who, as a school principal, has led practice and ideas in Indigenous education, and Christine Nixon, a woman who has also challenged ideas of leadership as Chief Commissioner of Police for the Australian state of Victoria.

THE IMPORTANCE OF BODIES

An example:

> Forums of political leaders held in parts of Asia and Oceania are often commemorated with 'class photos' of leaders in floral shared shirts. At the start of a recent meeting of Pacific Island leaders, Australian Prime Minister John Howard appeared in a casual polo shirt and jacket. There was no problem until he realised that other leaders were dressed in suits. After consultation with the forum Secretary-General, Mr Howard disappeared for fifty minutes or so. He then 'reappeared resplendent in a dark suit, white shirt and yellow-striped navy tie'.[3]

As the above example illustrates, bodies are not irrelevant in the construction of leadership's influence and effectiveness. The 'before' (polo shirt) and 'after' (suit) photos of the Australian prime minister accompanying this news story reveal a shift from a tentative persona to a striding and commanding presence, a shift captured in both the image projected in the media and the leader's own sense of power and importance.

Leaders and leadership gurus often pay great attention to the physical selves they project: their voices, what they are wearing, their gestures, and their command and use of the physical space available to them. When an esteemed leadership professor appeared for the first time before an audience of which I was part, he wore a suit over a black T-shirt. There was potent symbolism in this, and in the fact that he sat on the front desk cradling one knee with his arms. These physical manifestations conveyed, for example, that he did not wish to comply with business conventions of respectability, but that he was aiming for something looser and more intimate.

The accomplishment of leadership is often dramatic, and choreographed in an aesthetic sense. Peter Gronn's[4] research (discussed in Chapter 1), on Mussolini, Hitler and Stalin, shows how carefully body performance has been woven into the leadership mystique—from controlling the physical distance[5] from which leaders may be viewed to the use of make-up and photographs to accomplish a sufficiently awe-inspiring effect. The bodies of followers, audiences and organisations are also central, but rarely acknowledged in the accomplishment of leadership. Power relations are signified in the ways bodies are presented as well as in the ways they relate spatially to one another. Examples are found in the intricate physical rituals and norms of institutional settings: size of desk and office, accessibility or remoteness of managers, clothing, gestures and other features that indicate levels of power and the deference that each level demands.

Think of the scenes of many annual general meetings. The board sits on a stage elevated in a ballroom and magnified in a giant screen above—props designed to enlarge leaders to godlike proportions. Yet they are suited, faceless and (usually with the exception of the chair) speechless. In contrast are the shareholders, struggling up to the microphone, gamely and vainly seeking to have their grievances heard against an imperious gladiatorial gang. An implacable hierarchy of power is established in physical and bodily terms, even if thumbs don't literally go down.

Drawing on my own and other research, I have discussed elsewhere the ways in which leadership is also a performance and accomplishment of masculinity.[6] Strongly masculine performances are required for many leadership roles,[7] particularly in certain industries such as consulting and stockbroking. These may extend to sometimes sexually charged activities, such as the 'beauty pageant' in management consulting where hopeful recruits are tacitly graded on their bodies and physical confidence as well as on their case analyses: 'looking good' becomes synonymous with 'being good', and attractiveness is part of leadership potential.

There are also physically determined badges of status like the capacity to work 'all-nighters' or to work continuously around the clock for several days in order to deliver an important project. In her fascinating study of financial traders in the City of London, McDowell finds that a 'performance of youthful virility' comes to be naturalised and expected, charged with 'high testosterone' and evidenced by states of *déshabillé*.[8] In the National Australia Bank example described earlier where traders incurred a huge debt, the macho, 'do or dare' and 'work hard, play hard' culture was blamed for the scandal that was to elicit the resignation of the CEO and the board (see Chapter 4). Traders could never own up to mistakes or seek help, yet routinely operated far outside bank guidelines of loan limits.

WHY LEADERS HAVE BEEN SEEN AS BODILESS

Leaders and those who study them often seek to perpetuate the idea that leaders are special—if not immortal, then at least more in control and less marred by human frailty than the rest of us. Leaders' bodies become motifs for the mystique of flawless command. Leaders work inhuman hours, defy body rhythms, cross time zones and still turn up for a fourteen-hour day, thereby establishing their credentials for leadership. An English politician who gloated about his own diet and marathon performance asserted that a capacity to master your own body was evidence of a capacity to take charge of others.

By leaving the body out of accounts of leadership, we are encouraged to believe that leaders are without bodies and without the ailments that afflict lesser beings. At the most senior levels of organisations, leaders usually escape scrutiny as bodies. If male, powerful and senior, they are likely to be portrayed as bodiless—and it is important we notice this, understand why and see what effects this representation has.

At the same time, this impression of physical mastery is fragile. Executives admit they are driven to extraordinary lengths to maintain the illusion of impregnability (the antithesis of the feminine condition of pregnability). Leaders who are perceived as physically weak are suspect in leadership terms, and a great deal of 'spin' is often undertaken to overcome the impression of vulnerability. Body management can, then, become an obsession. One director I know confided that a board had been seriously occupied with the question of whether to get an executive's beard shaved off because it conveyed untrustworthiness. This preoccupation with conveying the right leadership image is rarely analysed explicitly in the theorising or teaching of leadership. Instead, it is passed over as 'image management' or spin-doctoring.

THEORISING BODIES

In sociology, cultural studies, philosophy and feminism, bodies have been discussed extensively.[9] Bodies also began to make their way into studies of gender and organisations in the early 1980s, with the work of people like Joan Acker. While most early work was focused on the constraints and discipline exercised on women's bodies in the workplace, studies of masculinities also brought male bodies into the gaze of organisational studies. In recent management literature, research has mapped the ways in which leadership is saturated with bodily performances, showing how dominant ideas about men's bodies limit what is seen as suitable behaviour for managerial men.[10]

However in some research, the more the body has been talked about, the more 'bodiless' it has become. Theorising has taken hold of the body and interrogated it to within an inch of its life, leaving it inert and parched. At the other extreme is the extensive interest in 'body language' and how to 'use' the body to execute a more masterful or influential performance. Such accounts treat the body as an instrument of the mind, an extra resource to harness the ego's efforts to be more attractive or powerful. These accounts are unreflective about the ends to which the body might be put, and usually oblivious to the way structural and societal circumstances determine how bodies are seen and interpreted. They are therefore unaware of the scope for individuals to stand outside of or escape these limitations. So my desire in this chapter is to steer between extremes while providing a serious account of embodying leadership, with its constraints, risks and possibilities.

Bodies are seen, appraised and responded to according to pre-existing cultural norms, institutional practices, and gender and racial regimes. These regimes ensure that we notice and *see* some bodies, while others experience relative invisibility. Thus, in male-dominated environments, women's bodies are noticed and evaluated. Similarly, bodies that are darker or lighter in skin and hair tones, or are clothed in culturally distinctive ways such as the hijab, attract instant and often unconscious interpretation.

The bodies of the two leaders discussed here—Chris Sarra, acclaimed Indigenous school principal and community leader, and Christine Nixon, a woman who is Victoria's highly successful Police Chief Commissioner—are already labelled by race and gender. Of course, the leadership of Sarra and Nixon is much wider than the body work described here.[11] However, I want to show that body practices have been important in the ways each of them has led change. Both have modelled a way of being in their bodies that subverted conventional norms and both have also been pressured by expectations to move back into more standard body spaces.

TWO CASE STUDIES OF LEADERSHIP BODY WORK[12]

Why these two leaders? Both called Chris, they are on the face of it very different. Among the leaders I research, however, they show important things about embodied leadership. I was intrigued by the ways in which gender (in the case of Nixon) and race (in the case of Sarra) seemed to allow a space for a different kind of bodily practice, which then became subject to discipline by the systems (or institutional bodies)[13] in which they were embedded. Both leaders were open, keen to experiment and not caught up by the need to conform.

As 'outsiders', they may have been afforded a little more discretion, although there is no doubt that both came under pressure to adopt more conventional leadership approaches. Despite their visibility, neither was compliant nor captive to the systems of which they were a part. Sarra and Nixon are rich leadership examples because their experiences show how bodies are sites of risk-taking and conformity, subject to discipline and available for experimentation. These two cases also offer general lessons about the issues faced by minority leaders. So, for example, Sarra's challenges are shared by leaders of many Indigenous communities worldwide and the obstacles to Nixon's leadership are replicated internationally for women and not just in policing or paramilitary organisations.

CHRIS SARRA

Chris Sarra[14] was appointed principal of the primary school in the remote Aboriginal town of Cherbourg, three hours' drive northwest of Brisbane, Queensland, in August 1998. Sarra had previously worked as a high school teacher, university lecturer and in a teacher-support role for Education Queensland, the body that administered schools in the state. There were no other applicants for the job of principal.

Cherbourg is a small Aboriginal settlement of less than 3000 people which has considerable social problems and high levels of unemployment. Its primary school was performing badly on almost every measure, including academic performance, rates of attendance and transitions to high school. Sarra, whose mother is Aboriginal, had some ideas about how to run a school in an Aboriginal community and wanted to try them in practice.

Aboriginal education is, in general, in a parlous state in Australia, having educational outcomes comparable with Third World countries. These educational conditions are, in turn, part of a complex picture of institutionalised discrimination against Indigenous Australians, and show up in much higher rates of mortality, disease and unemployment. Statistical surveys also show that the overall rate of Indigenous unemployment, at 26 per cent, is twice that of non-Indigenous populations. While 73 per cent of white teenagers finish Year 12 at school, only 32 per cent of Aboriginal children do, and while 10 per cent of the non-Aboriginal population have university degrees, only 2 per cent of the Aboriginal population graduate from university.[15] Further, recent

Chris Sarra with Indigenous children
Patrick Hamilton/Newspix

surveys show no incremental improvement over time, but rather a worsening on many social indicators.

Any leader seeking to make improvements to these conditions is tackling enormous, endemic issues. Because Aboriginals are only 2.4 per cent of the population, individuals who put themselves forward for leadership are swamped with tasks and requests to join committees and taskforces requiring Indigenous representation. Leaders find themselves quickly burnt out by the combination of high visibility and overburdening. They are not just doing their jobs (and they may be the first Aboriginal to occupy particular positions such as parliamentarian, judge, etc.), they are seen to be, and asked to be, spokespeople, representatives and agents of reform in undoing centuries of history. An additional complexity is that Aboriginals are typically very careful about speaking only for their own 'mob' or 'country' (area of land within Australia), rather than on behalf of all or other Indigenous Australians. White institutional practices that seek a single representative to act for Aboriginal interests are thus routinely making assumptions about leadership which are untenable for many Indigenous people.

Sarra's background

Sarra is the youngest child in a big family from the provincial Queensland city of Bundaberg. His father was of Italian origin and his mother from a local Aboriginal family. Sarra has nine older brothers and sisters, several of whom also went on to university studies and have become leaders in the local and wider communities. He was a talented football player and played in the school team, and with a Bundaberg team as well. 'They were happy to have me because I was good at sport, but no one was saying "You're pretty smart, you could do better",' says Sarra. Football had been an initial passport to success, but Sarra also found himself stereotyped by his physical prowess. He completed school with average results and scraped into university.

It didn't take him long to realise that the stereotyping he had experienced was part of a wider educational issue. Undertaking his Diploma of Teaching, he describes what he discovered:

> It came as a bit of a shock to see just how much I had been sold short by the school . . . and how I had sold myself short as a result of subscribing to other people's limited perceptions of who I was and what I could do . . . from then on I became determined to make other [Aboriginal] children see the realities that surrounded us.

It was this understanding of the oppressive processes by which Aboriginals are stereotyped as bodies without brains (athletes, runners, football players, boxers), and his determination to do something about it, that led to Sarra's PhD on Aboriginal education and identity.

Arriving at Cherbourg School and embodied leadership actions[16]

Sarra's memories of the damage done by his own lack of confidence greeted him at Cherbourg. The situation was embarrassing:

> When it came time for children to participate in the Years 3, 5 and 7 tests for literacy and numeracy, most would jack up and walk out of the room, or not bother to turn up for school in the first place . . . The Year 7 students left for high school like lambs to the slaughter, with no idea about how to conduct themselves in a regular classroom and nowhere near the personal skills, or the literacy or numeracy skills, to survive.

Bringing bodies into leadership

In this example and elsewhere, Sarra's use of physical imagery is powerful. He also has a commanding presence and, in many of the leadership challenges he describes, his physical power and presence are central to what he does. In the role of principal, he says:

> there are a lot of personalities to manage. Sometimes it makes you feel like a football coach. Cruising around the school, making sure everything is on track, keeping morale up. You don't feel like you're doing really hard work, but it's crucial. I'm not on the front line, but I need to be there to back the teachers up in the classrooms. They see me as a leader to turn to when they're frustrated or having trouble with parents. I've had parents say to teachers: 'If you pick on my kid again, I'll come in to school and bash you.' I've said we're not going to put up with that. They need to know I'm there backing them up.

Sarra's strong presence is undercut by a generally gentle voice and informal tone. He talks with frequent colloquialisms—some of them distinctively Aboriginal—and without educational or managerial jargon.

One of Sarra's first problems was literally one of bodies—namely, their absence. Absenteeism was rife at the school, and Sarra set about making the school a place where children would want to come, and stay for the whole day rather than go fishing—which many frequently opted to do. In morning assembly, with the kids sitting around on the floor, Sarra yells 'Good morning' to the kids and they yell back—as if affirming with the loudness of their voices the importance of their presence. He made sure the school was cleaned up, and addressed the vandalism problem so that it became a physically attractive place to be. This stands out in a community where there is widespread neglect of houses and buildings.

In his interaction with the children, Sarra engages in a lot of physical contact and acknowledgment of physical needs. He plays football at recess and worries about the little kids still milling about the school when it's dinner time and starting to get cold. He enacts physical authority: for example, when a student is congratulated at assembly, Sarra lifts them up and holds them across his shoulders; with others, he does a wobbly whole-of-body handshake. In a very different physical performance, he sits outside the classroom on the ground, joking with a group of young girls.

In terms of motivating, Sarra has focused on physical well-being. Meetings in the staffroom occur around food. Instead of penalising absences from school, kids who turned up were rewarded. The class with the lowest number of absences would receive 'iceblocks' or icy poles; then, at the end of the term, if their class had missed five days or less, they would go to McDonald's.

Central to Sarra's approach was the articulation of a new vision for the school: 'Strong and Smart'. 'Strong' bodies are positioned first—alongside and not subordinate to 'smart', in a way that is hard to imagine being articulated in a non-Indigenous school. Yet Sarra has been studiously careful to avoid the stereotyping into physicality that he experienced as a young Aborigine. He has worked hard, for example, to ensure that Cherbourg children, in spite of geographic isolation, are electronically literate. He appeals to the children's intellect, repeating that school will enable them to go on to do what they want in life. The 'Strong and Smart' vision and a jingle invented at Cherbourg are repeated often in public forums.

Sarra's physically visible and literally 'hands-on' style extends to an Indigenous approach to disciplining called 'growling'. It was this style of disciplining that created problems in 2004, when Sarra was the subject of a complaint to Education Queensland. He was accused of grabbing and roughly treating two students at the school. Australian newspapers and several television stations covered the complaint because of Sarra's high profile as 'Queenslander of the Year', an accolade that honours a person from Queensland who has made a significant contribution to public life. Sarra ruminates about dealing with bad student behaviour:

> I guess I had a choice. I could increase the intensity of their reprimand, or I could suspend them for six weeks, and I hate suspending children from school. So I . . . grabbed them by the arm, took them inside the classroom in front of the others. I growled them. What that means is I raised my voice at them. I went off, saying: 'We're not going to tolerate this from you. Other children here are working hard. Why should you be any different?' As I'm saying this, I'm banging my fist on the desk and the wall because I deliberately wanted to create a scene to increase the intensity of it all. If they played up in class and stopped other children from learning, I growled at them . . . or I would go and

see their parents and say: 'Look, your kid's playing up. We're trying to change where we're going with the school, we need your help.'

Sarra says his approach to leadership is firmly rooted in his Aboriginal identity. His values have encouraged a respect for the community and its elders, and a conviction that he couldn't be successful as principal of the school without the support of its community. Indeed, implicit in many of the changes Sarra has made is a very different model of how a school fits within a community. By supporting and involving the community, he has strengthened the school:

> One thing I know for certain is that I will always be an Aboriginal person who is the principal of a school. I will never be a white person. I will always exercise and value Aboriginal approaches to doing things.

At the same time, Sarra has also been careful not to position himself as a Cherbourg community leader because this brings its own expectations and problems:

> I'm from Bundaberg, not Cherbourg, which means something. There's something different about being brought up on the mission [Cherbourg was a church mission for many decades]. And that's something I can never pretend to understand fully.

Learning from Sarra's embodied leadership

After six years under Sarra's leadership, performance at Cherbourg State School improved dramatically. Vandalism at the school diminished to being a rare rather than a regular event. Absenteeism fell below the state average. Academic performance increased and student numbers at the school were rising. Sarra's work was being recognised and rewarded in the wider system. The school was being considered for an expansion plan which would see it being equipped to educate students beyond its current Grade 7 capacity up to Grade 9. In 2004 he won the Queenslander of the Year award, and in 2005 he was asked to become Director of a new Institute of Aboriginal and Torres Strait Islander Leadership, designed to train teachers and leaders throughout Queensland to work with Aboriginal communities for better educational outcomes.

Sarra went out on a limb to express leadership in physical ways appropriate to cultural circumstances, the needs of children at the school and his own Aboriginality. With the 'Strong and Smart' vision and rewarding children with food, his leadership was attentive to and caring for the whole embodied person. This lesson is particularly powerful in a system where the neglect of the physical (in bodies and in physical surroundings) has become normalised, where alcoholism, domestic violence and vandalism are routine. His firm self-identification as Aboriginal allowed him to follow Aboriginal ways of doing things rather than standard expectations of a school principal. Sarra presents as a holistic leadership package: head, heart, body, spirit, family, race, culture.

This embodied style has also created risks for him. It has provided ammunition for critics within the Aboriginal and non-Indigenous communities. Aboriginal communities typically have clearly delineated leadership responsibilities, and individuals who assume responsibility come under scrutiny. Sarra describes it with a quintessentially Queensland metaphor of mudcrabs:

> I guess it would have been naive of me to think that I could win such an accolade like Queenslander of the Year and enjoy such a great honeymoon with the media and everything would be great. It's probably naive of me to think that there wouldn't be someone out there trying to cut me down because in some ways it's part of blackfellas being crabs in the bucket, and [they've] got to pull each other down. There were questions about how I disciplined students and whether or not I was doing the right thing. And it just kind of blew up into a frenzy.

In his role from 2005 as Director of the Institute of Aboriginal and Torres Strait Islander Leadership, Sarra is expected to generalise and extrapolate from his experience—to distil, professionalise and impart knowledge about leadership that may be extracted from identity and context. It might be claimed that these approaches are fine for an Aboriginal school but wouldn't work anywhere else. Some may argue that physicality and body work suit the 'special needs' of Aboriginal education. But body work in leadership can take many forms. To provide a very different example, I now turn to Christine Nixon.

CHRISTINE NIXON

Christine Nixon was appointed Chief Commissioner of Victoria Police in 2001. She was the first female Australian police chief—and indeed there are few internationally. At 48, she was young, and she was an outsider, her career until then having been in the police force of a different state, New South Wales. When she was appointed by a relatively new and reforming Labor state government, she faced many obstacles—both inside the tradition-bound police force and in its heavily unionised workforce, and within political and bureaucratic quarters as well. She took on responsibility for a police force with 12 800 personnel, over 380 police stations and annual expenditure of A$1.2 billion. As evidence of her success, in 2006 she was given the additional responsibility for security during the 2006 Commonwealth Games in Melbourne, and her contract as chief commissioner was renewed for a further five years.

Boundaries and demarcations are very tight in police work: uniforms, titles and traditions usually reinforce a firmly maintained hierarchy. Because the police are an emergency service, there is a propensity for rigid procedures: human lives may be at stake, so discipline has to be

Christine Nixon at the Gay and Lesbian Pride March, 2002
Craig Wood/Newspix

tight with little room for discretion. But these protocols—some explicit, many tacit—have often become sacred cows and produced a high degree of bureaucratisation that is dysfunctional in the changing world of police work. Domestic violence, child protection work and cracking sophisticated drug rings require police forces to be closer to their communities, to build relationships rather than installing themselves behind dark glasses and in police cars. Christine's work with bodies has broken down boundaries such as a sharp separation between the community and police, and between uniformed and non-uniformed police.

How Nixon presents: Informality and opening up

Meeting and watching Christine, she looks firmly grounded, standing squarely and substantial in shape. Though not tall, this sense of solidity and groundedness creates a strong and reassuring presence. She is not intimidating, and has an open, welcoming face, her expression one of friendly interest. Audiences sometimes interpret these bodily features as evidence of softness or indulgence—everyone's favourite aunt. Sceptics—inside and outside of the police—have sometimes doubted that she was 'tough enough' for the job. Christine rarely explicitly counters the stereotype, but people, especially senior people, don't 'get away with much'.

I had met with and done work with preceding police commissioners. Though deemed effective enough, they typically remained behind their vast oak desks, in cavernous wood-panelled offices, on the top floor of tall buildings and behind many security checks. Visiting Christine (she is called that rather than the cumbersome 'Ma'am' by her staff) is easy by comparison. Her relationship with her support staff is collegial. The doors of her office and others surrounding it are open, with many people coming in and out. Because Nixon comes across as informal and relaxed, she puts people at ease. Once when I was waiting to see her, a senior detective was hovering and waiting to show her a ring he had made for his wife for their 30th wedding anniversary. She is disarmingly frank. On her relationship with government she says: 'I don't want to ride around in police cars with pollies [politicians].'

The physical openness created in police headquarters has also been mirrored in an opening up of the force to outsiders. A year into the job, Nixon set about restructuring the senior ranks. Many senior officers who had spent their whole lives in the force were required to apply for their jobs. The selection panel consisted of external people as well as police. Several of those appointed as new members of the management team were outsiders.

In 2004, when Nixon was weathering criticism over police corruption, she arranged for experts from around the world to come and discuss the issues. She also invited journalists, including her most vociferous critics, to spend a day discussing the problems. The approach of opening up to one's critics and giving them as much information as possible was remarkable, not only for itself but because of how different it was to traditional police caution and tightly controlled information.

Being out and about

Once appointed, and among her first actions, Christine set out to talk with and listen to almost anybody in the Victorian community who asked: from high-profile business breakfasts to Country Women's Association afternoon teas in remote towns. Within the police force, she talked individually with the top 60 officers, consulted with 3500 members and targeted the toughest and most difficult local police stations to do 'whiteboard exercises. Tell me what your concerns are.'

This process of intensive consultation looks so sensible as to be obvious, but it was unprecedented in the police context. Remoteness had been written into her predecessors' job description: 'There was actually a rule that said (to the members) you're not allowed to write to the Chief Commissioner.' She introduced an open email policy where any member of the force could email her with comments, complaints or requests and receive a response from her. She receives a large number of emails from all parts of the organisation.

Changing uniforms

Police uniform was an issue that quickly emerged from members' emails as emblematic of the top-down rules that had governed, and disempowered, rank-and-file police. Uniforms had been designed for a more 'uniform' force with few adaptations for diversity, particularly for women or, for example, conditions of pregnancy. Nixon herself has her uniform specially tailored. She tackled the challenge of changing uniforms with the characteristic no-nonsense style that echoed her mother's impatience, setting up a uniform committee with the instruction 'come on, fix this':

> The members had told me 'Why do we have to wear things up on the border where it is 40 degrees [Celsius], why can't we wear jumpers not jackets?' And so all of a sudden the uniform became a symbol of freedom for people. They wanted to wear baseball caps, and not have to wear their hat in the corridors . . . So, it was all of these things, and you could actually go 'Right!' Getting rid of those barriers to the point where they could make choices. They were adults after all.

She wanted the members to be more comfortable—and that meant women as well as men—and she wanted them to have choice. As on a number of other issues, Nixon brushed aside convention, identifying herself firmly with the underdog and not the hierarchy:

> I told the Assistant Commissioner 'You've only got a month, [you] figure it' . . . so he just went and collected a whole lot of good thinking that had been done by a variety of people over 10 or 15 years previously and just kind of said, 'Let's do it'. Got a good team of people together, a mixture, which was what he was told to do . . . Did a road show, went around the state: 'What do you think?' 'Looks good to us.' Put it on the intranet so people could see it and analyse it. Went to the manufacturers, put the tenders in. Get on with it!

Nixon has also experimented with uniform herself, regularly leaving her uniform at home and wearing a dress or suit. With these actions, she was sending a new message about how uniforms were to be used: to reinforce that police are part of the community, not above it. However, she has also come under pressure to uniform up, for example when traditional groups in the community have expressed disappointment because she arrives to speak or visit not in uniform.

Affirming diverse bodies and taking a stand on discrimination

Nixon has come face to face with discrimination on many occasions in her career, and is under no illusions about prejudice. Even with the authority of her current role, she knows 'some people prefer to deal with a six-foot-eight bloke, not small women like me'.

In March 2002, Christine was invited to attend and march with police in the annual St Kilda Gay and Lesbian Pride March. She agreed, wanting to support the gay and lesbian police members who had invited her. It generated a media storm and a flood of rumours, including about Nixon's own sexuality. Looking at footage of Nixon marching along, surrounded by gay police, transsexuals and others in police drag, her actions are remarkably subversive. The decision to march generated considerable criticism from the media and politicians, and Nixon has not done so again—though she has attended the parade.

Nixon has also been working to change the kinds of bodies represented in the Victoria Police. In the past it had been very homogeneous: predominantly males of Caucasian background who matched the narrow physical standards of strength that had historically been deemed necessary for police work. Picking up on a wider state government commitment, Nixon led the recruitment of a diverse force that reflected the community it policed and protected. The result was a flood of new members who included groups never before targeted, such as mature women returning to the workforce or switching careers.

Withstanding the weight of expectations

It is not coincidental that Christine struggles with her own weight—as if to ensure she is solid enough to shoulder the expectations that she will do everything, do it successfully, apparently effortlessly and without help. She was taken aback by these expectations at the first police graduation over which she presided:

> I went to the Academy [for graduation]. It's a bit like an amphitheatre. I get driven on, I was sent a video to see what I was supposed to do. All these people are there, waiting for me. I went, 'Oh my God! All waiting for me.' Most of the time, I was the one doing the work. 'Why doesn't anyone else do anything here besides me, salute, give a speech, talk to them, give awards?' I thought to myself, 'You could fall over here and they'd go, "What do we do?" . . . Gee this is a lot of weight here.' I do feel it in that physical environment. When you have lots of people who want to talk with you, have their photos taken with you. It just builds occasionally, the expectations.

Christine says that marriage, at 38, changed her. In fact, a whole set of factors came together to help her, in her words, 'lighten up'. Two fellowships during the 1980s (to Harvard and London) gave Christine respite from difficult experiences in the New South Wales Police, and they marked the start of seeing what she had to offer on a bigger canvas of leadership:

> I'd been away . . . I didn't have responsibilities. I could just wander around the London Met, none of the 'weight of the world' on me and it was wonderful . . . I just lightened up. I went to shows, concerts and stuff, didn't have to study or do homework. That lovely time of not having to front, be the one who was responsible all the time.

These experiences taught her not only that she didn't have to set such tough standards for herself, but that she could sometimes be a better leader by stepping back and adopting a lighter touch—on herself and others.

However, 2004, when a number of organised crime figures were murdered in Melbourne, was a challenging time for the Victoria Police and for Christine personally. Though she had worked hard to delegate and ensure that, when crisis hit, she wasn't the only one to 'front' the media, in this case she felt she had little choice:

> The personal stuff was really about having to front it myself. These were very critical issues. In a sense I am not the organised-crime person but it was a big organisational issue. My media person said you have to front this, up until that time it hadn't been me . . . as we got closer there was this personal sense of . . . I don't think I ever got afraid but if they were to take me out there would be a whole lot of disorganisation in the police that would occur. For a period of time I carried a gun . . . and would have used it. Had my security upped around the place. It wasn't much more than that. People got a bit concerned and so did I.

On almost all commonly used measures of performance, and some less common ones, Nixon has been highly successful. On the basis of her consultations, she set the force four key performance measures: to reduce crime, car theft and road fatalities and to increase community perceptions of safety. She has achieved on all targets and her performance has been rewarded by government with significant extra resources, increases in police numbers, and in 2006 a renewal of her contract.

HOW BODY WORK FOSTERS LIBERATING LEADERSHIP

Leadership, as I argued at the start of this chapter, has been constructed as an activity of brains without bodies. Yet the evidence is that bodies have always been part of leadership. The two leader profiles in this chapter have shown that thoughtful incorporation of body work in leadership can act to enliven change in ailing organisational systems.

Christine Nixon's example shows just how much body work can be involved in leadership, from meeting people through to presiding over graduations and managing threats to her life. These physical demands may be one reason why some leaders make themselves and their bodies scarce. However, both Nixon and Sarra created physical proximity[17] to instigate change. For Sarra, physical contact and confidence has been an accepted, though occasionally problematic, means of increasing his impact. For Nixon, reducing distance has taken the form of being seen by and accessible to the community. Rather than aiming for overt physical charisma, as many leaders do, Nixon has adopted a more subtle process of loosening and permitting, of opening up (her office, her meetings); encouraging connections between formerly impervious bodies (uniformed and non-uniformed police and in cross-agency taskforces on issues like domestic violence); using her own body to make a statement (marching in the gay parade); freeing up body regimes for others (allowing staff choice in uniforms); and bringing in outside bodies to puncture the tightly bounded police brotherhood (through changes in senior management appointment processes and in recruitment). Nixon has worked to make the police more open and flexible, perhaps paradoxically developing the capacity of the 'police body' to admit mistakes and to simultaneously become more robust.

The two examples here—an Aboriginal Australian and a woman police commissioner—have bodies which are in contrast to most in leadership, and are therefore already visible. For both leaders, an appetite to experiment with bodily conventions may have grown out of experiences of being an outsider. Already perceived as 'different', they may have felt less constrained in their body work, particularly as they also enjoyed success in the community's eyes. Yet their experiences also tell us much about how different body work is pressured to conform.

The selection of these leaders brings the risk that I have reinforced the very idea I have sought to reject: that white men don't have bodies and women and Aboriginals do. But the risks, I want to suggest, are counterbalanced by the freeing possibilities that emerge from embodying leadership. Leaders—men and women—are embedded in body regimes where certain performances are rewarded, others disciplined. In a fundamental way, it is freeing simply to identify how these regimes operate, rather than being captive inside them, to map the unmapped physical assumptions of leadership.

In my experience of leadership development, encouraging people to be in their bodies more consciously changes their mindset towards themselves and others. It can foster a capacity to read and feel more empathically what is going on for others as well as for oneself.[18] Body consciousness in leadership can also promote connection with others in the moment, rather than being preoccupied with worries about the future or regret for the past. Working with a sense of one's own body is a reminder of mortality and a check on feelings of invincibility and hubris. Awareness of bodily symptoms such as bowed posture or shallow breathing allows leaders to come into the present, to pay attention to others, to notice where they themselves 'are' physically and mentally, and to put issues into perspective. These are some of the conditions which allow for more mindful leadership, which I explore with the role of the breath in the next chapter.

7
Breath and mindfulness

⚸

Breathing, according to me, corresponds to taking charge of one's own life.

Luce Irigaray (2002)

In this chapter, I take further the idea that leadership has been constructed as a disembodied activity, to explore how a focus on something as simple as breathing might change the practice of leadership.

Breathing consciously offers both literal and symbolic ways of slowing down and opening up—physically and mentally. It also offers moments in which to give full attention to the present and to relationships with other people in that moment. In such ways, it can allow leaders literally to take a deep breath or two before acting, deciding, responding; to defer a knee-jerk impulse for greater control or mastery; to allow the attention to others that can engage them in the task of finding new solutions.

In most Western traditions of thinking, breathing is a bodily by-product, with little relevance to the conscious self or its reasoning. In Eastern traditions, the breath is a gateway to the mind, a link which connects and unifies that which Westerners so often dichotomise. In this chapter, I draw on examples from the intersection of my work in leadership development with my growing interest in yoga and the philosophy behind its breathing practices (*svarodya* and *pranayama*). I explore how breathing in a more conscious way can bring composure and attentiveness into leadership. Because breathing encourages us to become more aware of ourselves and our bodies in the here and now, the act of consciously considering our breathing connects us to life and to mortality. It reveals the extent to which we are containing ourselves, perhaps by shallow or held breathing, and invites us to reflect on what is going on for us while we are so unconsciously and tightly controlled. For these reasons, doing breath work can be disconcerting but may also be transformative.

Writing about breathing is a risky undertaking because it stands so far outside conventional views of what is relevant to leadership. Nonetheless, I introduce it here as an idea that has come to be important to me in my own leadership work, and in learning how to lead differently. In my experience, conscious breathing can profoundly change what happens in many leadership situations. The examples and research I offer here are from my own teaching, and from therapeutic, conflict-resolution and other contexts, rather than from more conventional business leadership situations. Although I am not aware of any research looking into the specific relationship between breath and leadership,[1] meditative practices are increasingly being introduced to leadership development, as I explore in Chapter 9.[2] So, in the tradition of Eastern philosophy, don't take my arguments about the breath on trust. Try it to see whether it makes a difference to how you feel, what you see, and how you lead or respond to leadership.

THE THEORY AND PHILOSOPHY OF BREATH

Knowing and controlling the breath plays a pivotal role in Eastern philosophies and practices such as yoga, as well as in derivations such as the martial arts and in approaches to medicine.

Breathing is the first and last thing we do in our life, and it is what keeps us going in between. It reflects states of mind and body. Breathing is also a bodily function that most of us do unconsciously, yet can learn to do consciously. In yoga, breathing is therefore regarded as the gateway through which advanced practitioners can access unconscious systems within the body, such as the autonomic nervous system, and bring them under conscious control. Most meditative traditions include systematic training in processes of breath control, including retention and being without breath for periods of time. I offer here a sample of what I have learned personally from reading, observing and practising breathing techniques. For the reader interested in a deeper understanding, authoritative references are available[3] as well as an increasing number of explorations of the impact of meditative activities on well-being.[4]

In the Western tradition too, in various streams of somatic psychology and psychotherapy, there are well-established practices of working consciously

Breath and mindfulness

with the breath—for example, in the way therapists use a client's pattern of breathing as part of a diagnostic tool, where shallow or fast breathing indicates patterns of apprehensiveness or fear. Mirroring the client's breathing can help to create empathy between client and therapist, and encouraging deeper and more conscious breathing can assist a distressed client to feel more grounded.

The breath is a physically controllable pathway to the mind. Breath work is used as a central part of holistic approaches to diseases such as cancer. There is documented evidence that breathing slowly and more consciously creates physiological changes. These include:

○ reducing the heart rate;
○ oxygenating the bloodstream and reducing acidity;
○ decreasing muscular tension;
○ increased blood flow to organs and facilitating digestive, absorption and elimination functions; and
○ reducing various stress reactions in the body such as inflammation (many of which cause or exacerbate serious illnesses such as heart disease, arthritis, and so on).

Researchers into the brain and into consciousness are increasingly seeking to map neural connections between psychological, emotional and physical conditions in the body. These studies show that techniques such as conscious breath work, meditation and mindfulness can successfully be used in the treatment of conditions such as depression and in the following section I overview some of this research.[5]

As well as these relations to body and mind, the breath is also linked, in many ancient traditions, to spirit or soul. The word 'spirit' comes from the Latin word *spiritus*, which also means 'breath'. So 'respiration' (breathing) and 'spirit' derive from this common root. *Pranayama*, the Sanskrit word for breathing, includes the word *prana*, which means both 'before breath' and 'spiritual life force'. French philosopher Luce Irigaray also remarks on the fundamental way in which breathing connects to soul:

The practice of respiration, the practice of diverse kinds of breathing . . . constitutes the mental in a different way. It grants more attention to the education of the body, of the senses . . . Without doubt . . . the soul still seems related to the breath, to air.[6]

BREATHING AND MINDFULNESS IN LEADERSHIP

Tuning into the breath has several important potential effects for leaders:

- changing one's relationship to oneself;
- changing how we are with others; and
- bringing us into the present.

Specifically, some of the effects of breathing more consciously can include:

- slowing the breather down;
- connecting the breather to body awareness—to physical signs of breath-holding, tension or impatience;
- stretching and changing the way the breather's body is consciously experienced;
- opening up the chest, the diaphragm, ribs and associated areas, literally and symbolically expanding the heart area;
- making one aware of thought's usual dominance, holding thoughts in abeyance, developing mindfulness;
- encouraging awareness of what is going on around the breather;
- fostering connection with others by hearing their breathing or lack of it—noting, for example, sighs and other indicators of states of mind; and
- enhancing the sensation of being alive, bringing perspective to one's activities and the importance of not taking life for granted.

The breath can be a vehicle for fostering particular feelings. For example, one meditation technique encourages visualisation of compassion to accompany breathing. On the in-breath, one visualises compassion for self, while on exhaling the visualisation is of compassion for others. The focus is as if the feeling of compassion is moving directly in and out of the area known as the heart (upper chest). Similarly, a Buddhist meditation technique called *metta* encourages the meditator to experience feelings of loving kindness towards strangers and enemies as well as self, friends and family. In another technique, one visualises breathing light and healing directly into those parts of the body that are stressed or suffering.

Attending to the breath also brings one firmly into the here and now. Another of the disciplines in Eastern thinking aims at encouraging one to cultivate 'being in the present moment'. It is difficult to let go of concerns about the past and apprehensions about the future, but if it can be done, it is liberating for both the breather and those around them. In being reminded about the value of the present, we are encouraged to focus our efforts on being open and compassionate in current interactions rather than seeing others as a means to some future end.

Many of the most stressed among us might be surprised to realise that we often function while consistently holding our breath, or breathing intermittently or in a shallow fashion. Holding the breath holds a person in a state of suspension, focused on waiting for what comes next. Shallow or intermittent breathing mirrors holding: a tightness in body and a closed state of mind. Such habits are usually deeply ingrained ways of coping with anxiety or stress, and we are rarely aware of them. But by not paying attention to such habits, they perpetuate, thus reinforcing feelings of being under intolerable pressure or out of control. By taking a moment to breathe, we actively take control and restore—momentarily at least—a feeling of greater balance.

Breath work is a discipline that is taught to help the meditator begin to separate themself from the thoughts that incessantly occupy and capture the mind. It is not until we sit in meditation that we realise how 'busy' our minds routinely are. The clutter of fears, anxieties and trivia that run over and over in the mind starts to reveal itself. A key instruction in meditation is to still the mind, to let go of this clutter of thoughts by focusing on some aspect of the breath. Different traditions encourage this in different ways. In some, it is the suggestion to focus on a particular point on the body—such as the spot where the nostrils meet the upper lip. In other traditions, there is an instruction to focus on a prolonged and complete exhalation in which, as the whole body relaxes, the mind releases the thoughts occupying it. With practice, meditation allows us to experience a separation and detachment from the doubts, fears, recriminations, plans and illusions that can often appear to be the sum total of our mind and therefore ourselves. This is one of the steps involved in cultivating a purer consciousness.

Since the early 1990s, these ideas about breathing and meditation have found increasing application in approaches encouraging 'mindfulness'. The application of mindfulness has been explored in a number of psychological, medical, therapeutic, managerial, learning and conflict resolution spheres.[7]

Mindfulness is broadly defined as 'paying attention without judgment' and usually includes encouraging a focus on the present moment (as opposed to allowing the mind to be preoccupied with the past or planning the future). Contrary to what might be understood, the idea of mindfulness does not mean having a 'full' mind—it means learning how to observe and detach from extraneous thought thus allowing a stiller, clearer consciousness, which in turn allows for less distraction and more presence. The idea of mindfulness comes from meditative traditions, and particularly Buddhism which provides a long history and extensive discussion about how and why to cultivate habits of mindfulness.[8] An important emphasis of these treatments is that mindfulness is a practice that is undertaken without expectation or without an outcome in mind. As I explore further in Chapter 10, as soon as we strive too much to *achieve* something through mindfulness then the very point is lost. Buddhist author and teacher Ayya Khema conveys this intent to 'be' rather than 'do' in the title of one of her books, *Being Nobody, Going Nowhere.*[9]

Mindfulness is finding increasing application in various contexts. It is a means of helping people—patients or clients—manage illness and deal with difficult life challenges. For example, Harvard-based psychologist Ellen Langer was among those who applied mindfulness—which she defined as the capacity to create new categories—to treat various health conditions but particularly those associated with ageing. Jon Kabat-Zinn has specialised in the use of mindfulness meditation to treat chronic pain and stress-related diseases.[10] Mindfulness training has been found to assist people with a range of mental and physical disorders including depression, cancer, eating disorders, arthritis and multiple sclerosis. It assists by supporting people to manage their anxiety and stress responses, enhancing their well-being and reducing incidence of relapse.

The use of mindfulness techniques has also been advocated in managerial and other professional settings where people need to respond to external demands and client needs in ways that are clear-sighted, fully present and non-judgmental.[11] For example, leaders need to be able to hold their psychological baggage at bay, particularly when they are working directly with clients in stressful situations. Negotiation specialist Tom Fisher has advocated the use of mindfulness in his own work as a mediator. Successful conflict transformation requires that the parties avoid being trapped in past or default ways of thinking. Such parties need conscious ways of not reverting to unquestioned expertise or past habits (e.g. 'I've always mediated this way'); to hasty assumptions (e.g. 'This dispute is about x'); or to self-protecting beliefs (e.g. 'Emotion makes me uncomfortable in dispute resolution'). Fisher advises on an array of strategies and habits that can foster this kind of mindful openness in the mediator. These include regularly practising 'S-T-O-P'—that is, Stopping what one is doing, Taking a conscious breath, Observing bodily sensations, and then Proceeding with whatever one was doing. Such practices provide a heightened state of awareness, 'a space or a wedge between my mind and whatever it is encountering'. They enable us to reduce our self-centred reactivity, enhance our capacity to connect with those around us, and act appropriately and skilfully, both as mediators and as human beings.[12]

To conclude then, in executive development programs of various kinds and targeted to leaders in the law, professions, in not-for-profit organisations, and those charged with improving corporate governance, these principles are being applied.[13]

SOME EXAMPLES

How might these ideas about breathing and mindfulness manifest in conventional managerial and organisational settings? I explore this below using some examples from my experience.

BEGINNING AN MBA CLASS WITH BREATHING

In my first example with an MBA class, breath work became a reasonably regular start to our sessions together. We met early in the morning and, depending on how the class seemed to be feeling, I would ask whether the students wanted to begin in this way. Almost always there was enough enthusiasm to proceed. This breath work usually involved standing and doing some simple movements with arms and body, such as stretching and bending forward or back, accompanied rhythmically by deep breathing, and encouragement to expand abdominal and diaphragmatic parts of the breathing apparatus, in addition to the lungs. The entire process would take about four to five minutes, and then I'd invite participants to resume their seats. I'd try to resist responses suggesting that we needed to hurry, that we must get down to the 'real' work. It generally took a good few minutes for people to get into it—to move past self-consciousness, embarrassment or a mechanical response.

I used my voice to mirror the sense of opening up, and of deepening the inhalation, as well as lengthening the exhalation, and to encourage a letting go or release of tightness and tension. I would vary the routine a little, being guided by what they seemed prepared to tolerate, what they seemed to need, and by what elicited the most voluble response of sighs and murmurs.

There was generally some ambivalence about this start. Many class members stumbled into the lecture room, simply relieved to have made it to this early class, coffee cup sometimes in hand. I sensed that some just wanted to plonk down and tune out for a while—not to be asked to do anything but sit. A few, once they knew we might start this way, deliberately came a little later to avoid it.

However, with most of the class—even the reluctant breathers—I noticed a real difference in the way the class then proceeded. There was more energy and focus. There was sometimes regret about resuming seats or sinking back into passivity. I believe these brief experiences of breathing and stretching came to act symbolically, and to reflect bodily the kind of engagement, openness and inclusiveness that I was seeking to establish in our class.

It was also relevant that the subject I was teaching was 'Management and Ethics'. There were strong differences of opinion in the class. I also sensed that some were beginning with the assumption that the class would consist of me telling them the right way to think and act. Instead I wanted to encourage them to listen to each other and themselves. I wanted to create a space in which they might move out of entrenched positions and be open to hearing and seeing different experiences of the world. I wanted them to value their own experience, their feelings and understanding, to develop the confidence to think ethical issues through for themselves, and to identify ways forward rather than memorise theories or 'decision trees' about 'right' actions.

I believe the experience of breathing together changed the group dynamics. Breath work gives us all an experience—in the moment—which is shared and significant. Often people come to class preoccupied with what is going on in the rest of their lives—worries about the day ahead, what they have to do, what they didn't do yesterday, how they are going to get through what today will bring. They are locked into their own head and their own preoccupations, and this means that most people are not listening to one another, and are listening to me only with part of their minds.

Stopping to breathe creates an interruption to this. As an initially unexpected and unaccustomed task, it requires attention—even if it is resisted—and this takes the student into the present. Usually I have not offered much in the way of rationale, and this is deliberate. This way I can interweave the exercise and the students' responses into class discussion. I might ask for people to use it to explore their own reactions to unexpected change, or to reflect on how work pressures discourage leaders from paying attention to their well-being.

As well as bringing students into the moment, breathing encourages sudden awareness of others. There is attention to how others are physically placed; there are the sounds of others sighing and breathing more audibly; and I think there is also a connection with others that the act of breathing together mediates. Generally, when we finish, there is a rush of talk and exchange, a repositioning of bodies that seems newly mindful of others, where they are at and what has just happened.

RESISTING BREATHING AS COERCIVE

In my second example, I introduced breathing into my first encounter with 40 or so middle-aged senior executives undertaking an EMBA (see discussion in Chapter 3). Here, my request for the group to breathe was fiercely resisted. It is worth noting some of the characteristics of this group, and why my request elicited such a hostile response. These executives were already feeling under intense pressure with a schedule that, in a very real way, did not give them time to breathe. They were already anxious and, perhaps some of the time, literally holding their breath. Inviting them to breathe was then a particularly confronting thing to do; it required them physically to act differently, to let go of some psychological armoury and loosen up within the collective space of a classroom of peers, among whom there were some guarded or ambivalent relationships.

In most other cases of doing breath work, I had waited until I had a relationship with a group of students after several sessions with them, but in this case I didn't. I made a decision that I wanted to do something unexpected and surprising. Because breathing and stretching immediately requires concentration, it gets people out of their heads. I wanted to create a distance from the regular practices and rituals of this group's time together so that we might begin to observe ourselves and our dynamic. In other cases where I had begun like this with a new group, it had worked effectively as a platform for new learning. However, in this case, I was new to the group but they already had well-developed norms and expectations, having worked together extensively already. The encouragement to stand, breathe and stretch was experienced by some participants as an arbitrary and inappropriate thing to do. I hadn't established myself with the group, and my credibility was already fragile as most of the other teachers on the program were men and the methods of teaching that they had experienced were more conventional.

The learning for me in this case was the need to pay greater attention to where participants are—psychologically, emotionally, bodily, individually and collectively—as well as to pay attention to understanding how they see me, and where I am in relation to them. In retrospect, I see that what I intended as an opening-out and freeing was experienced as heavy-handed and coercive. My own desires and ego took precedence here, and I overestimated my capacity to overcome constraints and anxieties when leading them into a new learning space. These experiences have shown me that breathing is powerful work, but it is also potentially confronting and cannot be rushed. One needs to proceed with humility, care and respect for where people are and what might be unleashed.

TEACHING YOGA AT THE BUSINESS SCHOOL

The third example comes from my experience of teaching yoga at Melbourne Business School. For several years, I have taught an hour's class once or twice a week, and it has slowly attracted a modest but regular following. The class is located within one of the business school classrooms and attracts a mixed audience of academic, managerial and administrative staff, and MBA students. This mix itself creates an interesting and potentially subversive atmosphere, as students, their teachers and support staff locate themselves around the room— casually clothed, with bare feet, on the same level (the floor).

I initiated the class because I wanted, as a newly qualified yoga teacher, to bring some of the benefits—mental and physical—that I had gained from yoga practice to my colleagues and students. It was only once I was launched and registering people's responses that I realised I had transgressed some boundaries. Taking a bodily practice seriously, I was flouting a norm. Even more, in creating a setting which holds students, and administrative and academic staff on the same level, I was removing status and power props, and reducing those who participated to a metaphorical nakedness—without their brainpower, and with just the raw material of the body.

From the attendees' perspective, there was initial tentativeness about presenting a different physical self within the school buildings. Although some of our students are full-time and therefore don't attend in suits, most people dress reasonably conservatively. Occasionally a student might arrive in cycling gear, but generally the dress 'code' is not flouted. When I first raised the idea of yoga classes, concern was expressed by senior staff about an undermining of the serious business atmosphere, by 'people running around in lycra'. Getting into yoga gear, such as shorts, tighter clothing or bare feet, therefore immediately invites attention. One yoga class member requested after class: 'Can we all go up in the lift together? There is safety in numbers.' Others have remarked on how different they feel walking around in bare feet— more relaxed, but also vulnerable. Bare feet brings up associations, for example of childhood and a freer time, but adults are also often self-conscious, even ashamed of their feet. Again, I have been struck by how quite modest acts can have big and confronting effects.

Initially, the most enthusiastic yoga attendees were the general staff of the school (not academics), and they have remained so. These participants are predominantly, though not exclusively, women, aged from their early twenties to their fifties. Perhaps because they are not so vested and tightly packed into their cerebral selves, they have been most ready to 'come out': revealing physical limitations or breathlessness, and conversely their appetite for stretching, relaxation and letting go. This has been a much harder thing for the men in the school to do, and particularly for the male academics, though I now have a small band of men, in both administrative and academic roles, and at varying ages and stages of fitness, who are 'regulars'. These regulars have developed a new network around this common interest which cuts across boundaries of, for example, administrative and academic staff.

I almost always begin with a series of breathing exercises, and these vary depending on the group I have and what I sense they need. These exercises can be as simple as lying on the back, knees bent and hands resting above and below the navel, and being encouraged to breathe more fully and deeply, first abdominally and then more completely diaphragmatically and with both lungs.

People's responses to this experience vary. A general trend is that the more stressed people are, the more they need to be held in this space of just breathing deeply. Yet the more stressed they are, the more impatient they are to get into physical exercise and *asanas* (yoga postures or poses), and the more important it is to hold them calmly in breathing, resisting the pressure to move on. If I can hold them for long enough (more than a few minutes), using my voice and my own breathing as a cue, then they start to 'get it'. You can feel and hear them finding a different, less pressured space to be in. If I don't succeed in doing this, people can spend the whole class in the mindset in which they arrived—rushing through, completing one more task for the day, their thoughts preoccupied with the afternoon's engagements, worrying about the morning's omissions or mistakes.

Despite the assorted resistances and obstacles I have encountered in teaching yoga, I have relished this experience. It has allowed me to feel more free and fluid in the spaces I occupy in the school, and has influenced the way I teach my MBA subjects. I seem to have acquired allies who, even though they may not attend, support my efforts to do something quite different within the institutional walls. The fact of the yoga class creates a small eruption in the norms that govern the environment: taking time out for oneself and doing something that is not about knowledge or careers or material values. Even if it is only a small gesture in the direction of taking well-being seriously, participants in the institutional culture are enlivened by it.

As their yoga teacher, my relationships with participating students and colleagues have changed, becoming more blurred but typically richer and more spacious. I gain great satisfaction from their increasing flexibility, watching them peel out of their bodily rigidity and supporting them to extend themselves—physically and emotionally. I also feel regret when I change out of my yoga clothes and back into formal clothes to give a lecture, as though I am relinquishing some freedoms.

Teaching yoga and utilising practices aimed at expanding body and breath awareness while quieting the mind has changed the way I approach my teaching and work generally. It has also shifted my intent towards promoting openness, growth and greater freedom in the people with whom I work.

BREATHING IN LEADERSHIP

Leadership is often distinguished as a force that opens up and illuminates a new path or possibility, compared with managerial activity, which controls the resources that are already there. In this chapter, I have argued that conscious breath work can assist leadership work of this kind. Breathing can remind us when we are holding our breath, intent on self-control, holding 'in' our anxiety in a kind of self-protection that can only be short term.

What is needed in leadership may be simply stated but is hard to give: the capacity to not react impulsively from our own immediate needs; to be really present for others; to relinquish our need for control or mastery to the requirements of the challenge in front of us. Breathing consciously supports a leadership that steps back to reprioritise and reframe. Conscious breathing provides a connection to constancy, but supports these sometimes subtle, but difficult changes.

There are many opportunities for leaders and managers to introduce into their work a conscious awareness of breath, for themselves and others. Such a practice might be completely invisible to others, or it might be a more deliberate strategy—a way of encouraging others to slow down, of connecting and fostering focus on underlying purposes or what is important in life.

The following are some suggestions about using breathing techniques.

In relation to self:

○   at the start of the day as a way of centring and reminding oneself about priorities;
○   before and during difficult or potentially stressful events such as public speaking or important meetings;
○   as preparation for counselling subordinates or colleagues;
○   as a way of feeling more energised and able to do things;[14] and
○   to enable one to step back from immediate reactions and gain perspective.

In relation to others:

○   stopping to breathe audibly oneself as a reminder of, or mirror to, others;
○   tuning into how others are breathing to guide actions and decision-making (e.g. taking a break and encouraging others to get up, stretch or walk around at regular points during long or difficult meetings);

- observing the way people breathe, and using this as a barometer of the pressure they are experiencing, the extent to which they are 'here' or preoccupied, and adapting how one responds—for example, by allowing more time for ideas to digest; and
- using the breath as a way of supporting people to notice their physical and emotional condition and to take action to support well-being.

The approaches explored in this chapter—to breath work, to mindfulness and to meditation—can, I have suggested, support a more liberating kind of leadership work. However, taken out of context they can be just tools or techniques to enhance one's status or efficiency. The approaches become part of the problem, an extra task on the 'to do' list, rather than a release from it. With the ideas introduced here and in the book overall, the fundamental point is to open up new ways of being in leadership. This includes being alert to the risks, such as misusing spirituality (an issue I discuss in the next chapters).

Breathing, and the way we breathe, affects our bodies, our emotions and our thinking about ourselves and others. How we breathe changes what we do and how we do it, how we relate to others, how we speak and how we inhabit the space we are in. Whether leadership is a process of directing one's efforts to important purposes or an aspiration to influence others, breath provides a means for doing so with heightened consciousness and connection. By working more consciously with the breath, leaders can gain greater insight into knowing themselves, into understanding and detaching from unconscious impulses activated in relations of power. In this way, breath work can help leaders and followers to be mindful, self-aware and connected to others.

Further, it appears to me in my interactions with all sorts of people—colleagues, friends, students and executives—that the major challenge most leaders face is how to prevent being taken over by the demands of their work and being driven by the wrong priorities. Many express a yearning to be able to lead in a deeper sense while not becoming burnt out from tasks of dubious value. They hope to learn ways to find ongoing satisfaction and inspiration in the work they do, and to help those they lead to find these too.[15] The solution, as I take up in the next chapter, is not a simple one of resolving to find more 'work–life balance'.

PART III
Going deeper

8

The identity work
of leadership

&

*The more individuals become preoccupied/obsessed with the
(illusory) search for a stable and solid sense of identity, the more likely
it is that subjectivity will indeed become a 'psychic prison'.*

David Collinson (2003)

*. . . it is useful to treat identity as a narrative, or, more properly speaking,
as a continuous process of narration where both the narrator and the
audience are involved in formulating, editing, applauding, and refusing
various elements of the ever-produced narrative . . .*

Barbara Czarniawska (1997)

Identity and the search for the self have become central concerns in Western societies.[1] Increasingly, these preoccupations have been reflected in writing, advice and education about leadership, which has advocated that people who know themselves make better leaders.

This chapter explores the contemporary conditions that have sent many on a search for reinvented leadership identities. How can we understand the pressures on leaders to find and know themselves, and what kind of identity work is required in leadership? In the early part of the chapter, I discuss some of the identity 'solutions' offered to individuals, including a better work–life balance, career reinvention and ways to find, assert or return to a more authentic identity.

As discussed in Chapter 4, effective leadership often rests on an understanding of one's appetites and vulnerabilities. Some self-awareness is vital to prevent, in Alistair Mant's memorable phrase, 'leaders spewing their neuroses all about them'.[2] I too suggest in this book that good leaders are those who reflect upon themselves as individuals, honestly and insightfully, particularly in relation to where they are leading people and why.

But this chapter, and those that follow, are not intended to help leaders 'find' themselves. Identity is not an individually crafted product, in spite of what some marketers of 'designer lifestyles' would have us believe. Leadership requires a different kind of identity work, underpinned by an understanding of the systemic ways in which identities are produced: where, for example, some performances of authenticity are applauded while others are sanctioned; where a leader feels pulled by conflicting identities; where the sense of having found oneself authentically in leadership may be fragile and fleeting. Leadership can benefit from work on identity, but only by stepping back and reflecting on all the influences—internal and external to the self—that produce identity formation. A more viable, critical and, in the end, freeing way through identity preoccupations is to see the search for the self as not just a personal or individual problem, but a negotiated process that takes place within a politically charged organisational and social space.

CRAFTING SELVES

The seductive power of contemporary ideas about identity is illustrated well in marketing media. Advertisements appeal to aspirations to 'be' someone by purchasing something: 'I am what I own.'[3] In the April 2005 edition of the *Australian Financial Review*'s magazine, *Boss*, an advertisement appeared for a large four-wheel-drive vehicle (or SUV). It is reproduced here. The advertisement is similar in type to many that target busy people with money to spend, so it provides insights into how identity is constructed and appealed to, particularly for an audience aspiring to leadership.

The advertisement takes up a double-page spread in the early pages of the magazine. The scene across the two pages is a frozen plain, an icy steppe (one imagines Russian or Nordic), with a blur of trees signalling the horizon where land meets snowy sky. The impression is of an uncompromising landscape. On the right of the picture is the car, pristine but for the slightest dusting of snow. The windows of the vehicle are tinted, obscuring the interior. The driver is enigmatic, the vehicle appearing to have got to this point by itself.

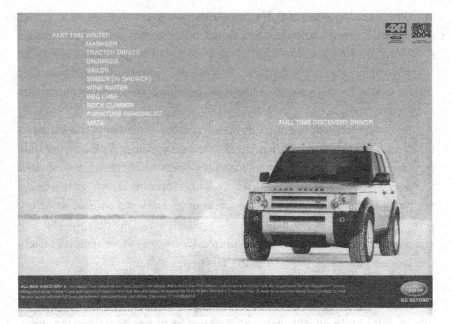

Land Rover advertisement, *Boss* magazine, April 2005
Copyright Land Rover; reproduced with permission

On the left page is the following text, laid out like this:

PART-TIME   WRITER

MANAGER

TRACTOR DRIVER

DRUMMER

SAILOR

SINGER (IN SHOWER)

WINE WAITER

BBQ CHEF

ROCK CLIMBER

FURNITURE REMOVALIST

MATE

On the right page, above the car, are the words 'FULL TIME DISCOVERY DRIVER. At the bottom of the page, in small letters, is the line: 'No matter how many lives you lead, there's one vehicle that's more than a match for them all.' The Land Rover trademark and slogan of 'GO BEYOND' also figures on the bottom corner.

What is being said here? The list on the left presents a list of identities which initially seems to have no apparent order or hierarchy. The identities seem jumbled, giving a pleasing impression of multiplicity, of many roles. The advertisement plays with identities: it offers the appealing proposition that each of us may be many people, rather than a single boring identity or boringly confined to one role.

Yet, on closer examination, there is a structure and order in this list, even though it looks thrown together. The first and second designation are artfully reversed, with 'writer' first and 'manager' second. There are presumably few people who write for a living who could afford this car, so what is being said with this reversal is 'I may be working as a manager for most of my waking hours, but in my heart I am a writer first'. This person—the one reading the advertisement—is not limited by his work role (and it is likely though not guaranteed to be a man that is appealed to).

Looking down the list, it then becomes apparent that the attractively diverse assortment of identities is actually qualified and narrowed down in other ways that appeal to a dominant masculine ideal. Look at the adjectives: not just a driver but a tractor driver; not just a waiter but a wine waiter; not just a chef but a BBQ chef . . . and so on. The list of adjectives specifying identity also clearly designates power and masculinity in this construction. The masculinity is firmly and indisputably established by the final 'mate', which also has the effect of culturally designating this identity as Australian.

The picture that emerges suggestively from this advertisement is that, for this kind of man, life is a rich mix of multiple roles, and there is an attractive playfulness and ad hoc quality to these. All the roles in the list are 'part-time'—though this is ambiguous, as if the driver can take them up and relinquish them as he desires. The busy car-driver can have many lives—exciting and even quirky, as with the singer in the shower. Endorsing the complexity and richness of this life project of multiple selves, the advertisement claims that only one vehicle is capable of 'matching' it (another competitive theme that appears subtly in a text designed to look non-hierarchical).

The advertisement described here appeals to the quintessentially post-modern view of identity, which is that it is not one but many. The postmodern individual dips into many selves and is continually engaged in the constructing of self from a smorgasbord of performances. This self is not limited by a work role, nor trapped by a single set of demands. The very charm of this self lies in its artful multiplicity.

Simultaneously though, in the list's very construction, in the appealing recipe of identity here, there is also predictability and conformity. In our very desire to position ourselves as outside societal prescription—as unique, unpredictable and playful individuals launched on our life project—our identities are all the more firmly anchored within a time, place, space and set of cultural concerns. The advertisement is emblematic of the tensions within identity—of seeking the thread of the authentic self alongside the desire to escape rigid categorisation and to play with identity. This echoes a key tension in contemporary theorising about identity: the extent to which individuals can craft and adjust their identities versus the extent to which identities are preordained by societal structures of power, class, gender, racial and other relations out of our control.

PRESSURES TO 'BE' OR FIND A SUCCESSFUL SELF

As leadership has gained currency and popularity as an idea, it has also become commodified—that is, it has become a product that is sought after, manufactured and traded. As part of this process, people face pressures to produce the 'right' leadership identity: confident and assertive, or in other circumstances, perhaps, reliable and without weaknesses.

There is also evidence from surveys of leaders that many feel they are losing themselves to their jobs. Very demanding roles require a single-minded focus on the task and disallow competing identities, such as father or hobbyist. Working hours have escalated so that people's capacity to pursue and invest in other life activities has become compromised.[4] Long working hours and norms of around-the-clock availability mean that many leaders feel there is no self other than the work self, that the 'real' self has vanished.

Identity pressures have also intensified with workplace conditions that routinise constant monitoring and evaluation of individual performances.[5] Performance management and '360-degree feedback' produce a regime of assessment considered normal in workplaces and by recruiters. Such extensive mechanisms of performance appraisal pressure some leaders into feeling they must turn themselves into someone else in order to succeed. While such practices may, or may not, be effective devices in improving performance and accountability of people in organisations, the point here is that these conditions have become an accepted part of institutional life, and we no longer see the pressure on identity that they produce. It is simply taken for granted.

The art of manipulating the identities of employees reached a crescendo in the 'managing culture' movement of the 1980s. In this trend within organisational management, of which strong remnants remain today, the identities of employees are massaged symbolically and tacitly. Indeed, as discussed in Chapter 2, one of the goals of transformational leadership is to mobilise employee aspirations and align them with organisational purposes. Through these processes, the identities of employees become interwoven with organisational interests. The leader is not outside this process, but enmeshed in it. Particular types of leadership selves are being produced and the selves are, in deep and self-disciplining ways, agents for maintaining the cultural status quo.

Further, some have argued that having people worry about identity may well allow for new methods of institutional and social control. As we become more used to seeking meaning through self-actualising work projects, rather than in religion or community, the self becomes more vulnerable. As we grow more concerned about our achievements, our career paths, our lifestyles, about how we present and 'come across' to others, we become more pliable to those who target our narcissism and vanity. These include not only marketers wanting to sell us cars and holidays, but also deeper ideological forces. We may seek to reinforce a sense of self by finding workplaces consonant with personal values, but those very workplaces, by reinforcing individualism and playing to anxieties, promote corporate goals. The organisations in which we work become the means by which we not only get paid but also gain self-esteem and realise our 'potential'. Organisations become the vehicle through which we know and feel secure—or insecure—about who we are.

Why worry about relying on workplaces to tell us who we are? One way to answer this question is to turn again to Michel Foucault, whose philosophical analyses have revealed insights about the forms of power and control that remain least obvious to us. Particularly relevant here are his ideas about discipline and surveillance, which he symbolised by the 'panopticon'—the surveillance tower in prisons, located so that all prisoners may be watched without knowing when or how, but ultimately compelling prisoners to take on the burden of disciplining themselves, as the authorities would have them do.[6] While few of us are literally incarcerated, the panopticon analogy captures the idea that we are nonetheless subject to inescapable surveillance and control of which we are unaware, but which we often obligingly self-police.

Surveillance is now extensive and routine in organisations. Video cameras, tracking of emails and electronic transactions, and embedded tracking devices establish new frontiers of surveillance. In a recent British report, up to 10 000 employees involved in trucking and warehousing supermarket goods have been required to wear tracking devices that inform management where they are. Unions have protested that these devices provide management with heightened levels of control while employees are treated like 'automatons'.[7] But Foucault's point is that self-disciplining surveillance can occur more subtly and powerfully, even at the highest levels of organisations. Here, the individual takes on the responsibility—rarely consciously—of producing an appropriate leadership identity for themselves—one that is consistent with institutional expectations.

Ideas about surveillance and regulation have been extensively investigated in contemporary organisational life.[8] One reason for the wide currency is that, though many do not work under overtly coercive conditions, employees fear that monitoring systems may be used inappropriately. Further, there is extensive evidence that individuals in work organisations not only become intensely self-regulatory, but also police their peers more punitively than any watchtower guard. Working conditions, systems of remuneration, career paths—in short, how we are at work seems increasingly to be under someone else's, or worse our own, punitive control.

People respond to these identity pressures with a variety of psychological defences. Some invest more deeply in work. However, as explored in Chapter 4, work that is driven by unconscious ego needs is risky because it can rarely suffice; instead, simply feeding addictive habits, we work harder and longer. Ego is the reason we find it hard to say no to things. Organisational change commentator Peter Block says that 'no matter how tough we think we have become, we look to bosses and others above us and hand them the power to determine . . . how valued we are, how secure we can be and how much freedom we have'.[9] A form of 'splitting' is also common where a tough, ultra-competitive and ruthless exterior is cultivated, and sustained by the idea that 'the real me' resumes outside work.[10] Another response, discussed in detail in Chapter 9, is that by bringing a deeper level of commitment to work, by drawing on a more spiritual kind of connection in the workplace, one might feel more wholeness and integration of self. Either way, processes of identity regulation continue to be pervasive. These conditions cause both psychic pain and the physical conditions that are its by-products, such as heart disease and stress-related disorders.

SOLUTIONS TO IDENTITY

Studies of managers support that the pressures described above are overriding concerns, yet they are often difficult to voice in organisational environments that seem intent on swallowing up every shred of emotional, intellectual and physical energy. Away from the workplace and colleagues, managers admit that their lack of work–life balance deeply worries them. In fact, it is one of the things that most worries them. The feeling that lives were completely imbalanced in favour of work has been found to be a major concern in a regular survey of Australian leaders.[11]

But, in spite of the resolutions leaders make to leave work early, or not to answer emails at home, by and large they feel powerless to change. And they drag families along in their tattered wake. Relationships crumble, kids become strangers, the good life gets put off for a few more years. As everything in the leader's life capitulates to this seemingly pre-eminent and irresistible force—work—there is a grasping for new and better solutions to identity.

In the next sections, I explore some of the solutions that have been offered to these dilemmas. I argue that such remedies often fail because they do not recognise the structural causes of identity pressures. Their effect is often to allow marginal changes around the edges but to forestall more serious questioning of the privileged place of work, corporate values and institutional power in our lives.

Work–life balance

If the problem is that the self has disappeared under the weight of work, one of the main solutions offered is better 'work–life balance'. A raft of books, programs and consultants advise on how to retrieve such a balance, including practices such as 'casual Fridays', where employees are encouraged to dress casually on Fridays so it doesn't feel so much like work, and programs aimed at helping executives manage their ageing parents ('elder care' programs).

What are we to make of this interest? Does it help, and if so, whom?

In the very term 'work–life balance' there is already embedded an equation: that work and life should be equally weighted, but also that they are opposites and distinct. Few people's experience of work or life is like this—the boundaries are much more blurred and permeable. Work is life and life includes work—though sometimes work can feel like it excludes life.

Another part of what's wrong with the idea of 'work–life balance' is how the problem is constructed. The words chosen to articulate it shape the way it is perceived. The ideas of post-structural theorists and linguists such as George Lakoff[12] are helpful because they encourage us to pay attention to how issues are located within discourse—that is, the ways they are framed and written about in the public domain, and what interests are served or left out by particular framings and articulations.

Through a 'discursive regime', a set of experiences comes to be defined as a problem, with an implicit solution. Before you know it, conferences are arranged on the subject, people become specialists or consultants in the field, organisations invest resources or resist doing so, policy-makers seek to influence outcomes. A regime has been created of truths, problems and remedies. In the case of 'work–life balance', the problem is located squarely on the shoulders of the individual—though with the institution standing by to provide the kind of help that makes it (the institution) look sympathetic to the problem while relieving it of more serious scrutiny.

In my observation of many leaders, getting caught up in finding 'balance' allows them to become more passively situated in a game in which someone else is setting the rules. Not only that, but in their preparedness to play by those rules, leaders become complicit in perpetuating them. When the company makes the odd concession or the leader adopts a stand, like once a week taking the kids to school before coming to work, this allows the overall system, in which work is privileged as the marker of identity, to be sustained—unexamined.

Reinvention

Another approach advocated for the resolution of conflict in identity arising from work is that of 'reinventing' oneself through reassembling one's professional capacities. This remedy dovetails with research by Charles Handy and others on the virtues of the 'portfolio' career, where individuals move through several careers throughout their lives. After early commitment to solid experience in corporations, leaders then move into more autonomous roles, including starting their own business—perhaps in a different field. Or, in later life, the transition may involve using skills in a different way—for example, as a coach, mentor or volunteer. Sometimes such reinvention includes 'downshifting': reducing working hours and perhaps relocating to an environment where commuting time is minimised.

In much of the writing about reinventing identity, the problem is again posed as the self and its packaging. The idea is that you top up—with extra skills and some small-business training, you repackage and, presto, the identity work is done. But this requires the discretionary space to work out what to do next, forgoing income in the meantime—a formula not possible for many.

It is also an illusion to think that reinvention will solve enduring tensions in the way we habitually go about things. If we are having trouble saying 'no' to requests, or in managing a workload, such issues are likely to resurface in a reinvented work life.

Finding 'authenticity'

The last few years have seen an explosion of interest in authenticity in leadership.[13] I interpret this surge partially as the result of leaders feeling under pressure with a loss of 'true' self in the highly monitored culture of corporate life. The remedy of authenticity is also consistent with the trends described earlier, which encourage us to cast identity as a product crafted individually rather than as a preoccupation mediated societally.

The 'authenticity' remedy for identity advocates emphasis on self-awareness and acting from self-knowledge. Examples are given of leaders who 'know themselves', who understand their talents, strengths, values and desires, and who demonstrate a consistency of behaviour and action around this authentic self. Such habits, often associated with integrity and good character, evidently seem a good thing in leadership, particularly given the examples of corrupted leadership described earlier (see Chapter 1), or in many other Australian and international cases where leaders publicly espouse commitment to high values while acting with duplicity and greed.

This authenticity ideal seems like an attractive proposition for leadership and is, on face value, consistent with the reflective approaches that I have been advancing in this book. However, there are several problems with the way that this approach has been elaborated and converted into advice for leaders.

Bruce Avolio and his colleagues define authentic leaders as 'those who are deeply aware of how they think and behave and are perceived by others as being aware of their own and others' values/moral perspectives, knowledge and strengths; aware of the context in which they operate; and who are confident, hopeful, optimistic, resilient and of high moral character'.[14] This definition is worrying both because of its complexity and its culture-centredness—that is, it appears to rest on culturally determined assumptions. It advances a value on self-knowledge that is not up for debate, nor put into historical or social context. The unquestioned elevation of the self is precisely the social preoccupation that Nikolas Rose powerfully calls into question. Why is self-knowledge so valorised in contemporary society, and specifically now in leadership? This question remains unconsidered in much of the material advocating self-aware leadership solutions.

The identity work of leadership

In the second part of Avolio's definition of the authentic leader, a roll-call of moral virtues is added. While these may be virtues in many societies, there is no recognition that these same qualities may be regarded as liabilities in other cultural contexts. In some Eastern societies, for example, qualities such as optimism and confidence can be read as indicators of arrogance, inappropriateness and insensitivity to context. Avolio's definition of authentic leadership is a culturally specific prescription rather than a universal or comprehensive one.

Further, for some members of society, being oneself in leadership may be a much more treacherous path than it is for others. Alice Eagly, in her discussion of authentic leadership, shows that the same behaviours are unlikely to produce an impression of authenticity *when used by female leaders*. When a white male like Bill Clinton shares a moment of weakness from his past, it might be read as authentic; when a female leader does the same, it is more likely to be read as inappropriately confessional. Similarly, there is extensive evidence that, when women 'act like one of the boys'—for example, being strongly assertive or jocular in socialising—they are judged as the opposite of authentic.[15]

So what are leaders who are also of minority status to do in pursuit of authenticity? In a rather breathtakingly simplistic piece of advice, Goffee and Jones urge that, unless female leaders acknowledge and validate some of the prevailing organisational norms surrounding gender roles, they will find it hard to obtain acceptance from male followers.[16]

Eagly's research helps to show that authenticity is not gender-neutral, that ostensibly 'authentic' behaviours and actions are read differently when they are delivered by male and female leaders. It also underlines that authenticity is always socially produced, not individually crafted. Authenticity is not just a matter of skilful individual performance: stereotypes, and cultural and social norms, play a role in determining whose performance of which authenticity is valued.

The authenticity solution has dovetailed with other forms of management advice designed to identify and develop the 'real' self. In many work settings, the drive for self-knowledge is translated into testing of one's personal, leadership or team 'style', and a structured regime of feedback as leaders are encouraged to continuously monitor themselves. This form of 'knowing' oneself—that is, of knowing one's place on a template—has the potential to play into a corporate agenda. The risk here is that, with the goal of 'being himself or herself', the leader gets locked into a regime of measurement and testing, a regime that already reflects social values about whose and what behaviour looks authentic, as well as corporate norms about what leadership should look like. Through such processes, an identity solution—greater authenticity—can become part of the problem, exacerbating anxiety about identity and increasing pressure on individuals to manufacture the right one.

These approaches often treat the 'problem' of the self and the solution—developing more authenticity in leadership—as a matter of individual willpower. In general, they ignore the fact that the norms by which authenticity is judged have deeply structural—social, economic, political—causes. To act as if this problem can be then solved by individual gestures towards authenticity alone allows deeper causes of disenfranchisement and alienation to be ignored.

Many of us, when facing new or difficult challenges—especially in organisational contexts—are given the advice 'just be yourself'. This can seem initially reassuring. 'Being oneself'—maintaining one's distinctive personal style and values in the achievement of group goals—may be a leadership strategy that works for some. However, my own experience is that being myself in professional contexts is risky and difficult, and sometimes I have felt punished for it. Similarly, among the leaders I have researched, there is often pressure for them to 'tone themselves down' or undergo a 'makeover' to cause less offence. For example, Lillian Holt, the Aboriginal leader I introduce in the next chapter, is a popular speaker but is also asked to not be so angry or confronting in her speeches. Particularly if leaders are already marked out as different from the norm because of their gender, race or bodily ability, being successfully oneself or one's authentic self can require a lot of camouflage.

A final risk of emphasising authenticity in leadership is that it can foster a preoccupation with the self rather than perspicuity in where one is taking others. Goffee and Jones[17] advocate the active management of the authentic self: the careful and studied selection of how the authentic self is performed and delivered. Self-knowledge and consistency are important, and so are selective self-disclosure, drawing on one's background, and being attuned to cultural and contextual cues.

While many of these ideas are welcome supports for reflection, the danger is that all this focus on producing a self can get in the way of good leadership. The crafting of authenticity can become an end in itself rather than a vehicle through which we promote leadership ends such as freedom or happiness. The search for authentic leadership can become one more platform for the fragile ego to shore itself up, to secure itself. This danger is described in Buddhism as 'spiritual materialism'—the misguided use of spiritual ideals to enhance ego needs. In the next two chapters, and this final part of the book, I show how and why leadership might require less—not more—preoccupation with self.

AN ALTERNATIVE VIEW OF IDENTITY WORK

In the preceding discussion, I have explored the identity pressures on leaders and some of the solutions offered for the loss of the self in the work of leadership. I suggest that, far from freeing leadership, many such solutions may lock leaders into more tightly prescribed performances. It is only by developing a wider and more critically informed understanding of identity formation that leaders may be able to navigate identity pressures more mindfully.

A leader's experience of her or his self, sometimes termed 'subjectivity', does not arise purely from individual, rational sense-making. Rather, economic and social conditions make available certain subjective positions or ways of thinking about oneself. It is from this already constrained repertoire that leaders perceive themselves and their choices—say, as tough enforcer, 'rainmaker' or change agent, as charismatic or as a 'people person'. While the subjective experience of individual leaders may be that they are 'free agents' making choices about their identities, careers and leadership, the reality is that they are actively inscribing themselves into predetermined positions within systems of power.[18]

Identity, rather than being authored in a vacuum by the individual, is constantly under construction in response to social ideas and pressures, constrained by power relations and shaped by dominant mythologies to which individuals subscribe, such as the idea of the 'self-made leader'. As we construct ourselves, we are also pinned into identities—some not the ones we want, while other sought-after identities may be denied us. People who present with hybrid, visibly mixed identities—especially identities not typical of the mainstream society—face challenges in leadership. For example, an audience may expect a great conductor to be a charismatic man, so when a women takes to the podium, there is dissonance.[19] Research has shown that this dissonance actually produces extra disturbance in the brain, where observers have to work additionally hard to overcome their preconceptions. In research on majority–minority relations, Elmes and Connelly show that 'individuals from lower status groups are faced with having to expend considerably more energy and effort managing the double binds and competing requirements of multiple group identities'.[20] For example, an African-American policeman may be faced in certain situations with the choice of acting as a policeman first or African-American first, and is also expected to demonstrate primary loyalty to both identities. Research on women leaders shows how women are locked into particular identities, such as nurturer and peacemaker, and it then becomes difficult for them to repudiate or act outside such identities without censure.[21]

Similarly, postcolonial writing describes the way in which the 'other' or the 'outsider' has been exoticised or imbued with an identity that forever prevents the possibility of being known in other ways—for example, by viewing people as 'oriental', 'exotic', 'heathen' or 'tribal'. The social and political processes by which 'other' is demarcated help to reinforce the undesignated position of the majority, the norm, those who are not 'other'. My research shows that Australian Aboriginal leaders face the continual burden of always being responded to *as Aboriginal* before the content of their words or the quality of their leadership is considered. Their Aboriginality precedes all other possibilities, and brings with it assumptions—for example, that they speak for all Aboriginals, that they have a particular commitment to culture, spirituality, land and so on.

In undertaking identity work, leaders need to step back and understand the wider processes by which certain identities may be assumed for them. They may actively seek to repudiate some identities or to cultivate unexpected ones—and this identity work is likely to be more onerous for those unconsciously assumed to be in predetermined identity positions—by ethnicity, gender, class or other categorisation.

Identity scripts that leaders also actively build for themselves can be an impediment to good leadership. For example, the identity of the 'self-made man' is often proudly sported by successful entrepreneurs. Here, the valued self, the most prized identity, is constructed around a narrative where the leader has built an enterprise. The individual identifies so strongly with this enterprise that they merge: the individual's interests become its interests; the leader *is* the enterprise. Such individuals can get sucked into the omnipotent fantasy: that they have done it all and can continue to do it all single-handedly—without setbacks or the effort and sacrifice of others.[22] The dangers of this identity script are most commonly revealed during enterprise phases such as succession-planning or entering a new growth phase, where the leader may experience relinquishing control as personal annihilation.

The individual leader can also suffer in such a self-made identity prison. Other selves—as partner, parent, friend, community member—are neglected and marginalised. The identity that promised so much becomes self-monitoring and excluding of other sides of the self. Despite all these risks, the idea of being 'self-made' is extraordinarily attractive to many leaders, and fits neatly with prevalent economic and managerial values such as individualism. Of course, there are entrepreneurs and leaders who can and do resist the fantasy that they can make a self and a successful enterprise in isolation. However, in leadership discourse—and particularly with the contemporary emphases on the self and the authentic self—it is essential for the leader, and the people working and living around them, that they don't fall for this self-authoring fantasy.

The ideas that we can simply orchestrate a better work–life balance, or reinvent or retrieve our authentic selves, have been shown to be overly simplified responses to identity pressures on leaders. In offering solutions such as reinvention or authenticity as matters of individual choice, they leave the wider system unnoticed. Searching for a 'truer' identity may have the effect of reinforcing rather than resolving the very insecurity these strategies were designed to overcome.

There is also an instrumental flavour to some of these solutions, despite the rhetoric. For example, corporate work–life balance programs are often designed to increase commitment. Indeed, research shows that employees who work 'flexible hours' or pursue work–life balance options feel more driven to work hard and deliver benefits, so as to repay corporate favour. Paradoxically— or perhaps not—such corporate innovations often keep people in the office longer and more willingly, trapped in repaying flexibility with greater loyalty.

But identity is a moving feast, as the advertisement discussed at the start of this chapter demonstrates. Appeals are increasingly made to our more complex and 'postmodern' appetites for identity—our desire to think of ourselves as not simply definable by one role. We prefer that we are multiple selves, surprising and defying categorisation. The overview of identity ideas in this chapter should show that, though this offers a more sophisticated 'take' on identity, it too is offering a solution that may turn out to be just as conforming, though the mechanisms may be more tacit. Societal conditions, power relations and our own desires collude to encourage our identities to be compliant extensions of the scripts offered to us. It is hard for us to stand back from the self offered to us—there may seem to be no other.

How might leaders work towards freedom and fluidity rather than entrapment? What might be more promising understandings about the identity work of leadership?

Social philosopher Anthony Giddens has proposed the idea of 'self-identity'[23] to explore the tensions between identity as simultaneously produced politically and as authored by the individual. Giddens is interested in how identity is shaped as a narrative as the individual consciously and unconsciously selects meanings and symbols, producing a sense of self. That self is not fixed, though there are continuities. The self is both disciplined and regulated, but also—usually—resistant and creative. Barbara Czarniawska captures the social and political nature of identity production as 'a continuous process of narration where both the narrator and audience formulate, edit, applaud and refuse various elements of the constantly produced narrative'.[24]

Organisational theorists Mats Alvesson and Hugh Willmott develop and apply Giddens's ideas to the managerial context, seeing identities there as improvised and accomplished rather than completely scripted. Identity, in their view, is produced in the dynamic tensions and interplay between self-identity, identity regulation and identity work. Their interest is not just in how organisations regulate identities, but in how individuals meet this regulation in identity work with managers and leaders 'continuously engaged in forming, repairing, maintaining, strengthening or revising the constructions that are productive of a precarious sense of coherence and distinctiveness'.[25] At any one time, organisational roles may provide 'a receptiveness to identity-securing positions'. Organisational conditions may also disrupt, so that 'being oneself' at work no longer feels secure, then eliciting feelings of anxiety or shame. Intensive remedial identity work follows where the leader may be open to take up new positions.

Systemically and politically mediated processes of identity formation are rarely total. People—including leaders—find ways to resist the processes by which their personhood, their experience of self, is defined for them. They do this, for example, through various forms of subtle, conscious and unconscious resistance: disbelief, incredulity, passivity, cynicism, avoidance, sabotage.[26]

Organisational researchers have become interested in mapping the dynamics of this 'micro-emancipation'. Despite pressure to produce acceptable identities, the evidence is that people find ways of dis-identifying and disconnecting their selves from these projects. Further, my argument in this book is that if leaders develop understanding of identity processes and make their own identity work conscious, they are not only in a better position to take up or resist identities for themselves, but also to make choices about whether and how they impose identities on others.

There are connections between the identity work I am proposing here and Eastern philosophies, which I detail in Chapter 10. In these philosophies, a preoccupation with self and identity is seen as a misguided illusion. The bundle of thoughts and emotions that we often perceive to be our identity is a manifestation of ego, and not in fact our true nature. Rather, by cultivating an understanding of connection with others and the world—seeing the self as a porous part of the whole—we allow a sense of self that is not continually needing to be preserved and defended. Identity work is not an end in itself, merely to secure the self, but a vehicle through which to better understand one's power, actions, vulnerabilities and possibilities.

By stepping back from the process of reactive identity search, we move towards untangling ourselves from the desire to 'be someone'. We loosen up our identity search. By understanding social processes of identity production, leaders become thoughtful about systemic constraints as well as the spaces and moments for resistance and 'micro-emancipation'. It is this awareness and experimentation, this kind of identity work, which promises greater freedom to leaders and the people who look to them for inspiration in their own identity work.

9
Leading
with spirit

&

When spirituality becomes popular we can almost be certain
that some vital elements . . . have been left out.

David Tacey (2003)

we can deceive ourselves into thinking we are developing spiritually when
instead we are strengthening our egocentricity through spiritual techniques.

Chögyam Trungpa (1973)

What are we to make of the surge of advice encouraging people to bring spiritual intelligence and 'soul work' to their approach to leadership? Is leadership a spiritual undertaking? If so, how might spiritual emphases show themselves in leadership?

For many people, the idea of spirituality has negative associations—either of institutionalised religion or New Age cultism. I begin this chapter by describing my own belated initiation into spiritual ideas. I explore the emergence of a new emphasis on spirituality in leadership, and suggest that much of it is unsatisfactory because it treats spirituality as a template or vehicle for individual advancement. Without a consciously liberating intent, and without mindfulness about one's power, spirituality is open to commodification—to being misused towards selfish, material or instrumental ends.[1]

But I also suggest that ideas about spirituality shouldn't be rejected simply because they have often been misused.[2] Canvassing new ways to think about spirituality can reveal new insights for liberating leadership. Drawing on two profiles of leaders whose work crosses social and corporate spheres, Lillian Holt and John Wilson, I show the rich and complex ways spirituality might be connected to, and animate, leadership. Far from the pious or elevated practices that are sometimes advocated, these forms of spirituality are rebellious and pragmatic. A spiritual interest is threaded through a life; it is an intent and an animating theme. By setting spirituality into the deeper context of the way life is lived and leadership practised, risks such as spiritual materialism may be minimised.

MY INITIATION IN SPIRITUAL MATTERS

I spent the first 50 years of my life confidently dismissing anything that looked even remotely spiritual. I pooh-poohed religious rituals, baptisms, communions, even weddings. I thought when we were dead we were gone. I was deeply suspicious, even contemptuous, of any scent of the sentimental. Faith was grasping at straws. I was not charitable about people who needed to make a deal with God. My strength—as I understood it—was a sharp intellect, and this had led to an ingrained position of deep scepticism. These habits of mind I had learned early, and I was deeply attached to them. My capacity to identify, acerbically inspect and then clinically assail cherished conventional wisdoms had been my path to success and an anchor for my identity.

My certainty started to crumble in 1996 with the death of my brother, Michael, at 45—the same age at which my father had died. Mortality stormed over the battlements of my nonchalantly constructed agnosticism. It was after Michael's death that I took myself off to learn how to meditate. Time off work, a new baby and a book followed in 1997, and these events marked the start of my own search for a different way to be.

Rapidly, though, my career cranked up again and from the late 1990s I began to feel increasingly 'driven'—by what, I didn't know, but to a place I was pretty sure I didn't want to go. Around me, people were facing serious illness. A couple of young students and friends died abruptly in their twenties and thirties. Meanwhile, others around me hardly paused for breath, clambering around each other and up ladders that led nowhere anyone would want to go.

Moving into my 50s, and as Carl Jung predicts, I started to see the world differently. I immersed myself in yoga and yoga philosophy. I read books about miracles and 'the soul's journey'. My armour of tough scepticism started to feel less necessary as I tentatively allowed myself to be more open, softer and more yielding. Through meditation, I began to see that what I had understood as myself—my cognition, body and ego—might not be the whole picture. There might be some transcendent essence or spirit that I shared with other living beings. And I was starting to experience the evidence, I became better at letting go of small hurts and minor grievances. I was feeling happier, more peaceful and loving.

This was a disconcerting process. On the one hand, I was becoming more open to the possibility of a spiritually enriched life. At the same time, I was encountering a burgeoning literature and interest devoted to spirituality and the soul in leadership, much of which made me deeply uneasy.[3]

When I talked to a well-read and religious friend about my own emerging interest in spirituality, he urged me to begin with a definition and referred me to William James's 1902 classic *Varieties of Religious Experience*. Part of my reluctance in beginning an exploration of spirituality was the feeling that I knew little about religion. How could I begin to acquaint myself with a body of spiritual thinking and writing that is centuries, if not millennia, old and deep? To understand or express what spirituality means seemed absurdly daunting. From where I stand, traditions of thinking about spirituality are vast and formidable, unconnected to my modest projects.

Traditions of spirituality have also, with some exceptions, been led by men—particularly the teaching and initiation. Or, more accurately, the spiritual writing that has been recorded, valued and available for us to draw on has been done by men. Many women have, with good reason, been made to feel inferior and marginal in many organised faiths, Western and Eastern.[4]

For many of us who are confident in our secular, rational spheres, 'spirituality' is suggestive of the conservative, institutionalised face of religion. Many readers will have experienced religion through the processes of schooling or church-going, and found it oppressive rather than freeing. So spirituality looks like part of the problem rather than a way out of it, and towards more liberating leadership. Yet, as David Tacey argues in *The Spirituality Revolution*, newer generations are expressing appetites for spiritual ideas that are uncontaminated by religious traditions.

My own experience showed that spirituality is a big and complex idea with many associations that may discourage its exploration. Yet I don't believe we should stand back and allow either spirituality experts or sceptics to monopolise understandings. I am not about to argue that the conscious adoption of a spirituality is central to good leadership. What I do want to suggest is that good leadership may be supported by diverse spiritual ideas and practices: the spirit to question, and to seek meaning and purpose beyond the surface which can be liberating for others as well as oneself.

SPIRITUALITY IN LEADERSHIP

The relation between religion and business has a long history: the two spheres have been integrally connected with good and bad effects in most societies. In spite of these interconnections, many mid-twentieth century management writers treated spirituality as incompatible with the rational, technical requirements of business.

However, beginning with the publication of Robert Greenleaf's influential book *Servant Leadership* in 1977, which advocated leadership as serving others, spirituality has increasingly become part of business and leadership discourse.[5] This interest has sprung from, and often overlaps with, emerging and popular themes in business thinking, including: concern about well-being and work–life balance; business ethics and governance; corporate sustainability and corporate social responsibility (CSR). It has also emerged from areas of leadership development concerned to create high-performing teams, and from scholars critical of a narrow focus on economic and material motivations in business. Each of these areas of research and attention has created pressures for a different kind of leadership. The CSR movement, for example, has grown into a 'must have' for many—particularly global—organisations. Corporate leaders are being encouraged to move from seeing CSR as basically good public relations to a deeper barometer of, and requisite for, corporate health. Yet there is no consistently clear message for leaders to follow. How do corporate leaders avoid the impression that CSR is an 'add-on'—or should they be up-front, as John Browne, chairman of BP, has been, and insist that CSR is simply essential to reputation and the continued 'licence to operate' supplied by communities to corporations?

The 'spirituality in leadership' genre then encompasses, at one extreme, robustly theorised critiques of global and postmodern capitalism, and at the other, prescriptive guides about how to inject spiritual feeling into dehumanised workplaces. The bulk of business writing comes from the United States, where spirituality sits comfortably with a confident religiosity.[6] The American appetite for all things 'New Age' also partly explains the enthusiasm with which American writers and companies have taken up ideas of spirituality and work.

Insights and teachings from various mystic and religious traditions have also entered the mainstream business literature.[7] In recent years, 'Spirituality and Business' conferences have started occurring regularly in Australia and the United Kingdom. In Australia, there is a Spirituality, Leadership and Management Network which first gathered in 1997 and has since held annual conferences. In 2000, the American Academy of Management—the most prestigious forum for business academics—launched a special-interest group entitled 'Management, Spirituality and Religion'. By the late 1990s, the spirituality discourse was well and truly established in academic and professional business and management contexts in Australia, New Zealand, the United States and the United Kingdom.[8]

The themes discussed in the spirituality and leadership literature weave a resonant and recognisable story which goes something like this. Since work has become so consuming (requiring long hours and becoming the main source of identity and relationships), employees have lost connection with families and communities. There is a vacuum of meaning in people's lives. Individuals in workplaces, including leaders, are seeking opportunities to bring their 'whole selves' to the workplace, to not leave their values at the door of the office, to be more 'authentic' in the way they operate at work. For example, in their book *Spiritual Capital*, Dana Zohar and Ian Marshall diagnose a failure in modern organisations, arguing—along with the Shell executive they quote—that corporate life is 'essentially dispiriting' because it is driven by the pursuit of money. They maintain that the old paradigm of self-interested capitalism needs to be abandoned for one in which organisations are operating from a 'deeper spiritual vision'. This spirituality 'in human beings makes us ask why we are doing what we are doing and makes us seek some fundamentally better way of doing it. It makes us want our lives and enterprises to make a difference.'[9]

In this argument, an emphasis on spirituality delivers individual happiness *and* business ends. Through organisations paying more attention to the spiritual needs of employees, work becomes more meaningful and transcendent, and employers tap new levels of commitment and 'spiritual intelligence' to direct towards organisational purposes. A 'win–win' situation is created where the employee and the organisation both benefit from more authentic relationships and deeper engagement of their people at work.[10]

RISKS AND RESERVATIONS

What does spirituality promise for leadership? And what is going on when business invests in 'enlightenment for leaders'?

Undoubtedly, the leadership and spirituality discourse is multi-faceted, covering a range of individual and organisational dilemmas to which spirituality might be applied, and with equally various prescriptions for how to do it. While it is too soon to assess precisely what all this interest in spirituality represents, it is important to explore its themes, why it has emerged now and what consequences it might have. I am suggesting that—whatever our findings—leadership will benefit from a more careful and critical appraisal of spirituality's potential.

I build on the work of critical scholars in pointing to three particular problems when spirituality is purposefully introduced into leadership:

○ the use of spirituality to purely material ends such as self-advancement;
○ the ways spirituality might be used to coerce and as an instrument of power; and
○ treating spirituality as a commodity for purchase—a new toolkit in the business of leadership development.[11]

Spirituality as a means to a material end

There is nothing new in approaches that treat spirituality as a means to an end, despite the contradiction at the heart of this. For centuries, churches and religions have exchanged spiritual offerings (forgiveness, salvation, an after-life, blessings on mercenary or political projects) for the favours of patrons and merchants. What is perhaps newer is the explicit encouragement by some in business and the leadership-development industry for leaders to tap into higher consciousness. Invoking soul has emerged as a legitimate way for leaders to develop themselves and simultaneously advance business interests.[12] Examples include the increasing incorporation into Western leadership development of learning from Eastern or Indigenous spiritual traditions. As I go on to discuss, this may promote a search for spiritual gratification that is often transitory or exploitative, in the process decontextualising and degrading spiritual practices from the traditions that shaped them.

Another recent advertisement for a luxury vehicle comes to mind here. This time the car is shown to be so easy to handle that even the most demanding driver—a Buddhist monk—can steer it through the night and be assured that no insects will be caught, or killed, by the front grille.

Using spirituality coercively

With a gush of enthusiasm similar to that which greeted organisational teamwork,[13] spirituality is assumed to sweep employees up into a more uplifting version of the organisation, one from which everyone can benefit. Building on a modern translation of the Protestant work ethic, work has been redefined as an intrinsically moral activity, tacitly and conveniently fusing individual searches for meaning and actualisation with capitalism's interests in efficiency and productivity.[14] In such ways, spiritual remedies often act as if developing the spirituality of leaders produces benefits for everyone: employee, leader, organisation. Yet look closer and such remedies may also increase the personal power of leaders vis-à-vis employees, and lend moral legitimacy to what are, in effect, perfectly ordinary corporate interests, such as selling more cola, fast food or fuel-dependency.[15]

In much of the spirituality literature, as in a considerable amount of that on leadership, the bias is individualistic and ahistorical, with little recognition of the structural forces at work in corporate life. Treating spirituality as a matter of private individual choice fails to acknowledge the political and structural forces which define and limit what employees—and leaders—are able to think and do. In acting as if individuals are completely free to develop their spirituality as they wish, this writing is part of a wider and powerful ideology: that individual self-development is an overriding moral value.[16] One risk is that, as individuals, we work away looking for meaning and developing our spiritual selves while Rome burns. Thinking about bringing more spirituality into leadership can look morally pleasing, but it may conceal tacit coercion of employees to subscribe, especially those at lower levels of the hierarchy.

Ideas of spirituality in leadership have gained currency among groups who are already privileged and powerful. The very language with which corporations and authors exhort the leader to find spirituality should provoke unease. Nikolas Rose argues that there are many examples in history where an elite has claimed 'lofty nobility and disinterest'[17] in its advocacy of certain projects or reforms, yet history has subsequently revealed that advocacy to have been driven by mundane self-interest. Spirituality can thus provide a mask for exploitation. In earlier centuries, the separation of church and state—the two great sources of institutional power—was viewed as a great triumph against tyranny. It is possible to read the enthusiasm for spirituality among corporate leaders as the thin but ominous beginning of a reamassing of economic, secular and spiritual power in the hands of an elite few.

Commodifying spirituality

There is considerable evidence of a commodification of spirituality in business environments where employees and their leaders are eager for new tools for success. For example, a number of instruments have emerged that assess an employee's level of spiritual 'intelligence' and consciousness, and imply that managers need to progress from a lower level of ignorance to an upper level of enlightenment. Not unpredictably, consultants are marketing new spirituality products. Emotional intelligence (EQ) has been joined by spiritual intelligence (SQ) as the essential leadership requisite.

Templates developed for testing spiritual aptitude can appear simplistic, both in their content and the route to improvement implied. In *Spiritual Capital* a 'Self-awareness Check' asks:

○   Do you have much sense of an inner life?
○   At the end of the day do you reflect on the day's events and experiences?
○   Do you have any sense of a deeper presence within you?
○   Are you comfortable with silence?
○   Can you confront uncomfortable truths about yourself?[18]

Surely it is a good thing for leaders to be encouraged to develop deeper awareness of their intentions and purposes? While such a list encourages reflection, it is entirely self-referential, and omits consideration of the effects of the leader's work on others, or on the wider world.

The point here is that, as in the field of emotional intelligence, quantification and measurement can convert a welcome emphasis into tools for surveillance and control, whereby employees are regularly assessed, judged and rewarded if they comply with a predetermined template of spiritual intelligence. Such instruments could conceivably be used in the coercion of employees whose motivation isn't elevated enough in just the same way as psychological instruments and feedback tools have sometimes been used to enhance managerial control. Quite soon, employees no longer need managers to control them because they internalise the need to demonstrate the desired qualities themselves.

A further concern is whether such initiatives to enhance spiritual capital in organisations or leaders can be read as 'add-ons'—that is, lending spiritual legitimacy to purposes or intentions that are already flawed. Companies including British Tobacco, BP, Coca-Cola and Hewlett Packard, and leaders such as Microsoft's Bill Gates, are often described as accruing spiritual capital through various charitable and other initiatives. Yet the same companies and leaders behave with profit-seeking single-mindedness in other contexts. For example, Gates has been lauded for his massive efforts on Third World health issues, yet criticised because, even in his philanthropy, he is seeking to be the backer of a big winner. Benevolence and apparent spiritual selflessness may also be seen from another angle as providing a platform for the elevation of leaders to saint-hood and as protection from scrutiny in other areas.

The argument is not to doubt all philanthropy or spirituality, but to carefully appraise how and why it is taken up. Genuinely spiritually driven leadership initiatives will be able to withstand such scrutiny. Actions do matter, yet actions undertaken to amass spiritual capital for purely material or personal gain should be questioned. While there may be nothing new or necessarily suspect about annexing spiritual ideas and techniques to leadership, we should always be alert to its misuse and assumptions. We should be concerned where what's good for the company and its leaders' spiritual well-being is automatically assumed to be good for other, less powerful, stakeholders. We should be especially concerned where, for example, these techniques are reserved for an elite or are shrouded in secrecy—sometimes spiritual leadership work is governed by codes of silence and talked about in hushed tones. In such cases, executives are literally 'initiated' into spiritual development, and may only speak of the experience with other initiates. These practices come together to create a set of understandings and language that are available only to those at the top, and so function to reinforce existing power relations.

TWO PROFILES OF LEADING WITH SPIRIT

In this section I provide profiles of two leaders to show how spirituality might operate differently in leadership. Neither Lillian Holt nor John Wilson claim to adopt a spiritual leadership style. Indeed, both are wary of the terms 'spirituality' and 'leadership' and how they are put together. Yet both are animated in how spiritual concerns influence the way they have done the work of leadership.

LILLIAN HOLT

I met Lillian Holt when she was director of the Centre for Indigenous Education (CIE) at the University of Melbourne (she is now Principal of Tauondi College, Adelaide). She attended a talk I gave to a conference that was addressing issues of reconciliatory leadership. An impressive Indigenous woman, she has short silver hair and a passion for dramatic jewellery. I was aware of her during my talk as she nodded and engaged with what I was saying. She approached me straight afterwards and we talked. I think the second thing she said to me was: 'Where did you get those deadly boots? [a compliment]'

I am relating the way I first experienced Lillian to reveal what I regard as important dimensions of her leadership. When she is present, she is really present—not there half-heartedly or with her mind on another meeting. Also, both consciously and less consciously, she does not behave according to the institutional script. She often finds institutional rituals and conventions oppressive, and she says so.

I have had many conversations and conducted several interviews with Lillian, initially as part of working with her on a research project on Aboriginal leadership. Right from the start, she was very uneasy about this word 'leadership'. She was worried about what designating someone an 'Aboriginal leader' meant, and was troubled by whether we should include the 'well-known' ones or the ones who are 'doing it differently'.

For Lillian, 'leadership' is a loaded word—negatively loaded. She gives many speeches, in Australia and internationally, about matters of leadership. She said that her speeches to young Indigenous people are often focused on rejecting Western models of leadership which 'steal your spirit'. In Indigenous Australian cultures, 'spirit' and 'spirituality' are terms with powerful meaning. Spirituality is one of the key ways Indigenous people know and identify themselves, connecting them to ancestors and ideas of country that are at the heart of their cultures. When Lillian argues that leadership steals your spirit, she means that institutional pressures change you; they erode your courage, passion and humour and wear you down so that important things don't get named and get overtaken by the trivial. In the following excerpts from one interview I undertook with her, Lillian elaborates why Indigenous Australians find it hard to speak out.

> There is a systemic blockage. Something happens to Aboriginal people who work in hierarchies, whether bureaucracy or academic . . . a bit like my own story of climbing the ladder of success. You get to the top and find it bereft, bereft of passion, bereft of intuition, of emotion. 'For God's sake don't talk about emotion in a place like this!'
>
> It leaves out a lot of stuff that Indigenous men and women could bring. I see it happening with white women. They become deferential in front of white males. It's wanting to be needed and approved of. I do it myself. I'm not saying I go in there guns blazing. You can't always do that because you have to apportion your emotional energy. I think

Lillian Holt, Principal of Tauondi College, 2006
Lillian Holt, personal collection

. . . oh really, that stiff upper lip, that anal retentive stuff, probably conserves your energies.

[There is a need to ask yourself:] 'What is it that limits us in the most essential and human way?' I am not talking about black stuff. I am not talking about white stuff.

What I'm saying is there needs to be a path opened up whereby people can actually speak into one another's spirit . . . and speak with passion, to speak with truth and to speak in their own voice, rather than having three references for every statement you make.

. . . I think what happens on the way to the top is you get burnt out or the system insidiously steals your spirit or your passion. It steals your courage and I think it takes great courage to speak out in a way that—in language that—is not acceptable. The safe language of leadership, the safe and secure language of leadership, which in relation to Indigenous issues is all about the statistical and historical: 'This happened to Aboriginal people, we're spending so many dollars.' It is all terribly, terribly controlled and precious.

Lillian's experience is that leadership, as it is commonly practised, comes at the price of spirituality. Her experience of so-called leaders is often a toadying conformity and a traitorous silence about the things that matter.

The opposite of pious, Lillian is a straight talker, unafraid to create discomfort with her honesty and humour. Along with some Aboriginal leaders such as Mick Dodson and Chris Sarra, whom I profile elsewhere in this book, Indigenous identity—including Indigenous spirituality—is integral to leadership. Leadership is not a purely rational or cerebral activity.

One of Lillian's leadership dilemmas is that she is in increasing demand as a speaker at conferences. She is a powerful speaker, and leaves few in her audiences unmoved. She explicitly refuses 'the language of leadership', which she describes as 'safe'; however, because she does not abdicate into safe territory, she becomes positioned as the 'Aboriginal' speaker. This tokenism is painful for her. She also comes under pressure to tone down her speeches, to be less confrontational. She is partly tempted by this—it would be a lot simpler and less exhausting to put on a mask and give a 'whitened' talk. White women in particular say to her: 'You always seem so frustrated' and then 'I want to help'. This is an example of many situations in which it is Lillian's intensity that is 'read' as 'the problem', in need of help to fix it so that it conforms more comfortably with white expectations. Lillian's response is: 'Didn't you hear what I said? I don't want you to help me. I want you to interrogate yourself. Your own whiteness.' As she notes: 'Leadership and human issues often get turned into race issues when advocated by Indigenous people.' Here she both advocates and models the reflectiveness that is at the heart of good leadership.

So how does Lillian Holt do a kind of leadership that allows her spirituality expression and enables her to resist the homogenising pressure to deliver the Aboriginal message that white audiences want to hear? In her leadership of the CIE, Lillian worked closely with Gary Thomas. When prompted, she explains he is formally her deputy, but that label is something she doesn't willingly use because she doesn't think about him in this way. They share a sense of humour, a capacity to support each other across gender and age differences, and commitment to what they want to achieve.

While working in the university, Gary had more of an appetite for bureaucracy and could ably go 'head to head' with the 'bean counters'.

Leading with spirit

Over several years, the two of them developed a formidable leadership approach which also delivered on the performance measures of recruiting and retaining Indigenous students. Lillian describes a conversation with Gary:

> I said to him last year when we were having a lot of politics here with all the players [in the CIE and university]. I remember saying to him in a pit of despair: 'I've actually lost my way. I don't know what my job is anymore.' He without hesitation said to me: 'Lil, you know what your job is. Your job is to dream this place into existence. To continue to dream it.' He said: 'When you're dreaming this place is flying . . . It is very powerful stuff when you communicate with people like that. You're one person who when you do, you really speak into the spirit of the other person.' And he said: 'You must continue to do that.' That's what he meant in the dreaming of it. 'When you're doing that, it is really flowing.' He said: 'You be the dreamer and I'll be the dream-catcher.'[19]

In this quote, Lillian identifies some ways she can do leadership without compromising her spirituality, which ends up meaning her commitment to the cause of supporting Aboriginal education in a way that doesn't lose sight of the value of the people and their culture. She has stood up to and extracted herself from bureaucratic requirements such as being the Aboriginal member of too many committees, in which her presence is all too frequently exploited—the means by which the committee itself appears 'inclusive' while practising the very rules of safety she so abhors. But she brings humour to this process. She describes:

> People here, in terms of being inclusive, of you as being an Indigenous person, they want you to go to everything. I said to Gary: 'How come these people want us to go to everything?' Gary said to me: 'Look Lil for them it's bonding. For us it's bondage.' [Laughs] So, you go along in that frame of mind. Have a laugh when you come back . . . but for us it's bondage. I find those administrative meetings terribly, terribly draining of the spirit.

In her leadership of the CIE, Lillian insisted on measuring against the most important barometers of performance for her: high-flying students attracted to the university, numbers retained and graduated. But it also matters that she and her small team created a cohesive and supportive environment for Indigenous students. She and the rest of the team knew them and what was going on in their lives. Students called in regularly and formed an informal support network that cut across what could otherwise feel a huge and impersonal set of faculties. The centre itself acquired a warm and welcoming feel, used as a meeting place with frequent gatherings around food:

> You need time for people to sit around and yarn and philosophise ... the First Europeans going to the Pacific, when they saw the natives sitting under a coconut tree, said: 'They're lazy.' What they didn't understand was that sitting around is an activity. I reckon that we do a lot of sitting around here ... I just say to them, grab a cup of coffee [and we have a] staff meeting that extends into morning tea.

Spirituality is manifested in Lillian's leadership in subtle and provocative ways: in the way she speaks publicly and what she speaks about; in the way she worked or 'dreamed' with her deputy and supported the students; in the way she challenged others to examine their assumptions and stereotypes before offering their 'help'.

Next I profile another leader, John Wilson. His interest in and practising of spirituality shares Lillian's appetite for robust challenging of convention, including the norms of piety.

JOHN WILSON

I first met John through his wife and my friend and co-author of *New Faces of Leadership*, Valerie Wilson. John ran his family's manufacturing and construction business from the age of 26 and later developed a reputation as a CEO to be brought in to turn around ailing Australian welfare organisations. He was appointed as the Founding CEO of Anglicare (an amalgam of three Anglican welfare agencies), CEO of the Brotherhood of St Lawrence (a well-regarded bastion of the welfare sector that had lost its way) and the Sacred Heart Mission (a Catholic agency working with the homeless and destitute).

At first John seemed—and I don't think he'd mind me saying this— rather eccentric. He is dynamic, full of energy and ideas, but shares with Valerie a capacity to see behind superficialities and an appetite to say what he sees there. He is alternately solicitous and frank to the point of coming across as shocking.

Leading with spirit

I wanted to talk with and interview John because he seemed to encapsulate some of the complexities around spirituality and leadership that I was increasingly keen to explore. He always struck me as a person with a conviction about the importance of spiritual ideas. I assumed—wrongly—that he had had a traditional and intense religious upbringing, and that he 'knew a lot' about spirituality from having been steered firmly into faith by various parents, teachers and mentors.

I was interested in how John's spirituality intersected with and informed his leadership roles, and vice versa. Does having a sense of spiritual vocation make you do the job differently? Does it create conflicts—for example, between the need for a bottom-line focus and the need to nurture staff—and how are these conflicts managed? Is there a hierarchy in spiritual values? Is there a series of stages of 'progress' along a spiritual path in leadership (like Elizabeth Kubler-Ross's stages of mourning)?

Once I started talking with John, these seemed rather naive questions. Up front, John declared 'the concept of spirituality is too vague for me'. He prefers terms such as 'values', 'vocation', 'theology'

John Wilson and his artwork, 2006
John Wilson, personal collection

and 'self-identity' to capture a process of 'finding yourself through others', or that 'oceanic feeling' that comes with identifying with all of the living world. Spirituality is for him both external and internal, a private and public activity: 'You need both legs to make it stand up.'

In fact, rather than religion, perhaps the strongest theme emerging from his childhood was a flair for running businesses. John grew up in an agnostic household. From Scottish stock, his mother was a fourth-generation businesswoman with an Angloceltic/Jewish heritage. His father was not religious either, but was a lawyer not much interested in material things. So, although there were strong traditions of social service paternalism on both sides (John remembers delivering boxes of food to the homes of his parents' employees), his was a secular upbringing.

It was also a relatively bleak existence after he was sent to boarding school at the age of eight, along with an older brother. As the smallest boy with an interest in artistic matters, he learned how to survive at school, but also developed a strong distrust and dislike of authority: 'If you're small you learn that authority doesn't do anything for you—you are more likely the object of male aggression or female spite.'

At seventeen, as he was approaching the end of his schooling, John took the unexpected step of writing to all the bishops in the region north of Australia requesting that he be considered for posts as an Anglican missionary. He took up the first positive response and went to the Solomon Islands. After spending a very difficult year there, he was enrolled in law at the University of Melbourne by his father, who died not long after.

During his twenties and thirties, John finished his law degree, later added an MBA, pursued his interest in theology (doing parts of a Diploma of Theology), and ran the family business, 'making it profitable while my mother looked on disapprovingly at everything I did'. There was not much admiration forthcoming for his business acumen, just the expectation he'd get on and do it.

Through this period he had a strong sense of vocation, alongside the pursuit of his eclectic interests in business and art. But it was a very solitary path with 'no guide'—'I had to work things out for myself.' Through his 'attempt to construct an adult faith', he knew he didn't want to be a priest. He came across many priests: some looked defeated, others were too punitive, and others just 'seemed to like dressing up'.

All the while, John was honing his business skills and his vision for how organisations should operate. His nascent spirituality sat alongside a fascination for human behaviour and an instinct for business and managing money. He was, and remains, in his words, 'a pillar of pragmatism'—which caused some tensions when he started to manage welfare agencies in the 1990s.

John's style in running these agencies was unsentimental and businesslike. He had no qualms in dealing with a newly elected state government intent on privatising and contracting out welfare: 'I was an expert at the tendering process, had done it for years.' He was also ruthless with people who, he felt, were bleeding the system and not working hard enough for clients. 'I turned the temperature up and closed the tea-rooms.' In one agency which was at crisis point, he got rid of the marketing department and there was an almost complete turnover of senior staff: 'After which I got to a point where I had an effective team, including some good "jam jar" accountants . . . I am a relentless bar-raiser.'

In the midst of his focus and tough-mindedness, John found that the values and 'spiritual engagement' of many of those working for welfare agencies delivered excellent value for clients. His experience was that, with some exceptions, 'social workers made better people managers than accountants'. Far from heavy-handed about his own faith, John fervently believes that working in a values-based way can change what happens in workplaces. He says:

> To me the key point about spiritual engagement is that it connects to passion, and passion to energy and creation, and creation to entrepreneurialism. It makes the person bigger than they are. They transcend themselves. Working in values-based NGOs, this is very, very apparent. People continue to do more for less because they believe. [These kinds of organisations] could and should and did produce better results for their clients than the government department doing the same job.

In terms of leadership style, John says he couldn't 'give the rousing speeches', inspiring others with rhetoric. But he could win tenders and deliver results. He also cared deeply for the people working for him, and many of them were at the front line of welfare, working with the desperate and suicidal. 'If someone [a client] died, everything would stop and I would go to that employee … There is a communion in being with somebody totally.'

Throughout the periods when he was a CEO, John was also 'growing myself theologically', taking himself off to retreats and being exposed to lots of faiths and religious systems. Though an Anglican himself, he despairs of predictable rituals such as 'the four hymn-sandwich service'. Disheartened by the pomposity and rigidity of much institutionalised religion, he is more at home with the 'earthy and direct' Catholics working on the front line of need. He developed a new sense of Christ as an 'ordinary guy in an ordinary world', a 'small figure' who lived a short life. His conviction was that the extraordinary was located in the ordinary. All the while, the old anti-authoritarianism would be bubbling along, prompting him to 'always go back to basics' and 'ask why I was doing things'. Faith is never comfortable or unquestioning. Within this spirituality, there is discomfort, 'a lot of wilderness' and dry periods that continue for years. Because he holds no church post, his faith cannot hold him hostage, but is rather a catalyst for discovery. It is driven by a 'yearning for metaphor and richness in life that [otherwise] isn't there'.

John maintains that it is Christianity, rather than increasingly popular faiths like Buddhism, that has most to offer people like him. Because Christianity arises out of his own culture's history and society, spirituality can be 'studied' by looking at 'how real people have struggled in real times with everyday life'. There are 'glimpses of God' in this process that sees the inner work of faith and values directly link with the outer work of leadership.

In the leadership work of both Lillian Holt and John Wilson, spirituality appears in ways different to that advocated in the leadership literature. Spirituality is not an 'add-on' or template, but an integral part of their culture and life history. In both cases, spirituality is not without conflict or contradiction, and it often supports an interest in interrogating and usurping the status quo, in the interests of clients or those lower down various hierarchies. Spirituality plays out in pragmatic ways, often being less about introspection and more about concrete methods of interacting with and mobilising others. Though spirituality is acknowledged by both Holt and Wilson as deeply significant in making sense of what they do, and how they go about it, it is not an overblown claim. There is humour, frankness and humility in these two leaders' accounts of leading with spirit.

RETHINKING SPIRITUALITY IN LEADERSHIP

Spirituality is a potentially valuable set of insights to bring to the study of leadership; however, much of the existing writing which connects these two ideas is prescriptive and commodifying. It advocates spirituality for material or questionable ends, treats it as a resource for leaders which can have coercive and oppressive effects, and behaves as if there are universal sets of spiritual ideas that can be applied across cultures and societies. I have argued the need to adopt a critical eye on the emergence of this literature and to ask: 'What is this literature doing?' 'Why is it emerging now?' 'Who benefits?' and 'To what end?' There is something in the observation of a friend who had been schooled in a particularly rigid convent environment. Teaching leaders to be more spiritual looked to her like a grab by a masculine elite to repossess and technologise ways of thinking and practising that have been marginalised as feminine but have now emerged as increasingly influential—for example, among young people.

Silvio Berlusconi, the Italian political leader, was quoted as saying, at the outset of his campaign to be re-elected prime minister: 'I am the Jesus Christ of politics. I am a patient victim. I put up with everyone. I sacrifice myself for everyone.'[20] As we observed in the 2006 Italian elections, the majority of the electorate did not see him in this way—as having a direct connection to God. History is full of examples of corrupt leaders who believed they had a special relationship to God, and who marketed their spirituality as part of their leadership. We should be wary of leaders with institutional power—either in politics or in business (Berlusconi had both)—who then additionally annex religion or spirituality to support their own ambitions.

In this chapter I have drawn on the work of two very different leaders, Lillian Holt and John Wilson, to reveal some of the complexity, tensions and dynamism that are part of leading with spirituality. I summarise some of these tensions below.[21]

○ *Spirituality as biography*: each journey as different and arising in response to families and testing circumstances.
○ *Spirituality as inner and outer work, reflection and action*, including the tensions where these things come into conflict.
○ *Spirituality as embedded in power relations*, not somehow immune or separate from them.
○ *Spirituality as ordinariness*, a way of struggling with everyday things but with greater awareness.

○ *Spirituality as something that can come and go*, that feels interrupted and empty as well as substantial.

○ *Spirituality as awareness of connection with others*—that you lead only because of others' respect for you.

○ *Spirituality as passionate and embodied*, potentially rebellious and loud rather than pious.

○ *Spirituality as made up of contradictory experiences*:
   – internal reflection and external connection;
   – discipline and serious commitment alongside the capacity for humour, lightness and release;
   – ritualistic and with substance;
   – richness, metaphor and symbolism with rawness and grit;
   – passion and reason;
   – faith and doubt;
   – embodied yet transcending the material.

In his 2003 book, *The Spirituality Revolution*, David Tacey maps the huge shift in many Western societies in the last decades away from institutionalised religion towards diverse notions of spirituality. The evidence is that—particularly among younger generations—there is an appetite for connecting spiritual ideas, such as working to a higher purpose or finding meaning in connection with a greater whole, to work and to leadership.

In suggesting a role for spirituality in leadership, it is important to resist pressures to codify or justify its benefits to the bottom line. What might leaders do instead? They can, as Lillian and John do, talk about their own spiritual experience. They might, through their own example and through leadership practices, make space for people to explore and validate ideas around values, purpose and meaning in their workplaces. Rather than instructing people in what to do to pursue a spiritual practice, leaders can model its importance in their way of relating to others.

There are many spiritual currents in leadership, evident in small acts of connection or courage as much as in ritualised observances. Drawing on spiritual traditions and ideas can allow us to understand leadership possibilities in a broader way, beyond the limiting discourse of business and the bottom line. How can such ideas be incorporated in leadership in ways that do not distort or misuse but open new awareness and new freedoms for leaders and the people around them? It is to this question I turn in the final chapter.

10
Less-ego leadership

⚘

The problem is that ego can convert anything to its own use.

Chögyam Trungpa (1973)

Only leaders who recognise their fallibility and operate on that basis are likely to succeed in the long run.

Keith Grint (2000)

How can people do leadership in a more consciously liberating way? In this chapter, I build on the deeper understandings of identity and spirituality that have been explored in the preceding chapters, to suggest that sometimes the obstacle to doing leadership differently is oneself. Our attachment to particular understandings of ourselves—our identities—and the ego's need to protect those selves, is the problem. The human need for approval, for control or affirmation of a self, can become the dominating impulse: leaders may be captured, diverted or swamped by ego needs.

But insights about identity and the ego also hold a solution to the challenge of change. More liberating effects—for followers and leaders—may flow from learning *how to do leadership with less ego*. By releasing oneself from the need to *be* someone, to prove our value, we become available to lead in a truly different way.

But what do I mean by 'less ego'? *Less-ego leadership* explores the possibilities in leadership of:

○ a relationship with ourselves that is reflective but not preoccupied with securing self, or with personal rewards;

○ less striving towards goals and struggling to prove ourselves, which takes us away from the present moment;

○ being with others in ways that do not use them for our own purposes;

○ less narcissism and vanity;

○ knowing self but so as to be a platform for release from the anxiously self-scripted life;

○ through awareness, abandoning the search for leadership as a greater self so as to open up to new ways of being;

○ an appetite for doubting simplistic solutions, particularly those we devise for ourselves, but also those offered to us by others;[1] and

○ a commitment to practical implementation and to the test of daily conduct.

Less-ego leadership is the opposite of what is often urged in writing on leadership. Partly because of strong values of individualism (discussed in Chapter 2), leaders are often encouraged to invest time and effort in themselves and in acting out their 'true' identity—perhaps inviting self-absorption or grandiosity. Some self-knowledge is necessary, but it should be with the intent of freeing and releasing rather than self-advancement.

You will notice that I am not advocating *egoless* leadership: egolessness is probably an impossible ideal for most of us. Some form of self-belief may be required if we are to accept opportunities to influence others, and self-belief can clearly coexist alongside humility, as examples such as Gandhi and the Dalai Lama show.

While I still have much to learn and understand about Eastern philosophies,[2] these guide my thinking about leadership, and in particular less-ego leadership, offering an antidote to the cult of the individual and hero worship that permeates much leadership literature in the West. Eastern ideas suggest that the most transformative leadership may come not from working to build one's leadership persona, but from working to release oneself from 'the bureaucracy of the ego'.[3] This sort of release is what I describe as less-ego leadership.

LEARNING ABOUT EGO FROM EASTERN PHILOSOPHIES: MY INTRODUCTION

I came to the study of Eastern philosophy—especially Hinduism and Buddhism—through the physical practice of yoga. I felt my body was a problem, not able to withstand the stresses of working intensive, long days. I turned to yoga to refine and strengthen my physical body, thinking that this would put me back 'in control', back in the driver's seat of my life.

The physical pursuit of yoga stimulated other changes, largely independently of my conscious will. It was as if the physical discipline and regularity ushered in a gradual shedding of personal preoccupations (and some, though far from all, vanities and insecurities), and stimulated a search of a different kind. I started to want to inhabit the world differently from the way I'd done in my first 50 years. Instead of careering along, being part of a system that induced a lot of stress *for myself and others*, I wanted to be *with others* in a way that was better—happier and supportive of growth—for us all. To do this, I had to start with myself.

In my initial flirtation with Buddhism, I couldn't believe my luck. I thought religion had to be punishing, yet here was the Dalai Lama fervently advising us to pursue our own happiness! I found, as I started to read more and practise the ideas, that not only did these deliver feelings of greater personal contentment, but my capacity to give to, and to forgive, others increased. The simple idea that one's capacity to feel compassion should in some way start with oneself has been both a life-changing and a very practical insight for me.

Opening myself to these ideas felt risky. My stern self was intermittently scathing about such 'self-indulgence'. Initially I stayed firmly in the closet and divided my life into two parts: 'business school and leadership' and 'yoga and Eastern thinking'. As I continued my study and practice,[4] however, I came to see that, rather than living in two worlds, I could make connections between the two that might be valuable to others. It also seemed from my research that thoughtful leaders are often approaching the challenges that Eastern thinking addresses—for example, how to be and how to influence so as to promote greater well-being and fulfilment for those around one.

For centuries, many European writers and philosophers have been inspired by Eastern ideas, the wisest taking pains to acknowledge rather than simply exploit these influences on their own thinking.[5] Yet many other Western scholars have cast a doubtful eye in the direction of Eastern philosophies—particularly as they have been popularised and transformed by Western interest.[6] While such reserve is entirely appropriate, in my experience, Western critical thinking and Eastern philosophies share a deep, critical sensibility. They both argue against fashion, and warn against slavish obedience to people presenting as gurus and offering the truth. Both offer ways of stepping back from what is taken for granted, including the role of leadership.

Further, there is a simplicity and accessibility in many core ideas of Eastern thinking that is not accidental. These ideas, originally transmitted orally, are designed to be available for everyone rather than being embellished into large, forbidding treatises. Much of this thinking does not discriminate by requiring resources, status or trained intellect in order to put its tenets into practice. In their very accessibility, these teachings are a deliberately political and democratic act.

The key aspects of less-ego leadership that I am concerned with here are:

○ liberating intent;
○ being reflective with less ego;
○ connection with others; and
○ cultivating a sceptical perspective.

A LIBERATING INTENT

In the first part of this book I described the importance in leadership of reflecting on one's intent or purpose. Leaders need to ask: 'What is my leadership for?' Often this question doesn't get asked, or the answer is an impoverished one that overemphasises material goals and neglects what happens to lives in their pursuit.

As discussed in Chapter 3, ideas of freedom are complex and contested. It was towards the end of a lifetime of investigating power, knowledge and identity that philosopher Michel Foucault explored relations between concepts of 'care of the self' and practices of freedom. Foucault points out that in Greek and Roman philosophy, 'in order to practice freedom properly, it was necessary to care for the self, both in order to know one's self . . . and to improve one's self, to surpass one's self, to master the appetites that risk engulfing you'.[7] In an interview in 1984 entitled 'The ethic of care for the self as a practice of freedom', Foucault explores central elements of such practices including 'getting free of oneself'—'an act of self upon self by which one tries to work out, to transform oneself and to attain a certain mode of being'.[8] He argues that the practices of freedom are more important than defining an end state of liberation, because such a state inevitably opens up new power relations which then in turn require further liberating practice. Foucault's work underlines the complexity in working towards freeing practices: power is always present, even when conditions and individual participants seek to free.

Yet the idea of leading with the intent of freeing people has a long history in diverse traditions of philosophy, religion, law, international relations and politics. By seeking to be freeing in one's stance and influence, we are also consciously thinking about power, and the purposes to which our own and others' power is put.

In practice, leadership might seek to free by:

O listening to people and encouraging greater self-governance in workplaces and communities;

O educating for greater awareness of structural, political and economic forces and their effects;

O providing skills and resources for greater self-direction;

O fostering questioning of the status quo;

O having faith and trust in others to take responsibility and exercise it compassionately; and

O encouraging people to be mindful about their power, influence and urge to control and use others.

An example of a leader who built leadership on empowering the most powerless is Kiran Bedi, appointed in 1993 as the Indian Inspector-General of Prisons. In her role as Governor of Tihar Jail in New Delhi, Bedi was responsible for over 9000 prisoners and a prison system that was deeply corrupted and dehumanised.[9] In the past, the approach had been to punish with an appalling regime of violence, fear and neglect, on the assumption that, if it was bad enough, people would do anything to avoid reimprisonment after release. There was no evidence that this technique worked.

The radicalism of Bedi's approach lay in her attitude towards both prisoners and prison guards. Informed by her own spirituality and traditions, Bedi's approach was to foster a kind of freedom for prisoners and guards: to see the potential for goodness in them; to nurture self-respect; to offer mental stimulation; and to support them to reform themselves. Bedi introduced educational opportunities, such as access to Open University courses, self-governing structures for the prisoners, and proper medical support for drug addicts and those suffering mental illness.

The most powerful of Bedi's leadership interventions was to introduce *Vipassana* meditation. Bedi made *Vipassana*—a way of thinking and conducting oneself in life—available to prisoners and prison officers. The technique, while not easy, can be learned by anyone, and provides a potentially lasting means for people to change themselves. The *Vipassana* system requires participants to meditate for ten days, largely in silence. Participants are supported by training and techniques to help them work through the intensely inward process that unfolds.

Kiran Bedi with pigeons
Dinodia Photo Library

When Bedi was transferred from Tihar Jail in 1995, inmates went on a hunger strike. She said of the prisoners: 'They loved me and I loved them . . . The experience of Tihar can be universal. Wherever combined determination is based on innate goodness . . . anything is possible.'[10]

Bedi has had critics, and after her departure from Tihar many of her reforms unravelled. We could argue that this leadership approach was too idiosyncratic to endure, that her followers could not sustain a different way of being without structural support and continued leadership commitment. However, this might be to miss the point. This example shows the significance in leadership of the underlying intention and a faith in people's humanity. Confronted with an apparently irredeemable system, leadership here was aimed at supporting people to free themselves—not physically, but with techniques to help them acknowledge what they had done, and to make choices about how they would continue to live. Underpinned by respect for basic human rights and the conviction that people could change the condition of their lives, this leadership approach had an intent of liberation.

BEING REFLECTIVE, WITH LESS EGO

As discussed in earlier chapters, much of the writing on leadership promotes reflection and self-awareness. Reflection is the basis of learning and change. However, in this book I am arguing for a particular kind of reflection—one in which we reflect in order to reduce rather than reinforce the power of ego on the way we operate.

Reflection is often justified on the basis of self-improvement. We reflect to understand ourselves better or to do better in our lives. Yet, in this quest, what sometimes happens is that reflection is used to prop up the self: to be more successful, more popular, more desirable, to discover a better self. All of these efforts are designed to serve, at some level, a needy ego.[11]

Building on evidence assembled in earlier chapters, I am suggesting that many initiatives designed to promote self-awareness in leadership actually take leaders in the wrong direction. Striving towards being an aware, actualised or authentic leader may encourage preoccupation with self, rather than release from egoistic concerns. The mind and the ego can be obstacles to, as well as tools of, self-awareness.

So how might leaders work towards less ego? Eastern thinking—particularly Buddhism—is again helpful in guiding reflectiveness that does not feed ego-centredness. A key Buddhist teaching is that life is suffering. One source of suffering is attachments. We are attached to a false self, attached to a limited understanding of life, attached to our tendency to use others and things to validate ourselves. The more we cling to these illusions—of ourselves as independent of other living beings; of seeking to find ourselves through attachment to things and people; and of confusing ego as the start and end of the self—the more we suffer.

In such Eastern models, the mind is understood as many-layered and as both an impediment to, and a vehicle for, enlightenment. Most of us spend much time captive to the lower levels of consciousness, distracted by endlessly replaying thoughts—regrets and doubts about the past, fears and anxieties about the future. As anyone who has tried meditation knows, the rule of these thoughts is tyrannical and ingenious. The result is that many of us come to believe that the thoughts that fill our minds represent the whole—that our thinking is who we are, our ego is us.

However, in traditions of mindfulness and meditation, we are encouraged to step back and allow a space in which we are not captured, or defined by, our thoughts. We are able to become more mindful and aware of the present, to make more of a choice about if and how we react to and interpret experience. Such techniques offer a way of seeing the self without getting trapped into defending self.

Eastern thinking also encourages us to see the ego, and our conscious sense of ourselves, as not the whole self. Just as people sometimes confuse the physical body (the bundle of bone, tissue and water) with the self, there is a danger that we begin to believe we are *what we think of as ourselves*. The narrative going on now in my head—about me, my identity and history, my needs and desires—is mistaken as my entire self. Rather, Eastern thinkers suggest we can create space between ourselves and our egos, so that we can observe the ways in which the self invents the self, and then swallows that self whole—more or less undigested.[12]

How can such awareness of ego, and detachment from preoccupying and colonising thoughts, play a part in better leadership?

Less-ego leadership: An example from the classroom

The first time I put experiential learning right at the heart of the curriculum for MBA students, it felt risky for me as the teacher because I did not know, from one class to the next, what would come up—whether we would find ways of learning from our own experience and, indeed, what we would learn.

Among the students there were many who were significant to this story, but two were particularly important. The first was a mature-age student from India who had held a lot of responsibility in his previous managerial roles and had previously largely accepted how things were done. By the time he entered my subject, he was starting to look deeply into his life for a greater sense of meaning. He had read many spiritual books and had a thoughtful and introspective demeanour. Also though, he had become attached to the idea that the only worthwhile leadership came from completely dissolving the ego, like a truly enlightened being. He was idealising a kind of selfless leadership which he felt was very far from himself. He would often appear rather forlornly in my office, and it didn't seem possible for me to find anything that would 'cheer him up'. There was a paradox here which is important to acknowledge: that in the very striving after the goal of egolessness, personal ego needs may be being reinforced.

The second student I want to mention was anointed informally as a leader right from the first class. While not overly approval-seeking, this student was certainly conscious of his impact. He dressed in a counter-cultural way and clearly enjoyed his status in the class. For him, leadership was primarily a one-person show, and he wasn't doing much listening. His contributions were powerful but thoughtful, and he quickly developed a capacity not just to act but to step back and experiment with how he positioned himself. About two-thirds of the way through our subject, we did some reading and work on narcissism.

This research and class feedback allowed him to see himself, and his own addiction to self-validation. For him, the challenge of leadership became to leverage himself out of constantly looking at himself, so that he might find ways to be with others, hearing and learning from them.

It was coming to the end of the subject, and I was not sure how we were going to draw together what we had learned. The students were all working hard, but many were struggling. One woman, who worked for a large and overstretched local government authority, asked: 'But how can I go about putting these new ideas of leadership work into practice, in an organisation like mine?'

To understand how our insights were to be applied in practice was a crucial test. We charted the ideas diagrammatically on the whiteboard. The charismatic student volunteered that he was wrestling with the intensely egocentric and narcissistic position he characteristically tended to occupy. We indicated this at one end of the continuum on the whiteboard. Then the Indian student reluctantly admitted that he might have to move away from complete selflessness or egolessness—in this life, anyway. This we marked as the opposite extreme of the continuum. We began an exploration of all the positions, behaviours, outlooks and interventions that might sit between these two extremes: thinking about one's effect on others; really listening; finding out that others might have something to teach us; discussing how to ensure there is sufficient respect for this to happen; understanding that achievements are often truly collective; taking time to value the present process and relationships—all this rather than being trapped into striving only to reach our own individual goals.

This is what I began to understand as the territory of 'less-ego leadership'.

Practices for leaders

For leaders in organisations, a less-ego approach might rest on being adept at noting and observing when various parts of one's own ego show themselves: the needy or striving self, the disapproving or punishing self. By detaching and observing, we can establish a distance—however slight—between that needy or striving self and another experience. Such a stance allows us, even if only gradually, to tame an ego intent on controlling others, or inflating or justifying the self.

The path starts with oneself and one's own practice in ways that require few resources—only disciplined practice and commitment. It is a practical approach: one in which the individual should not take things on trust but try them out and see whether they make a difference. It is also advisable not to undertake this process entirely on our own. Leaders too often expect themselves to be 'lone rangers'—omnipotent, or at least self-sufficient. In contrast, what I am suggesting here is leadership which is open to feedback and learning, through structured opportunities such as coaching and guided reading and exploration.

The idea of letting go of the self more—of not endlessly striving towards an improved self—seems to be the opposite of the confidence-boosting or assertiveness that is sometimes preached in managerial literature. Yet the idea of *letting go* is not *giving in* or *being soft*. As described in Buddhist teachings, letting go requires fearlessness and an absence of aggression.[13] Ian Johnson quotes Kearney, another lay Buddhist teacher, to reveal the difficulties we often have in ceasing craving:

> If we are striving for enlightenment, then that very striving indicates that what we are after is not right here, right now. We are looking for it in the future. But reality is not located in the future; it is located right here, right now. Therefore our searching results in the endless postponement of our finding. We are always looking elsewhere for what is right here and as long as we do so, we are guaranteed never to find it.[14]

In my interpretation of such Eastern philosophies, the first steps toward change are typically around patiently establishing discipline and good habits. In observing these, other changes begin subtly to occur. For example, in yoga 'the eight-fold path' begins with one observing the restraints (*yamas*), including avoiding things such as violence (*ahimsa*), stealing (*asteya*) and untruthfulness. The observances (*niyamas*) follow, including being pure and disciplined in one's ways of life, and avoiding attachments and fear of death in the pursuit of study and higher purposes. These two stages are followed by physical practice and purification (*hatha yoga*), the discipline of breath (*pranayama*), and then increasingly focused practices of refining consciousness including withdrawal of the senses or reducing reactions to sound and light, concentration and meditation.

Practices of mindfulness and meditation also have a role in less-ego leadership.[15] My most recent meditation teacher advised that it wasn't until you had practised uninterruptedly daily for at least a couple of months that the mind said to itself: 'Oh well, I see that she is serious about this.' Until this amount of disciplined commitment to practice, the 'lower' mind is dancing around, tolerating one's trifling efforts, but all the time knowing that it won't last. A day's practice will be missed, one will be 'too busy', other engagements will crowd in. The status quo will be restored, and nothing needs to change.

My teacher was right about this. Our minds are clever, seeing through and outwitting our fragile resolve. For leaders, the way to show that we are really serious about change is to practise, and to *commit to* that practice. After a while, the simple truth of this becomes clear. Meditation encourages a detachment from the self in order to see how the mind acts as master and servant, prison guard and escapee. It encourages a detachment from attachment—that is, enables us to see that our feelings towards others are often clinging and instrumental rather than the expressions of love or concern we claim. Meditation encourages us to move from a stance of needing others to validate ourselves to a condition of non-judgmental compassion towards self and others. Meditation, in most traditions, is also supportive of efforts to expose the limitations of thinking—of illusions and false dichotomies. By dispassionately watching and then detaching from the mind, there is movement towards a purer, less cluttered sense of being. The sharp boundaries of 'self' become less important, replaced by a sense of connection with the whole.

These practices may sound esoteric, but there are leaders working in this very way. Sogyal Rinpoche is a Tibetan Buddhist master and author of *The Tibetan Book of Living and Dying*. For the last five years or so, he has visited Australia to conduct retreats for leaders focusing on meditation practices that foster compassion and clarity, and redirect narcissism or spiritual materialism. Regular participant Gordon Cairns, former CEO of the major Australasian wine and beer company Lion Nathan, says that these retreats have dramatically changed the way he leads—from being a 'horrible boss' who was bad for himself, his company, his subordinates and his family, to someone who spends half his time mentoring and caring for the dying, activities which give him the 'most joy and meaning'.[16]

The idea of stepping back from a striving self in order to provide better leadership is being applied in other areas of professional work. Stuart Twemlow[17] is a Professor of Psychiatry and advanced martial arts teacher, who draws on Zen philosophy and techniques in his work with psychotherapists and teachers in schools seeking to reduce bullying. Twemlow argues that Zen, with its principles of impermanence, non-attachment, attention (mindfulness) and compassion, provides psychotherapists with ways of working effectively with clients which are healthy for client and therapist. In some of his other work with schools, Twemlow has applied his insights to building student leadership, particularly the intervention of the 'helpful bystander'. Instead of supporting the more traditional conception of student leadership—sports captains and prefects, who are often too busy to notice what is troubling other students—Twemlow shows schools how to build the capacity of bystanders as leaders.

This view of the work of leadership as including the capacity to 'step outside the protective cocoon of the self' is also a theme of the American philosopher Al Gini. According to Gini, it is an unchallenged and partially unconscious preoccupation with our own survival and material well-being that makes us 'moral slaves to the system that sustains us'.[18] Gini explores reasons why 'it's hard to be good', and in particular why so few people show the courage to act or speak out when terrible things happen. According to both Twemlow and Gini, useful leadership work in institutional life involves releasing or 'shedding the burden of the self' in order to work effectively for others and towards valuable purposes.

A CONNECTED RELATIONSHIP WITH OTHERS

By becoming reflective and beginning to recognise and detach from the ego's activities, we also start to identify themes in the way we have scripted our lives. Once it becomes possible to see these patterns, we are able to imagine another way of being. In engaging in this personal reflective work, we not only liberate self; we also begin to see others differently, as not simply 'there' for us or for what they 'do' for us.

Without this self-insight, we react to people in our lives as satisfiers of needs, or as obstacles to be controlled and changed. It is not unusual for us to see others—subordinates, peers, bosses, partners and even friends—as frustrating us from doing what we want, as resisting the plans and ideas we lovingly slave over. Our thinking often goes: 'If only they would be different, then our plans could progress, dreams be realised, lives be fulfilled.' Our efforts to secure our own identity render others as bit players in our big drama.

The trap here is investing so much of our time in the mirror, in seeing ourselves interminably reflected in others' opinions. If we are constantly absorbed in this, and in reacting to various opinions, we are not able to concentrate practically on the needs of those whom we lead. Organisational theorist John Roberts is interested in what is left when a leader *can* escape this egocentrism—a kind of forgetting of self, a letting go of the all-important personal narrative, which can allow one to be with others without looking for gratitude, or for the self to be reflected heroically through the eyes of others. It is also then 'helpful to know that I am not the entity that I mistake myself for'.[19]

Researchers David Knights and Majella O'Leary, in their article on ethical leadership, draw on the work of ethicists and philosophers to explore the tensions between acting for self or acting for others, and whether it is possible to transcend the duality usually assumed between the two. Knights and O'Leary also argue that our abiding preoccupation with the self can preclude ethical leadership. As a legacy of Enlightenment thinking, 'the other' tends to be defined and experienced first in relation to self, and actions, even if labelled moral, are always acts of power. Because of this, 'leaders become preoccupied with their own image as leaders rather than with their ethical responsibility to others'. These researchers draw on the philosophy of Levinas to suggest further that 'the heart of ethics rests in the face-to-face interaction with the Other', that it is in allowing connection with others to precede and interrupt our sense of our autonomous selves that true moral responsibility may be possible.[20]

Stepping back from the ego therefore requires both knowing yourself and letting go of yourself. Letting go of these personal scripts has powerful liberating effects. When we cease trying to control others, we find freedom for ourselves as well as for them. By allowing others priority, less-ego leadership becomes possible.

To look at the application of some of these ideas, I have drawn inspiration from studying Australian Aboriginal leaders. Aboriginal culture[21] places a strong value on the group—or their 'mob', as Aboriginal people often call their own group. Leadership is not an individual performance, but the work that members of their mob do together to achieve meaningful outcomes, such as regaining title to land.

When you talk to senior Aborigines, they often repudiate labels like 'leader'. Chris Sarra, the Aboriginal school principal introduced in Chapter 6, describes his role as one of 'engaging in meaningful dialogue with the community', including working with a particular elder in the Cherbourg community who is passionate about improving education for Indigenous children. Sarra writes:

> Mrs Long was my eyes and ears to the community . . . While she may not have had any formal educational qualifications, she had something that was far more valuable at the time—she was highly respected and knew the community inside-out. Any new principal should find their own Mrs Long before doing anything else . . . And don't worry if you are not sure how to find them. They will probably find you first. Just be ready to recognise them and their extreme value.[22]

In Sarra's account, the achievements at Cherbourg State School are there because of the community's efforts. He listened and respected, worked with and consolidated. For Sarra, conventional ideas of leadership do not adequately reflect the complexity and richness of this process of connection.

Mick Dodson[23] is also Aboriginal, a professor at the Australian National University and widely regarded as an important Australian and international leader.[24] Yet he doesn't like the idea of 'leadership'. He responded to a request for advice to aspiring young leaders only after a long pause, saying:

> I don't call myself a leader really. I think you've got to never give up. You need to hang in there, but I'm not much of a leader. Good advice is you've got to try and be competent, I've been so darned incompetent. Now, I'm just trying to be competent most of the time.

When asked about his greatest achievement, Dodson volunteered this image:

> I really loved seeing traditional owners getting the title to their land back. I loved being there. There was an old blind bloke who was just crying. He had the title back to his country. I cried with joy with him . . .
>
> This was no easy task, after years of getting over hurdles, brick walls you've got to climb . . . but it isn't an individual achievement, there's a whole team involved from the lowliest employee, the cook and field officers through to the Chairman. It's all the people themselves in a joint effort to get through those land claims.

In an interview with me, Mick elaborated somewhat reluctantly on some of the things he'd learned about leadership:

> I see so-called leaders trying to race around and do everything themselves and that is really bad—poor leadership. I mean, one of the really good characteristics, I think, of leadership is the capacity to delegate—delegate properly and confidently, to people you know you trust to know what they are doing.
>
> And you don't hit the nail on the head every time. You fail yourself. I think one of the . . . central principles behind the capacity to delegate [is] . . . understanding your own strengths but more importantly knowing what your weaknesses are and, moreover, knowing what to do about that. Not trying to battle through. Actually getting help or getting expertise. Don't try and fill shoes you can't fill . . .

Mick Dodson in a sea of reconciliation hands
Sean Davey/Fairfax Photos

A leader is not a boss or manager: 'You do what I tell you to do.' An important part of leadership is inclusiveness. [You say:] 'Why don't we do this?' 'What do you think of that, Joe?' They say, 'Well, I think that's a really dumb idea, Mick.' I say, 'Well, why?' They say, this, and this and this . . .

When I was younger, I worked as a consultant. People would ring me up and say, 'Mick, we want you to do such and such'. I can say to them, straight out to them: 'I suggest you go and ring Bill Bloggs. If he's not there he might be able to put you onto somebody—but I can't do this.' They say, 'Oh yes you can.' I say, 'No I can't, I'm sorry. You won't be getting your money's worth out of me.' And that's about honesty, that's about integrity.

If I can't do it, I say no. That's leadership . . . The capacity to say no and for good reasons . . . Usually because I don't have the time to do it but sometimes there are things I don't think I should do because I don't agree with them or it offends my sense of decency . . .

You don't always succeed, you know, you don't always stick to these rules. You're as frail as any homo sapiens. And you make mistakes and you do some really dumb things. But I notice as you get older you don't do them as frequently. You don't make these mistakes as frequently.

The last thing Mick Dodson, Chris Sarra, Lillian Holt and other Aboriginal leaders would want is to be beatified. Yet my research shows that such individuals provide examples of leadership which is less captured by ego and more connected with others. They show how leadership work might grow out of respect and commitment to the group. And they show a healthy realism about their own frailties and capacity for mistakes, and how to acknowledge and work with them.

Leadership research is increasingly exploring ways to work from a position of compassion and connection with others.[25] In the central chapters of this book, I discussed other leadership practices which, in my experience, foster a sense of respect for and connection with others. Simple practices like paying attention to breathing and to bodily possibilities in leadership can open up leaders to less instrumental ways of being with others.

CULTIVATING A SCEPTICAL VIEW

I have described throughout this book a drift in the literature towards construing the leadership quest as one of personal betterment. This view generally neglects the structural nature of the conditions of people's lives and the significance of collectively organised action and resistance. The idea of lone agents able to shape their individual destinies is rejected in both the contemporary Western critical traditions and in the Eastern philosophical tradition. Subjectively experienced realities are shaped by wider power relations, and it is through such power relations that our sense of ourselves—our identity—is constructed and limited (see Chapter 8).

The risk of ego-centredness does not mean that we should dispense with explorations of self-awareness and spirituality in leadership, but that we should be heedful of the trap of 'spiritual materialism'—using spiritual insight to prop up a needy ego. In Buddhism, the *bodhisattva* vows are part of making a commitment to being open and compassionate without feeling the need to prove anything, without keeping count or demonstrating to any audience how far you've come. Eastern teachings are also eloquent on the need to be wary of seductive ideas and people presenting themselves as gurus.

As in critical theory, the advice of much of Eastern philosophy is antiauthoritarian in stance and egalitarian in the remedies offered for resistance. It takes a position of initial scepticism about those who purport to offer us the best or only definition of reality. Far from recommending cult-like worship or abdication from reasoned analysis, critical and Eastern thinking are equally dubious about those with power who promise to use it for our betterment. A core teaching of the Buddha advises us not to believe in anything just because it has been written down, or recited, or been handed down, or because it is believed by many, or is told by teachers, or comes from someone inspired. Rather, Buddhism suggests that you always apply for yourself the test of disciplined, experiential investigation and I have sought to write this book in a way that invites such practical personal engagement.

RESUMING THE PERSONAL

Not long after I had returned to my work at the business school in 2004, I wrote in a paper called 'Renewal':

> Lately I have been looking out on the world with new eyes. Where once my job seemed laden with stressors, I now feel lucky to have the opportunities I do. I used to walk into my office and feel burdened—the checklist of 'to dos' in priority order in my head, my heart sinking as the emails loaded into the in-box, the phone-light blinking with messages. I often walked into an MBA class feeling as though I was preparing for battle, armoured with the answers to any smart-arsed comment.
>
> Now I look out onto Leicester Square, breathing in the beauty of where I am, physically and metaphysically . . . I feel differently about my students, the classroom experience, my work and life.
>
> What's changed? Although it was initially tempting to think that I had just landed an unusually pleasant bunch of students (and they are, I think), that the people around me were just being nicer to me (and they are, I think), it has gradually become apparent that I have changed, that I am in a new place. And it literally feels like I am sitting inside new skin looking out with new eyes.[26]

My previous experience was that the big obstacles I had perceived in my career and life were elsewhere—in my institution, my bosses, my peers, my students. Through yoga and Buddhist studies, I came to understand that the obstacles were in me and in how I reacted to things. I learned to recognise when I descended into this old way of thinking—into projecting my problems onto everyone else—and I gradually started becoming more responsible for myself and my own happiness.

I have also learned to be conscious of the ways I get hijacked by my ego. My need to secure my identity in the approval of others, my need to *be* someone all slowly and irrevocably showed up in meditation practice. Like a parade of unwanted but all-too-familiar characters, these needs for approval kept reappearing and doing their tired curtain calls. The art became to not castigate myself for this shambling cast of insecurities and vanities, but just to note them. Once allowed to surface, they slackened their hold at least for a time.

People approach the work of leadership from many directions. All sorts of experiences open up people to thinking about doing leadership in new and different ways. It might be a sense of duty—religious, political or parental—or a desire to give back or to serve others, or to help others and oneself find greater happiness and sustainability in ways of working. The search for meaning or greater authenticity in the way one lives and works can also fuel an appetite to do leadership in a different way.

My argument in this chapter is that sometimes the obstacles to these new forms of leadership are inside oneself. In finding new ways forward, efforts to placate a driving or unforgiving ego can prevent us from finding space for compassion, connection and being in the moment. *The ego is not the whole self.* It is freeing to find ways to put a space between one's ego and one's self, in order to do the work of liberating leadership.

Epilogue

&

Be the change you want to see in the world

Mahatma Gandhi

In leadership, there is a paradox. Leadership is adulated as a remedy to all sorts of societal problems but routinely disappoints us. Ideas and practices of leadership may simultaneously seduce, enslave and ultimately fail us. There is mixed evidence about how much leaders influence organisational fortunes, and perhaps we should be relieved about this. Yet I have also shown that the power of leaders is frequently overestimated. The popularity of leadership is part of wider economic and cultural ideologies in which heroic leadership functions as a panacea, more likely to prevent than foster diverse, valuable, adaptive, collaborative leadership work.

Most traditional approaches to learning about leadership are flawed on many counts, as argued in the first three chapters of the book. Leadership development often assumes that leadership is a good thing and teaches that the task of a leader is to emulate successful CEOs. Too often we get caught up in heroic and gendered narratives about generals and adventurers, swallowing the leadership mantra rather than asking deeper and more important questions about what or who leadership is for.

So, part of our task in learning about leadership is not to learn how to do it, but to learn how myths of leadership have come to have a hold on us. Our task is not to perpetuate an unthinking set of assumptions about what makes a leader, but to probe deeper into where our hungers for leadership come from and what effects they have.

Better leadership will not come about simply by individuals resolving to be more courageous or more collaborative in their approach—though such emphases may indeed be welcome in situations where leadership is often equated with 'doing more with less' or delivering relentless increments in the share price.

Leadership can only become more freeing once we've made the effort to see how it functions as a social idea, a dominant motif of our times, bringing with it many unspoken intents—for example, the value of material outcomes—and often silently serving powerful interests.

Yet adopting such a critical approach is not straightforward. People have a lot vested in leadership. Many executives have spent their careers working towards it, investing time and energies cultivating it. Family life, health and personal interests have been sacrificed in order to fill leadership responsibilities. This long and arduous leadership road may leave little appetite for questioning the end that is finally in sight. Yet my argument here is that merely following leadership orthodoxy is, by definition, not leadership. And it is unlikely to elicit the kinds of outcomes that many well-intentioned leaders have in mind.

At a societal level, initiatives undertaken under the banner of leadership generally enjoy status. I learned early in my academic career that when I wrote papers on and talked about gender or ethics or change in business, there was mild interest. Yet when I started working on leadership, my ideas gained greater power and legitimacy. When I have started to question leadership in groups that I work with, they often react with anger, and the more senior the group the stronger their outrage. Criticism of leadership is experienced as an attack (and some take particular offence when it is a woman doing the questioning), or an effort to undermine, rather than a way to make leadership ideas more meaningful.

At the same time, my research and experience suggest to me that many people are disaffected with prevalent leadership ideas and are open to the kinds of deeper and more challenging insights that I introduce through the central section of the book. New views of power, of bodies, breath and mindfulness, of the role of identities and personal histories in leadership, have the potential to give us a much richer and more rounded account of our own and others' leadership experiences. These views offer more powerful explanations of the obstacles to change—in social structures, in stereotypes, in language and discourse, and in our own frailties. Leadership can only become freeing once we've taken the time to reflect on and explore the ways in which our identities and egos get caught up in playing a performance. Doing this different kind of identity work enables leaders to find space to open up to new sources of power and different ways of being.

I have spent much of the last ten or so years experimenting with creating and exploring with students and colleagues this different kind of leadership space. Here I have had direct experience of being captured by my own hungers: Will they (students and managers) like me? Will they give me good evaluations? Will I be shamed in front of my colleagues? Will they approve of me enough? If I am honest, I admit to an enduring fantasy that they will all love me. When they don't (alarmingly sometimes the reverse), I have wrestled with the leadership dilemma of being courageous and hopeful, while not quarantined in my ego's dance of neediness.

So how do I situate myself and the way I want to work within the dominant norms of leadership? A common assumption is that one can only do a leadership job 'full-time'. Leadership is all-consuming; one has to be available and visible around the clock. Can leadership be done 'part-time', in a way that does not completely consume the life of the person leading, and indeed those of the people surrounding that leader? Can leadership be done without a formal role, title or mandate to exercise it? Can leadership be done by simply being with people in a different kind of way, encouraging questioning but also supporting them to take their and their colleagues' value and well-being seriously? I believe the answer to these questions is a cautious 'yes', and this book offers ideas that have been helpful to me and others in thinking about how to do leadership in this different kind of way.

In Part III, I have argued that leadership requires less, not more, preoccupation with self. A serious risk of emphases on, for example, authenticity or spirituality in leadership is that they can foster the very striving which much spiritual teaching warns against. These endeavours in learning to lead can become one more vehicle through which the fragile ego shores itself up.

My experiences working with managers, students and colleagues are of people frequently under intense pressure. Big things happen to them—they form relationships and then experience their breakdown; they start families, endure illness, suffer the passing of people they love; they get retrenched and face unemployment. Yet most of the literature does not allow that these experiences are often central to leadership learning. Rather leaders are often expected to ignore such events, fitting them into the corners of an already pressured work life, hastily getting 'through' them in order to resume business, or life, 'as usual'.

In my life and work I have learned most by paying attention to the whole person and the things happening to them in every part of their life. A practice of leadership is needed that supports the individual at all levels—physical, emotional and spiritual as well as intellectual—to free themselves to do meaningful, connected transformative work. I hope this book offers some guidance in doing so.

Amanda Sinclair

notes

Introduction

1   I use the term 'valuable purposes', rather than objectives, goals or outcomes, to encompass the great breadth of ways 'value' can be defined and delivered, and to acknowledge that value is not always instantly or readily measurable. My colleague John Alford (2002) has written cogently on how this kind of 'public value' in public-sector and not-for-profit contexts is often 'co-produced' with clients.

2   See Grey (2005) for a lucid and readable account of the flaws of this and other managerial assumptions.

3   Asking such questions and making these calculations is a time-honoured philosophical means of deciding on an ethical course of action. Calculating the benefits and costs, and to whom they accrue, is a central part of utilitarian or teleological thinking. More recent philosophical approaches have argued that there should be a shift from a focus on rights towards calculations of suffering—see, for example, Shklar (1984).

4   It is worth pausing to note this word 'vision' that is so widely and carelessly used in the leadership literature. Originally applied to mystics able to make contact with other worlds, a discourse analysis suggests that it may be another one of the ways that leaders are put into the special or immortal category, having special 'seeing' and foretelling powers.

5   Keith Grint (2000) provides a detailed and compelling analysis of this speech as a piece of leadership.

6   See Heifetz and Linsky (2002).

7   Denhardt (1981).

8   Rose (1989).

9   Gemmill and Oakley (1992) describe leadership as an 'alienating social myth', a 'social hoax aimed at maintaining the status quo'.

10 On the case to write differently, see Grey and Sinclair (2006).

11 Watson (2003, 2004) provides many examples of this and shows the costs of routinely using dreadful, meaningless language.

Chapter 1

1   So described by Paine Webber, cited in O'Reilly (2000).

2   Data for this vignette has been gathered from original and secondary sources

including *Fortune* magazine, 5 August 1995; 31 March 1997; 13 April 1998; 24 January 2000; 17 April 2000. Secondary sources include McLean and Elkind (2003), Wheen (2004), Tourish and Vatcha (2005).

3   The stories of these two whistleblowers are told in McLean and Elkind (2003), their film *The Smartest Guys in the Room* and Swartz with Watkins (2003).

4   Gronn (2006).

5   Lindholm (1988); Meindl et al. (1985) on 'the romance' of leadership.

6   Chris Grey initially pointed this common origin out to me. Marta Calas and Linda Smircich (1991) also note it.

7   Irving Janis coined the term in *Victims of Groupthink* (1972).

8   For a discussion and examples of this sentiment, see Sinclair (1994).

9   See, for example, Denhardt (1981); Mant (1983); Kets de Vries and Miller (1984); LaBier (1986).

10 See Chapter 4 for a detailed discussion of the importance of backgrounds.

11 Manfred Kets de Vries has written extensively about this mystique and how it traps leaders: see, for example, Kets de Vries (1994).

12 Gabriel (1997).

13 Heifetz and Laurie (1999), p. 56.

14 Dr Pat Seybolt undertook the research and prepared this Melbourne Business School case study: 'Steve Vizard', unpublished. Information and quotes from the case and used here are all from published sources. I am indebted to Pat's work and insights about this case and on the seductive processes in leadership.

15 Elias (2005).

16 For the assertion that Vizard received 'special treatment' because of his status see, for example, Mitchell (2005), Maiden (2005), Hughes (2005), Trounson (2005); and Hewitt (2005) on the fact that he escaped a jail sentence.

17 Shand (2005).

18 Mitchell (2005).

19 Ibid.

20 Gronn (2006).

21 See Collinson (2005b) on the importance of maintaining physical distance in leadership.

22 Brad Jackson's book (2001) provides some powerful examples.

23 This story and some others about leadership development are elaborated in my article 'Seducing Leadership: Stories of Leadership Development' (Sinclair, forthcoming), which will appear in a special issue of the journal *Gender, Work and Organization*.

24 Meindl et al. (1985); Lindholm (1988).

25 Kellerman (2004).

Chapter 2

1   Gronn (2003), p. 269.

2   David Collinson (2005a) has applied a dialectical framework and drawn on non-leadership discourses of power, resistance, control and gender to challenge and extend boundaries in the study of leadership.

3   The history I offer here reflects my own reading of the study and application of leadership ideas, and undoubtedly my political and psychoanalytic biases. I have also

Notes

drawn on histories by other scholars, including Bryman (1992, 1996), Gronn (2003) and Grint's (1997a, 1997b, 2000) often funny takes. For recent overviews see Rickards and Clark (2005) and Storey's (2004) edited collection, especially the first two chapters.

4　Lasswell (1930) was a pioneer of political psychology, a field continued by Australian scholars such as the late Alan Davies and Graham Little, who were also my teachers.

5　For a fascinating biography exploring Follet's contribution, as well as her exclusion, see Tonn (2003).

6　Barnard (1938), p. 284.

7　See Alvin Gouldner's (1950) edited collection *Studies of Leadership* and his introduction to that volume for a very useful overview of the trait approach and the reasons to take a more sociological view of leadership.

8　For example, Adorno et al.'s (1950) famous *The Authoritarian Personality*, also Gilbert (1950) and Hoffer (1951) on followership.

9　The publication of exhaustive studies such as those cited in Ralph Stogdill's (1974) *Handbook of Leadership* are widely seen to have supplied no evidence for traits; however, subsequent analyses provide some evidence (see e.g. Kirkpatrick and Locke (1991)) and recent leadership writing shows a resurgence of interest in traits.

10　See Baritz (1960) for a prescient warning about the role of science and particularly social sciences in supporting capitalism's rise; also Locke (1989, 1996) and Burnham (1962) for authoritative histories of the ascendancy of management as a science. More recently Rose (1989) pursues the 'governing' of the soul that psychological and social scientific methods have allowed.

11　Baritz (1960), p. 3.

12　See Sharon Beder's (2000) fascinating history of the Protestant work ethic in America.

13　Reproduced with permission. I am indebted to Andrew Pirola-Merlo for drawing the *Songbook* to my attention via his paper, 'Moral Leadership is an Oxymoron'.

14　William Whyte published his critique of 'the organization man' in the 1950s.

15　See Locke (1989, 1996).

16　Rose (1989, 1996).

17　For example, Abraham Zaleznik wrote a controversial and influential article in *Harvard Business Review* in 1977 arguing for renewed focus on leaders.

18　Gouldner (1950), pp. 10–11.

19　See the work of Meindl et al. (1985).

20　A ten-year survey conducted by the UK National College of School Leadership (2006) concluded that transformational leadership was easily the most popular area of journal articles on leadership.

21　Burns (1978), p. 4.

22　The organisational benefits of measuring transformational leadership are described in Bass and Avolio (1994).

23　Hampden-Turner and Trompenaars (1993).

24　For more on this dichotomy, see Gronn (2003).

25　Bennis and Nanus (1985), p. 218.

26　Quinn and Snyder (1999), p. 169.

27　Joel Bakan's book *The Corporation* (2004) offers a compelling argument from a legal point of view as to why managers and companies can never be expected to behave in a socially responsible fashion and why we need to start from this premise rather than the misguided hope that they will.

28   Conger and Kanungo (1998), p. 17.

29   Many techniques of modern organisation originated in the Prussian army, and Peter Gronn advises me that selection techniques and assessment centres were developed in the English War Office.

30   For example, a lack of interest in documented failures of military leadership—such as the Australian *Voyager* disaster, where navy command united to support a demonstrably flawed commander/leader.

31   See Grey (2001) for a critical reading of what's going on when 'relevance' is being demanded.

32   Watson's books *Death Sentence* (2003) and *Watson's Dictionary of Weasel Words, Contemporary Clichés, Cant and Management Jargon* (2004) provide copious and sobering examples of the spread of managerial jargon into all corners of public life.

33   Ritzer (2000).

34   Conger et al. (1999), p. 15.

35   There are important exceptions to this general neglect—for example, the work of Alistair Mant (1983, 1997) on childhoods and leadership. This research is discussed in Chapter 4.

36   This table has been compiled drawing on sources concerned with critical perspectives in general and specifically leadership. They include Knights and Willmott (1992), Fournier and Grey (2000), Czarniawska and Wolff (1991), Alvesson and Willmott (2002a), Gronn (2003, 2006), Grint (1997, 2000) and Collinson (2005a).

37   Calas and Smircich (1991).

38   Fletcher (2004), p. 648.

39   Ibid., p. 653.

40   Ibid., p. 656.

41   Foucault (1977, 1981), and see also Bernauer and Rasmussen (1988).

Chapter 3

1   Eveline (1996) explores the pervasiveness of phallic imagery in management discourse, for example 'the worry of "going limp"'.

2   Sinclair (1995a, 2000a, 2004b).

3   Belenky et al. (1986).

4   See, for example, Luke and Gore (1992); hooks (1994); McWilliam and Jones (1996); McWilliam (1999); Gallop (1995).

5   For a discussion of the midwifery and banking metaphors, see Belenky et al. (1986).

6   Lather (1991), pp. 163–4.

7   See, for example, Daloz Parks (2005).

8   For an interesting example see Blackler and Kennedy (2004).

9   Daloz Parks (2005).

10   The Tavistock Institute regularly conducts Group Relations conferences which are entirely experiential, and the Australian Institute for Socio-Analysis (AISA) has also conducted similar courses and conferences which I have attended.

11   See also Hirschhorn (1997) for the importance of resisting dependency in leadership.

12 Sinclair (2005a).
13 See Grey (2005); Fournier and Grey (2000); Grey et al. (1996); Reynolds (1999); Perriton and Reynolds (2004) specifically on the value and challenges of critical management pedagogy.
14 See particularly Foucault's *Discipline and Punish* (1977) and *The Final Foucault* edited by Bernauer and Rasmussen (1988).
15 Bourdieu et al. (1999), p. 607.
16 See for example the work of Knights and Willmott (1992), Collinson (2005a) and Jones (2005).
17 See Judi Marshall (1999) for a discussion of the limitations of 'teaching' to encompass the work of less conventional classrooms.
18 A version of these experiences appears as 'Teaching Leadership Critically to MBAs' in *Management Learning*, Sinclair (forthcoming).
19 Ibid.
20 Raab (1997).
21 See Luke and Gore (1992), particularly Walkerdine's chapter; hooks (1994); Howie and Tauchert (2002): chapters by Morley, Hughes and others.
22 See research by Marshall (1984, 1995); Martin (2006); Eagly (2005): and my own work, especially *Doing Leadership Differently* (Sinclair 1998, 2004c).
23 Ellsworth (1989).
24 Walkerdine (1992), p. 16.

Chapter 4

1 See McLean and Elkind (2003); also Tourish and Vatcha (2005) for accounts of the backgrounds of the key figures in the Enron story.
2 Ignominious childhoods are also a feature of dictators such as Mussolini and Stalin. See Gronn (2006) for connections to biographical accounts of such leaders; see also Gilbert (1950) on Hitler's childhood, and Burns (1978).
3 A phrase explored by Ron Heifetz and Marty Linsky (2002).
4 Some of these ideas are described ably by Valerie Wilson in the book we wrote together, *New Faces of Leadership* (Sinclair and Wilson 2002). The book also provides examples of how the openness and trust demonstrated by some corporate leaders can be mapped back to childhood experiences.
5 Zaleznik (1977), p. 67.
6 See, for example, Collins (2005) and Goffee and Jones (2005, 2006).
7 Exceptions include the extensive work of Manfred Kets de Vries, Michael Maccoby and Douglas LaBier, as well as a small number of scholars drawing on psychoanalytic perspectives in their study of organisations—for example, Howard Schwartz.
8 See, for example, a special issue of *Leadership Quarterly* on authentic leadership development: vol. 16, no. 3, June 2005.
9 This is an idea to which I was introduced by the late Alan Davies and Graham Little, my doctoral supervisors, who wrote extensively on the connections between childhood and leadership styles. See O'Donnell (2006) for an exploration of the origins of political conservatism or progressiveness in the families of American political leaders.
10 See Gardner (1995) and Mant (1983).
11 Gardner (1995).

12 See Popper and Mayseless (2002) for a review of some of this argument; also Steyrer (2002). Kets de Vries (1994, 2006) provides a lengthy and vivid account of antecedents and forms of narcissism.
13 Gardner (1995), p. 32.
14 Mant (1983).
15 For general discussions of birth order, see Grose (2003), Richardson (1995) and Kluger et al. (2006); and for birth order and leadership, see Sulloway (1996), Stewart (1992), Andeweig and Van den Berg (2003) and Steinberg (2001).
16 Steinberg (2001).
17 Grose (2003), p. 56.
18 Sulloway (1996).
19 Quoted in Gardner (1995).
20 Implicit leadership theories (ILTs) is a construct that has been used in applied psychological and leadership studies, particularly to identify the way national cultures socialise people to make assumptions about leaders which are activated unconsciously in institutional settings. See House et al. (2004) for a cross-cultural application of ILTs.
21 Fletcher (1999); Meyerson (2001).
22 See Eagly (2005) for a detailed account of this case.
23 For a more detailed analysis of these processes, see my *Doing Leadership Differently* (Sinclair 1998, 2004c).
24 Heifetz and Linsky (2002).
25 'Groupthink' was a term originally coined by Irving Janis to describe examples of disastrous public policy decision-making. See also, for example, Maier (1997) for an exploration of how dominant masculinities contribute to concurrence seeking.
26 See Gabriel (1997), also Hirschhorn (1997) for an extensive discussion of the dynamics of dependency.
27 For example, Little (1985, 1988).
28 Heifetz (1994); Heifetz and Linsky (2002).
29 Detailed accounts and analyses of these events appeared in the press—see, for example, Williams (2004).

Chapter 5

1 Hirschman (1970).
2 I have written extensively about these issues—for example, Sinclair (1995a, 2000a, 2004b).
3 In the organisational field, the first major collection to begin to map processes of resistance was Jermier et al. (1994).
4 Foucault (1981), p. 94.
5 There is a large body of writing about women and power which I will only gesture to here. Some of the managerial literature rests on the argument that women are more uncomfortable with power and use it differently. While not wishing to discount this possibility, I do not want to simply argue that women 'do' power differently, nor to suggest that women need 'help' to exercise power more assertively or effectively.
6 See McIntosh (1988) for a stunning account of the invisibility of white power and privilege.

7   There is a significant feminist literature which explores the trap of white women believing that they can speak for black women, and that their common gender overrides racial experiences. In the Australian context, see for example Moreton-Robinson (2000).

8   For an excellent review of ideas about power see Hardy (1998).

9   Kotter and Schlesinger (1979); see also Dunphy and Stace (1988).

10 See Casey (1995, 1999).

11 Jermier et al. (1994) provides some wonderful examples of the powerful practice of resistance.

12 See Collinson (2005a) for a development of this argument.

13 Blackmore (1999).

14 Meyerson and Scully (1995); Meyerson (2001).

15 Fletcher (1999).

16 Frost (2003) provides many examples of this toxicity.

17 See Bradshaw and Wicks (1997); Collinson (1994); Jermier et al. (1994); Meyerson and Scully (1995).

18 See Van Nostrand (1993) for many examples.

19 Meyerson and Scully (1995), p. 594.

20 Collinson (1994), p. 25.

21 Krantz (2006), p. 222.

22 Ibid., p. 223.

23 See Ciulla (1998) for a thoughtful analysis of the problem of 'bogus empowerment'.

Chapter 6

1   This chapter has been adapted from an article that appeared in *Leadership* vol. 1, no. 4. It is used with permission from the publishers, Sage.

2   Profile means a description in words, but it is also a metaphor meaning physical outline.

3   Excerpted and adapted from Nicholson (2005).

4   Gronn (2006).

5   See Collinson (2005b) for an analysis of the role of physical separation in leadership.

6   Sinclair (1995c, 1998).

7   See Still (2006) for a poignant account of how older leaders struggle to maintain their physical invincibility in the face of ageing.

8   McDowell (1997), p. 169.

9   See, for example, Turner (1984); Scott and Morgan (1993); Grosz (1994); Gatens (1996); Acker (1990).

10 Collinson (1992); Collinson and Hearn (1996); Kerfoot and Knights (1996); Kerfoot (2000); McDowell (1997).

11 Further descriptions of the leadership actions of both leaders are available in case studies. For Chris Sarra, these are Cherbourg State School A and B case available through the Australian and New Zealand School of Government (ANZOG) Case Library. For Christine Nixon, there is a personal profile and a case study of cultural revolution soon to be available in the Melbourne Business School Case Library. On Nixon, see also Prenzler (2004). Chris Sarra (2003) has written a compelling account of the challenges and some of his leadership initiatives at Cherbourg.

12   These case studies have been undertaken as part of my general research on leadership and I draw on my primary research here as well as secondary sources including two episodes of *Australian Story* produced and shown by the Australian Broadcasting Corporation (2002, 2004). I know Christine Nixon well, and have been working with her since 2002—not long after she took the job as police commissioner. I have spent weeks 'shadowing' her at various times, conducted formal interviews, and had many discussions with her. I have sought to provide a 'rounded' account of her leadership here and elsewhere, wanting to avoid lists of responsibilities (for 'men, money and machines') or achievements against performance measures. My desire to 'write' Nixon's leadership differently has itself been tricky because it is possible that my account (especially within a discussion about bodies) may be read as reinforcing gender stereotyping rather than focusing on her very substantial achievements, which I clearly want to avoid. I have also been watching Chris Sarra for several years, though I have never met him. I have followed his career, talked to people who know him, watched videos of him and communicated with him by email. I have also been engaged in a related research project on Indigenous leadership.

13   Andy Sturdy pointed out that these institutions can also be understood as bodies (e.g. the police body). The National College of School Leadership Research Advisory Forum to which I presented an earlier draft of these ideas, and of which Andy was a part, reminded me that all performances are embodied—it is only that we selectively notice some.

14   I wish to acknowledge Chris's permission to use material for this profile, material that was originally gathered and compiled into a case by Tim Watts, whom I also wish to acknowledge.

15   A recent survey by the Australian Institute of Health and Welfare (2003) paints an even darker picture, showing that—despite three decades of government policy and interventions—there has been no discernible improvement in educational outcomes for Aboriginal students.

16   For additional information on actions undertaken at Cherbourg, see Sarra (2003).

17   Collinson (2005b).

18   Sinclair (2005a).

Chapter 7

1   If we were to include leadership in the spiritual traditions, then there is certainly research linking advanced meditation practices and leadership: see, for example, Rama (1978, 1988). Also, some work focusing on the performance skills of leadership such as public speaking and image management includes attention to breathing.

2   See Goleman (1998, 2003) and, for example, Loehr and Schwartz (2001), who incorporate meditative techniques in cultivating executive 'high performance', and more recently Smith (2006).

3   Rama et al. (1979) provides a comprehensive account of the physical mechanics of respiration as well as a means of higher spiritual awareness. Also, Rama (1988) provides guidance on advanced practices of *pranayama* and *svarodaya*.

4   Goleman (1998, 2003).

5   For example, Segal et al. (2002); Goleman (2003); Brown and Ryan (2003).

6   Irigaray (2002), p. 50.

7   For a summary of applications of mindfulness-based therapies such as cognitive therapy (MBCT), and an analysis of the psychological and biological mechanisms which determine their effectiveness, see Melbourne Academic Mindfulness Interest Group (2006). Also a special issue of *Psychotherapy in Australia* (2006) is devoted to 'Making Sense of Mindfulness'.

8   Thich (1991, 1999).

9   Khema (1987).

10 Langer (1989); Kabat-Zinn (1994, 2003).

11 Gerzon (2006).

12 Fisher (2005).

13 For example, the 'Spirit in Action' programs being run at Harvard Law School. See also Smith (2006) for a discussion of executives who meditate and the improvement in their performance.

14 Loehr and Schwartz (2001) describe the importance of 'recovery' techniques in high performance among athletes and executives, arguing that these should occur every 90 to 120 minutes.

15 For my own take on these issues see Sinclair (2004a).

Chapter 8

1   For a critical history on the search for and production of the self, see Rose (1989, 1996).

2   Mant (1983).

3   See Gini (2000, 2006).

4   See Hochschild (1983, 1990, 2003); Edwards and Wajcman (2005); also Beder (2000).

5   See particularly Townley (1994, 1995); also Garsten and Grey (1997).

6   Foucault (1977).

7   Report at the GMB 2005 Annual Conference, cited in *The Guardian*, 7 June 2005, p. 1.

8   See for example, Knights and Willmott (1989); Casey (1995, 1999); Jacques (1996).

9   Block (1993), p. 78.

10 Collinson (2003).

11 Morley (2005). See also Edwards and Wajcman (2005) for a British and European perspective.

12 Lakoff (2005).

13 See *Leadership Quarterly*, Special Issues on Authentic Leadership; Goffee and Jones (2005, 2006).

14 Avolio et al. (2004), pp. 803–4.

15 Eagly (2005).

16 Goffee and Jones (2005).

17 Ibid.

18 See Alvesson and Willmott (2002b) and Collinson (2003) for particularly clear accounts of identity theory and work in managerial contexts.

19 This effect was so powerful in musical accomplishment that, when one symphony orchestra held auditions behind a screen in order to ensure they recruited the best musicians, women were much more strongly represented.

20 Elmes and Connelly (1997), p. 159; see also Bell and Nkomo (2001).

21 Fletcher (1999); Meyerson (2001).

22 See Mulholland (1996) for a wonderful analysis of the 'self-made' narrative.

23 Anthony Giddens (1991) has been an important contributor. Drawing extensively on Foucault's work, Nikolas Rose (1989, 1996, 1999) has provided critical accounts of modernism's obsession with the self.
24 Czarniawska (1997), p. 49.
25 Alvesson and Willmott (2002b), p. 626.
26 See, for example, Collinson (1992, 1994); Jermier et al. (1994); Fleming and Spicer (2003).

Chapter 9

1 Trungpa (1973).
2 For an overview of the re-emergence of spirituality and its relationship with religion, see Tacey (2003).
3 Some examples in order of appearance include Conger and Associates (1994); Bolman and Deal (1995); Barrett (1998); Lewin and Regine (2000); Zohar and Marshall (2000, 2004).
4 See, for example, the account of Buddhist nun Tenzin Palmo's experiences in MacKenzie (1998). Also, for an Anglican perspective, see Porter (2006). Tacey (2003) contains many examples of university students' search for spirituality despite bad experiences of religion.
5 For overviews of the 'spirituality at work' literature, see *Journal of Organizational Change Management* (1999), vol. 12, no. 4, including articles by Butts, Cavanagh, Delbecq and Burack; *Journal of Management Inquiry* (2005), vol. 14 no. 3; see also Giacalone and Jurkiewicz (2003); and, for the connection to leadership, see Cacioppe (2000a, 2000b).
6 See Sharon Beder (2000) on American connections between the Protestant work ethic and religious morality; also Elmes and Smith (2001) on American spiritual ideals and workplace practices.
7 See for example, Kaye (1996); Roach (2000); Kets de Vries (2005).
8 Casey (2004) provides an excellent overview of developments in spirituality in organisations. Also, Joanne Ciulla (1998) documents the extent of the 'race for the worker's soul' as it has played out in many large American firms.
9 Zohar and Marshall (2004), pp. 27–9.
10 See Zohar and Marshall (2000, 2004); Barrett (1998).
11 Excellent critical analyses of the spirituality trend include Calas and Smircich (2003); Bell and Taylor (2003, 2004); Casey (2004); Mitroff (2003).
12 Barrett (1998).
13 Sinclair (1992, 1995b).
14 Beder (2000) and Bunting (2004).
15 Bell and Taylor (2003), p. 336.
16 Rose (1996).
17 Ibid., p. 18.
18 Zohar and Marshall (2004), p. 85.
19 Dreaming and ideas of 'the Dreaming' have special significance in Aboriginal culture. The Dreamtime is the origin of history and creation stories, which are central to ancient and modern ritual. For further detail, see Hammond (1991) and Tacey (1996).

20 Berlusconi also undertook to abstain from sex during the election campaign, a promise perhaps offered to reinforce an image of ascetic and self-disciplined commitment to the task of being re-elected. I am indebted to Peter Gronn for alerting me to the *Inquirer* article in which this quote appeared, reproduced in *The Weekend Australian*, 18–19 March 2006.

21 See also Mitroff (2003) for an argument for more encompassing understandings of spirituality and not equating religion with spirituality.

Chapter 10

1   See Jacques (1996) for a powerful sceptical argument.

2   The term 'Eastern philosophies' is full of problems. There is no unitary or agreed collection of thinking traditions that fits into this category, and Eastern philosophies have often been understood only in contrast to Western. However, in the interests of economy, I use this term to encompass thinking in the Buddhist and Hindu or Vedantic traditions that derive from the Indian *Upanishads* or sacred texts. Yoga philosophy also derives from these original sources. For an extensive discussion of the themes and derivations of Eastern philosophy, see Ram-Prasad (2005).

3   This is a phrase used often in Buddhist teaching but see for example, Conradi (2004).

4   The process of study, practice and learning that I describe here represents an idiosyncratic and elementary understanding. I first started studying and practising meditation in 1996, in the Sri Chin Moy tradition. I renewed my yoga practice around 2000 and started studying yoga texts in 2002 as part of training to be a yoga teacher. During this time, I also became interested in Buddhism. For the insights offered here, I draw on books that have been recommended by my teachers and by Buddhist Institutes I have visited. They include the teachings of Patanjali, as described in various books such as *How to Know God*, which is a translation of and commentary on Patanjali's work by Swami Prabhavananda and Christopher Isherwood (1953, 1981) and *The Hathayogaprad īpikā* (ed. Kunjunni Raja 1972). In the case of Buddhism, I have drawn on written and oral teachings by H.H. the Dalai Lama (1998, 2003), oral teachings by His Eminence the 7th Dzogchen Rinpoche, Jigme Losel Wangpo, and by Buddhists in Melbourne and Cambridge, and various written work including Thich Nhat Hanh (1991, 1999), Pema Chödrön (1997), Ayya Khema (1987), Chögyam Trungpa (1973), Sogyal Rinpoche (1992) and Ian Johnson (2002).

5   For example Jung (1995) and more recently Irigaray (2002).

6   Zizek (2001), p. 15, argues that 'western Buddhism' is a fetish which has helped adherents to 'fully participate in the frantic pace of the capitalist game while sustaining the perception that you are not actually in it'.

7   Bernauer and Rasmussen (1988), p. 5.

8   Ibid., pp. viii and 2.

9   For this profile, I draw on Bedi's (1999) book *It's Always Possible*, an article by C. Kremmer (1999) and a video on the application of *Vipassana* meditation techniques in prisons in the United States and India.

10 Kremmer (1999), p. 5.

11 See Trungpa (1973) for a beautifully lucid account of the ways spiritual practices and aspirations can become misdirected into the service of ego.

12 This term comes from Sharon Gray, in an article on meditation she wrote for the Melbourne *Age*.

13 Trungpa (1973).
14 Kearney quoted in Johnson (2002), p. 101.
15 See Goleman (1988, 2003); Fisher (2005); Johnson (2002). For fascinating profiles of leaders who are also Buddhists reflecting on their leadership work, see Mac-Kenzie (2001).
16 Cairns is quoted in Macken (2006); see also Smith (2006).
17 See Twemlow (2001) on incorporating Zen into psychotherapy training and Twemlow (2000) for a discussion of his work helping schools with bullying.
18 Gini (2006).
19 Roberts (2003).
20 Knights and O'Leary (2006), p. 133.
21 There are risks in talking about Aboriginal culture as if it is unitary and coherent. Of course it is not, and it is always evolving. However, among Aboriginal communities, there has historically been an emphasis on identity through the group and distributed leadership in the group, in contrast to the individualism of white Australian society.
22 Sarra (2003), p. 6.
23 Information for this profile draws on, among other things, an interview conducted with Mick in 2004 as part of my research on Aboriginal leadership, research into and observations of his speeches, and a radio interview, broadcast on Awaye, ABC Radio National, 10 February 2006.
24 Mick Dodson is Professor of Indigenous Studies at the Australian National University. He was awarded an Order of Australia for his work in Indigenous Affairs, particularly land rights, social justice and international affairs. He is a member of the United Nations Social and Economic Council's Permanent Forum on Indigenous Issues Council which deliberates and advises on matters related to economic and social development, culture, the environment, education, health and human rights.
25 See, for example, Frost (2003) and Fineman (2000) on working with compassion, as well as Joyce Fletcher's (1999) work on relational leading.
26 Sinclair (2004a).

bibliography

This book spans a broad area of thinking, beyond what is usually encompassed in a leadership book. Each chapter provides an introduction to a much wider literature and, accordingly, the notes and bibliography are designed to assist readers to further explore these areas and their connection with leadership. I have designated some *leadership* articles and books with an asterisk, because they provide, in my view, particularly cogent or valuable accounts.

Abrahamson, E. (2004) *Change without Pain*, Boston: Harvard Business School Press.

Acker, J. (1990) 'Hierarchies, jobs, bodies', *Gender and Society*, 4(2): 139–58.

Adorno, T., Frenkel-Brunswik, E., Levinson, D. and Sanford, R. (1950) *The Authoritarian Personality*, New York: Harper.

Alford, J. (2002) 'Why do public sector clients co-produce?: Toward a contingency theory', *Administration and Society*, 34(1): 32–56.

Alvesson, M. and Willmott, H. (eds) (2002a) *Studying Management Critically*, London: Sage.

—— (2002b) 'Identity regulation as organizational control: Producing the appropriate individual', *Journal of Management Studies*, 39(5): 619–44.

Andeweig, R. and Van den Berg, S. (2003) 'Linking birth order to leadership: The impact of parents or sibling interaction', *Political Psychology*, 24(3): 605–23.

Australian and New Zealand School of Government (2005) 'Chris Sarra and the Cherbourg State School' (A) and (B).

Australian Institute of Health and Welfare (2003) *The Health and Welfare of Australia's Aboriginal and Torres Strait Islander Peoples 2003*, Canberra: Australian Bureau of Statistics.

Australian Story (2002) 'The Nixon Years', first shown 22 April 2002, Australian Broadcasting Corporation.

—— (2004) 'Good morning Mr Sarra', first shown 4 October 2004, Australian Broadcasting Corporation.

Avolio, B., Gardner, W., Walumbwa, F., Luthans, F. and May, D. (2004) 'Unlocking the mask: A look at the process by which authentic leaders impact follower attitudes and behaviors', *Leadership Quarterly*, 15: 801–23.

Avolio, B. and Yammarino, F. (eds) (2002) *Transformational and Charismatic Leadership: The Road Ahead*, Oxford: JAI Press.

Bakan, J. (2004) *The Corporation: The Pathological Pursuit of Profit and Power*, New York: The Free Press.

Baritz, L. (1960) *The Servants of Power: A History of the Use of Social Science*, Connecticut: Wesleyan University Press.

Barnard, C. (1938) *The Functions of the Executive*, Cambridge, MA: Harvard University Press.

Barrett, R. (1998) *Liberating the Corporate Soul: Building a Visionary Organisation*, Boston: Butterworth-Heinemann.

Bass, B. (1985) *Leadership and Performance Beyond Expectations*, New York: Free Press.

Bass, B. and Avolio, B. (eds) (1994) *Improving Organizational Effectiveness through Transformational Leadership*, Thousand Oaks, CA: Sage.

Beder, S. (2000) *Selling the Work Ethic: From Puritan Pulpit to Corporate PR*, Melbourne: Scribe.

Bedi, K. (1999) *It's Always Possible: Transforming one of the Largest Prisons in the World*, Briar Hill, Vic.: Indra Publishing.

Belenky, M., Clinchy, B., Boldberger, N. and Tarule, J. (1986) *Women's Ways of Knowing: The Development of Self, Voice and Mind*, New York: Basic Books.

Bell, E. and Taylor, S. (2003) 'The elevation of work: Pastoral power and the New Age work ethic', *Organization*, 10(2): 329–49.

—— (2004) '"From outward bound to inward bound": The prophetic voices and discursive practices of spiritual management development', *Human Relations*, 57(4): 439–66.

Bell, E.E. and Nkomo, S. (2001) *Our Separate Ways: Black and White Women and the Struggle for Professional Identity*, Boston, MA: Harvard Business School Press.

Bennis, W. (1989) *Why Can't Leaders Lead? The Unconscious Conspiracy Continues*, San Francisco: Jossey-Bass.

Bennis, W. and Nanus, B. (1985) *Leaders: The Strategies for Taking Charge*, New York: Harper and Row.

Bennis, W. and Thomas, D. (2002) *Geeks and Geezers*, Boston: Harvard Business School Press.

Bernauer, J. and Rasmussen, D. (eds) (1988) *The Final Foucault*, Cambridge, MA: MIT Press.

Bion, W. (1961) *Experiences in Groups*, London: Tavistock.

Blackler, F. and Kennedy, A. (2004) 'The design and evaluation of a leadership programme for experienced Chief Executives from the Public Sector', *Management Learning*, 35(2): 181–203.

Blackmore, J. (1999) *Troubling Women: Feminism, Leadership and Educational Change*, Buckingham: Open University Press.

Block, P. (1993) *Stewardship: Choosing Service over Self-Interest*, San Francisco: Berrett-Koehler Publishers.

Bolman, L. and Deal, T. (1995) *Leading with Soul: An Uncommon Journey of Spirit*, San Francisco: Jossey-Bass.

Bourdieu, P. et al. (1999) *The Weight of the World: Social Suffering in Contemporary Society*, trans. P. Ferguson et al., Oxford: Polity.

Bowell, R. (2004) *The 7 Steps of Spiritual Intelligence: The Practical Pursuit of Purpose, Success and Happiness*, London: Nicholas Brealey.

Boyatzis, R. and McKee, A. (2005) *Resonant Leadership*, Boston, MA: Harvard Business School Press.

Bradshaw, P. and Wicks, D. (1997) 'Women in the academy: Cycles of resistance and compliance', in P. Prasad, A. Mills, M. Elmes and A. Prasad (eds), *Managing the Organizational Melting Pot*, Thousand Oaks: Sage, pp. 199–225.

Bridges, W. (2001) *The Way of Transition: Embracing Life's Most Difficult Moments*, Cambridge, MA: Perseus Publishing.

Brown, K. and Ryan, R. (2003) 'The benefits of being present: Mindfulness and its role in psychological wellbeing', *Journal of Personality and Social Psychology*, 84: 822–48.

Bibliography

*Bryman, A. (1992) *Charisma and Leadership in Organizations*, London: Sage.

*—— (1996) 'Leadership in Organizations', in S. Clegg, C. Hardy and W. Nord (eds), *Handbook of Organizational Studies*, London: Sage, pp. 276–92.

Bunting, M. (2004) *Willing Slaves: How the Overwork Culture is Ruining our Lives*, London: HarperCollins Publishers.

Burnham, J. (1962) *The Managerial Revolution*, Harmondsworth: Penguin.

Burns, J.M. (1978) *Leadership*, New York: Harper and Row.

Cacioppe, R. (2000a) 'Creating spirit at work: Re-visioning organization development and leadership, Part 1', *Leadership and Organization Development Journal*, 21(1): 48–54.

—— (2000b) 'Creating Spirit at Work: Re-visioning organization development and leadership, Part 2', *Leadership and Organization Development Journal*, 21(2): 110–19.

Calas, M. and Smircich, L. (1991) 'Voicing seduction to silence leadership', *Organization Studies*, 12(4): 567–602.

—— (2003) 'Introduction: Spirituality, management and organization', *Organization*, 10(2): 327–8.

Casey, C. (1995) *Work, Self and Society: After Industrialism*, London: Routledge.

—— (1999) '"Come join our family": Discipline and integration in corporate organizational culture', *Human Relations*, 52(2): 155–78.

—— (2000) 'Sociology sensing the body: Revitalizing a dissociative discourse', in J. Hassard, R. Holliday and H. Willmott (eds), *Body and Organization*, London: Sage, pp. 52–70.

—— (2004) 'Bureaucracy re-enchanted: Spirits, experts and authority in organizations', *Organization*, 11(1): 59–79.

Chödrön, P. (1997) *When Things Fall Apart: Heart Advice for Difficult Times*, Boston, MA: Shambhala Publications.

Ciulla, J. (ed.) (1998) *Ethics, The Heart of Leadership*, Westport, CN: Praeger.

Collins, J. (2005) 'Level 5 leadership: The triumph of humility and fierce resolve', *Harvard Business Review*, July–August.

Collinson, D. (1992) *Managing the Shop Floor: subjectivity, masculinity and workplace culture*, Berlin: Walter de Gruyter.

—— (1994) 'Strategies of resistance: Power, knowledge and subjectivity in the workplace', in J. Jermier, D. Knights and W. Nord (eds), *Resistance and Power in Organizations*, London: Routledge, pp. 25–68.

—— (2003) 'Identities and insecurities: Selves at work', *Organization*, 10(3): 527–47.

*—— (2005a) 'Dialectics of leadership', *Human Relations*, 58(11): 1419–42.

—— (2005b) *Questions of Distance: Leadership*, 1(2): 235–50.

Collinson, D. and Hearn, J. (eds) (1996) *Men as Managers, Managers as Men: Critical Perspectives on Men, Masculinities and Managements*, London: Sage.

Conger, J. (1992) *Learning to Lead: The Art of Transforming Managers into Leaders*, San Francisco: Jossey-Bass.

Conger, J. and Associates (1994) *Spirit at Work: Discovering the Spirituality in Leadership*, San Francisco: Jossey-Bass.

Conger, J. and Kanungo, R. (1998) *Charismatic Leadership in Organizations*, San Francisco: Jossey-Bass.

Conger, J., Spreitzer, G. and Lawler, E. (eds) (1999) *The Leader's Change Handbook*, San Francisco: Jossey-Bass.

Conradi, P. (2004) *Going Buddhist: Panic and Emptiness, the Buddha and Me*, London: Short.

Czarniawska, B. (1997) *Narrating the Organization*, Chicago: University of Chicago Press.

Czarniawska, B. and Wolff, R. (1991) 'Leaders, managers, entrepreneurs on and off the organizational stage', *Organization Studies*, 12(4): 529–46.

(His Holiness) the Dalai Lama (2003) *Lighting the Path: The Dalai Lama Teaches on Wisdom and Compassion*, trans. and ed. Geshe Thupten Jinpa, South Melbourne: Lothian Books.

(His Holiness) the Dalai Lama and Cutler, H. (1998) *The Art of Happiness: A Handbook for Living*, New York: Riverhead Books.

Daloz Parks, S. (2005) *Leadership Can be Taught: A Bold Approach for a Complex World*, Boston: Harvard Business School Press.

Denhardt, R. (1981) *In the Shadow of Organization*, Lawrence: Regents Press of Kansas.

Du Gay, P. and Salaman, G. (1992) 'The culture of the customer', *Journal of Management Studies*, 29(5): 615–33.

Dubouloy, M. (2004) 'The transitional space and self-recovery: A psychoanalytic approach to high potential managers' training', *Human Relations*, 57(4): 467–96.

Dunphy, D. and Stace, D. (1988) 'Transformational and coercive strategies for planned organizational change', *Organization Studies*, 9(3): 317–34.

Eagly, A. (2005) 'Achieving relational authenticity in leadership', *Leadership Quarterly*, 16(3): 459–74.

Edwards, P. and Wajcman, J. (2005) *The Politics of Working Life*, Oxford: Oxford University Press.

Elias, D. (2005) 'The man who knew everyone', *The Age*, 9 July.

Ellsworth, E. (1989) 'Why Doesn't This Feel Empowering? Working through the repressive myths of critical pedagogy', *Harvard Educational Review*, 59(3): 297–324.

Elmes, M. and Connelly, D. (1997) 'Dreams of diversity and the realities of intergroup relations in organizations', in P. Prasad, A. Mills, M. Elmes and A. Prasad (eds), *Managing the Organizational Melting Pot*, Thousand Oaks: Sage, pp. 226–54.

Elmes, M. and Smith, C. (2001) 'Moved by the spirit: Contextualizing workplace empowerment in American spiritual ideals', *Journal of Applied Behavioural Science*, 37(1): 33–50.

Eveline, J. (1996) 'The worry of going limp: Are you keeping up in senior management?' *Australian Feminist Studies*, 11(3): 65–79.

Fineman, S. (ed.) (2000) *Emotions in Organizations*, London: Sage.

Fisher, T. (2005) 'Beginner's mind: Cultivating mediator mindfulness', *ACResolution*, Fall: 28–9.

Fleming, P. and Spicer, A. (2003) 'Working at a cynical distance', *Organization*, 10(1): 157–79.

Fletcher, J. (1999) *Disappearing Acts: Gender, Power and Relational Practice at Work*, Cambridge, MA: MIT Press.

*— (2004) 'The paradox of postheroic leadership: An essay on gender, power and transformational change', *Leadership Quarterly*, 15: 647–61.

Foucault, M. (1977) *Discipline and Punish: The Birth of the Prison*, trans. A. Sheridan, London: Allen Lane.

— (1981) *A History of Sexuality, Volume 1: An Introduction*, trans. R. Hurley, Harmondsworth: Penguin.

Fournier, V. and Grey, C. (2000) 'At the critical moment: Conditions and prospects for critical management studies', *Human Relations*, 53(1): 7–32.

Freire, P. (1972) *Pedagogy of the Oppressed*, trans. M. Ramos, New York: Herder and Herder.

Frost, P. (2003) *Toxic Emotions at Work*, Boston: HBS Press.

Gabriel, Y. (1997) 'Meeting God: When organizational members come face to face with the supreme leader', *Human Relations*, 50(4): 315–42.

— (1999) 'Beyond happy families: A critical re-evaluation of the control–resistance–identity triangle', *Human Relations*, 52(2): 179–203.

Bibliography

Gallop, J. (1997) *Feminist Accused of Sexual Harassment*, Bloomington, IN: Duke University Press.

—— (ed.) (1995) *Pedagogy: The Question of Impersonation*, Bloomington, IN: Indiana University Press.

*Gardner, H. (1995) *Leading Minds*, New York: Basic Books.

Garsten, C. and Grey, C. (1997) 'How to become oneself', *Organization*, 4(2): 211–28.

Gatens, M. (1996) *Imaginary Bodies*, London: Routledge.

*Gemmill, G. and Oakley, J. (1992) 'Leadership: An alienating social myth', *Human Relations*, 45(2): 113–29.

Gerzon, M. (2006) *Leading Through Conflict: How Successful Leaders Transform Differences into Opportunities*, Boston, MA: Harvard Business School Press.

Gettler, L. (2005) *Organisations Behaving Badly: A Greek Tragedy of Corporate Pathology*, Brisbane: John Wiley & Sons.

Giacalone, R. and Jurkiewicz, C. (eds) (2003) *Handbook of Workplace Spirituality and Organizational Performance*, Armonk, NY: M.E. Sharpe.

Giddens, A. (1991) *Modernity and Self-Identity*, Cambridge, MA: Polity Press.

Gilbert, G. (1950) *The Psychology of Dictatorship*, New York: The Ronald Press Co.

Gini, A. (2000) *My Job, My Self: Work and the Creation of the Modern Individual*, New York: Routledge.

—— (2006) *Why It's Hard to Be Good*, New York: Routledge.

Goffee, R. and Jones, G. (2005) 'Managing authenticity: The paradox of great leadership', *Harvard Business Review*, 83(12): 86–98.

—— (2006) *Why Should Anyone be Led by You*, Boston, MA: Harvard Business School Press.

Goleman, D. (1998) *Meditative Mind*, Hammersmith: Thorsons, HarperCollins.

—— (2003) *Destructive Emotions*, London: Bloomsbury.

Gouldner, A. (ed.) (1950) *Studies in Leadership*, New York: Harper.

Greenleaf, R. (1977) *Servant Leadership: A Journey into the Nature of Legitimate Power and Greatness*, New York: Paulist Press.

Grey, C. (2001) 'Re-imagining relevance: A response to Starkey and Madan', *British Journal of Management*, 12, Special issue: S27–232.

—— (2005) *A Very Short, Fairly Interesting and Reasonably Cheap Book about Studying Organizations*, London: Sage.

Grey, C., Knights, D. and Willmott, H. (1996) 'Is a Critical Pedagogy of Management Possible?', in R. French and C. Grey (eds), *Rethinking Management Education*, London: Sage, pp. 94–110.

Grey, C. and Sinclair, A. (2006) 'Writing differently', *Organization*, 13(3): 443–53.

Grint, K. (1997a) *Fuzzy Management*, Oxford: Oxford University Press.

*—— (ed.) (1997b) *Leadership: Classical, Contemporary and Critical Approaches*, Oxford: Oxford University Press.

*—— (2000) *The Arts of Leadership*, Oxford: Oxford University Press.

*Gronn, P. (1998) *The Making of Educational Leaders*, London: Cassell.

—— (2002) 'Distributed leadership as a unit of analysis', *Leadership Quarterly*, 13(4): 423–52.

*—— (2003) 'Leadership: Who needs it?' *School Leadership and Management*, 23(3): 267–90.

—— (2006) 'Aesthetics, heroism and the cult of "the leader"', in E. Samier and R. Bates (eds), *Aesthetic Dimensions of Educational Administration and Leadership*, London: Routledge, pp. 191–204.

Grose, M. (2003) *Why First Borns Want to Rule the World and Last Borns Want to Change It*, New York: Random House.

Grosz, E. (1994) *Volatile Bodies*, Bloomington, IN: Indiana University Press.

Hammond, C. (ed.) (1991) *Creation Spirituality and the Dreamtime*, Newtown, NSW: Millenium.

Hampden-Turner, C. and Trompenaars, A. (1993) *The Seven Cultures of Capitalism: Value Systems for Creating Wealth in the United States, Japan, Germany, France, Britain, Sweden and the Netherlands*, New York: Doubleday.

Hardy, C. (1998) 'The power behind empowerment: Implications for research and practice', *Human Relations*, 51(4): 451–83.

Hassard, J., Holliday, R. and Willmott, H. (2000) *Body and Organization*, London: Sage.

*Heifetz, R. (1994) *Leadership Without Easy Answers*, Cambridge, MA: Belknap Press.

Heifetz, R. and Laurie, D. (1999) 'Mobilising adaptive work: Beyond visionary leadership', in J. Conger, G. Spreitzer and E. Lawler (eds), *The Leader's Change Handbook*, San Francisco: Jossey-Bass, pp. 55–87.

*Heifetz, R. and Linsky, M. (2002) *Leadership on the Line: Staying Alive Through the Dangers of Leading*, Cambridge, MA: Harvard Business School Press.

Hewitt, J. (2005) 'This sentence ends with a question mark', *Australian Financial Review*, 30 July.

Hirschhorn, L. (1988) *The Workplace Within*, Cambridge, MA: MIT Press.

*—— (1997) *Reworking Authority: Leading and Following in the Post-Modern Organization*, Cambridge, MA: MIT Press.

Hirschman, A. (1970) *Exit, Voice and Loyalty: Responses to Decline in Firms, Organizations and States*, Cambridge, MA: Harvard University Press.

Hochschild, A. (1983) *The Managed Heart: The Commercialization of Human Feeling*, Berkeley: University of California Press.

—— (1990) *The Second Shift*, New York: Avon Books.

—— (2003) *The Commercialization of Intimate Life*, Berkeley: University of California Press.

Hoffer, E. (1951) *The True Believer: Thoughts on the Nature of Mass Movements*, New York: Harper and Row.

hooks, b. (1994) *Teaching to Transgress: Education as the Practice of Freedom*, New York: Routledge.

House, R., Hanges, P., Javidan, M., Dorfman, P. and Gupta, V. (2004) *Culture, Leadership and Organizations: The Globe Study of 62 Societies*, Thousand Oaks, CA: Sage.

Howie, G. and Tauchert, A. (eds) (2002) *Gender, Teaching and Research in Higher Education: Challenges for the 21st Century*, Aldershot: Ashgate.

Hughes, C. (2002) 'Pedagogies of, and for, resistance', in G. Howie and A. Tauchert (eds), *Gender, Teaching and Research in Higher Education*, Aldershot: Ashgate, pp. 99–112.

Hughes, G. (2005) 'The bank, the police and fame', *The Age*, 6 August.

Irigaray, L. (2002) *Between East and West: From Singularity to Community*, New York: Columbia University Press.

Jackson, B. (2001) *Management Gurus and Management Fashions*, London: Routledge.

Jacques, R. (1996) *Manufacturing the Employee: Management Knowledge from the 19th to the 21st Centuries*, London: Sage.

James, W. (1902) *Varieties of Religious Experience*, New York: Longs, Greens.

Janis, I. (1972) *Victims of Groupthink: A Psychological Study of Foreign Policy Decisions and Fiascoes*, Boston: Houghton, Mifflin.

Jermier, J., Knights, D. and Nord, W. (eds) (1994) *Resistance and Power in Organizations*, London: Routledge.

Bibliography

Johnson, I. (2002) 'The application of Buddhist principles to lifelong learning', *International Journal of Lifelong Learning*, 21(2): 99–114.

Jones, A. (2005) 'Developing What? An anthropological look at the leadership development process across cultures', *Leadership*, 2(4): 481–98.

Jung, C. (1995, edited with an introduction by J. Clarke) *Jung on the East*, London: Routledge.

Kabat-Zinn, J. (1994) *Wherever You Go, There You Are: Mindfulness Meditation in Everyday Life*, New York: Hyperion.

—— (2003) 'Mindfulness-based interventions in context: past, present and future', *Clinical Psychology*, 10: 144–56.

Kahn, W. (1992) 'To be fully there: Psychological presence at work', *Human Relations*, 45(4): 321–49.

Kaye, L. (1996) *Zen at Work*, New York: Crown.

Kearney, P. (1999) *Meditation in Eastern Religions*, Brisbane: University of Queensland Press.

Keefe, K. (2003) *Paddy's Road: Life Stories of Patrick Dodson*, Canberra: Australian Institute of Aboriginal and Torres Strait Islander Studies Press.

Kellerman, B. (2004) *Bad Leadership: What it is, how it happens, why it matters*, Boston: Harvard Business School Press.

Kenway, J. and Modra, H. (1992) 'Feminist pedagogy and emancipatory possibilities', in C. Luke and J. Gore (eds), *Feminism and Critical Pedagogy*, New York: Routledge, pp. 138–66.

Kerfoot, D. (2000) 'Estrangement, disembodiment and the organizational other', in J. Hassard, R. Holliday and H. Willmott (eds), *Body and Organization*, London: Sage, pp. 230–46.

Kerfoot, D. and Knights, D. (1996) '"The best is yet to come?" The quest for embodiment in managerial work', in D. Collinson and J. Hearn (eds), *Men as Managers, Managers as Men: Critical Perspectives on Men, Masculinities and Managements*, London: Sage, pp. 78–98.

*Kets de Vries, M. (1994) 'The leadership mystique', *Academy of Management Executive*, 8(3): 73–92.

—— (1999) 'What's playing in the organizational theatre? Collusive relationships in management', *Human Relations*, 52(6): 745–73.

—— (2005) 'Leadership group coaching in action: The Zen of creating high performance teams', *Academy of Management Executive*, 19(1): 61–76.

*—— (2006) *The Leader on the Couch: A Clinical Approach to Changing People and Organizations*, San Francisco: Jossey Bass.

*Kets de Vries, M. and Miller, D. (1984) *The Neurotic Organization*, San Francisco: Jossey-Bass.

Khema, A. (1987) *Being Nobody, Going Nowhere: Meditations on the Buddhist Path*, Boston: Wisdom Publications.

Kirkpatrick, S. and Locke, E. (1991) 'Leadership: Do traits matter?', *Academy of Management Executive*, 5(2): 48–60.

Kluger, J., Carsen, J., Cole, W. and Steptoe, S. (2006) 'The new science of siblings', *Time*, 168(2): 30–9.

Knights, D. and O'Leary, M. (2006) 'Leadership, ethics and responsibility to the Other', *Journal of Business Ethics*, 67(2): 125–37.

Knights, D. and Willmott, H. (1989) 'Power and subjectivity at work', *Sociology*, 23: 34–58.

—— (1992) 'Conceptualising leadership processes: A study of senior managers in a financial services company', *Journal of Management Studies*, 29(6): 761–82.

Kotter, J. and Schlesinger, L. (1979) 'Choosing strategies for change', *Harvard Business Review*, March–April: 106–14.

Krantz, J. (2006) 'Leadership, betrayal and adaptation', *Human Relations*, 59(2): 221–40.

Kremmer, C. (1999) 'The caged bird sings', *The Age*, 13 March.

Kunjunni Raja, K. (ed.) (1972) *The Hathayogapradīpikā of Svātmārāma*, Chennai: The Adyar Library and Research Centre.

LaBier, D. (1986) *Modern Madness: The Emotional Fallout of Success*, Reading, MA: Addison-Wesley.

Lakoff, G. (2005) *Don't Think of an Elephant!: Know your Values and Frame the Debate*, North Carlton, Vic.: Scribe.

Langer, E. (1989) *Mindfulness*, Reading, MA: Addison-Wesley.

Larkin, P. (1974) 'This be the Verse', *High Windows*, London: Faber and Faber.

Lasswell, H. (1930) *Psychopathology and Politics*, Chicago: University of Chicago Press.

Lather, P. (1991) *Getting Smart: Feminist Research and Pedagogy With/In the Postmodern*, New York: Routledge.

Leadership Quarterly (2005) Special Issue 16(3).

Lewin, R. and Regine, B. (2000) *The Soul at Work*, New York: Simon and Schuster.

Lindholm, C. (1988) 'Lovers and leaders: A comparison of social and psychological models of romance and charisma', *Social Science Information*, 27(1): 3–45.

Little, G. (1985) *Political Ensembles: A Psychosocial Approach to Politics and Leadership*, Melbourne: Oxford University Press.

—— (1988) *Strong Leadership: Thatcher, Reagan and an Eminent Person*, Melbourne: Oxford University Press.

Locke, R. (1989) *Management and Higher Education Since 1940: The Influence of America and Japan on West Germany, Great Britain and France*, Cambridge: Cambridge University Press.

—— (1996) *The Collapse of the American Management Mystique*, Oxford: Oxford University Press.

Loehr, J. and Schwartz, T. (2001) 'The making of a corporate athlete', *Harvard Business Review*, January: 120–8.

Luke, C. and Gore, J. (eds) (1992) *Feminisms and Critical Pedagogy*, New York: Routledge.

Machiavelli, N. (1984) *The Prince*, ed. and trans. P. Bondanella, Oxford: Oxford University Press.

Macken, J. (2006) 'Meditate on this', *Australian Financial Review*, 18 February.

MacKenzie, V. (1998) *Cave in the Snow: A Western Woman's Quest for Enlightenment*, London: Bloomsbury.

—— (2001) *Why Buddhism? Westerners in Search of Wisdom*, Sydney: Allen & Unwin.

Maiden, M. (2005) 'The Shame Game', *The Age*, 30 July.

Maier, M. (1997) 'We have to make a MANagement decision: Challenger and the dysfunctions of corporate masculinity', in P. Prasad, A. Mills, M. Elmes and A. Prasad (eds), *Managing the Organizational Melting Pot*, Thousand Oaks: Sage, pp. 148–67.

*Mant, A. (1983) *Leaders We Deserve*, Oxford: Blackwell.

—— (1997) *Intelligent Leadership*, Sydney: Allen & Unwin.

Marshall, J. (1984) *Women Managers: Travellers in a Male World*, Chichester: Wiley.

—— (1995) *Women Managers Moving On*, London: Routledge.

—— (1999) 'Doing gender in management education', *Gender and Education*, 11(3): 251–63.

Martin, J. (2003) 'Feminist theory and critical theory: Unexplored synergies', in M. Alvesson and H. Willmott (eds), *Studying Management Critically*, London: Sage, pp. 66–91.

Martin, P.Y. (2006) 'Practising gender at work: Further thoughts on reflexivity', *Gender, Work and Organization*, 13(3): 254–76.

Bibliography

McDowell, L. (1997) *Capital Culture: Gender at Work in the City*, Malden, MA: Blackwell Publishers.

McIntosh, P. (1988) 'White privilege and male privilege: A personal account of coming to see correspondences through work in women's studies', working paper, Wellesley, MA: Center for Research on Women, Wellesley College.

McLean, B. and Elkind, P. (2003) *The Smartest Guys in the Room*, London: Penguin.

McWilliam, E. (1999) *Pedagogical Pleasures*, New York: Peter Lang Publishing.

McWilliam, E. and Jones, A. (1996) 'Eros and pedagogy', in E. McWilliam (ed.), *Pedagogy, Technology and the Body*, New York: Peter Lang.

Meindl, J., Ehrlich, S. and Dukerich, J. (1985) 'The romance of leadership', *Administrative Science Quarterly*, 30: 78–102.

Melbourne Academic Mindfulness Interest Group (2006) 'Mindfulness-based psycho-therapies: A review of conceptual foundations, empirical evidence and practical considerations', *Australian and New Zealand Journal of Psychiatry* 40: 285–94.

Meyerson, D. (2001) *Tempered Radicals*, Boston, MA: Harvard Business School Press.

Meyerson, D. and Scully, M. (1995) 'Tempered radicalism and the politics of ambivalence and change', *Organization Science*, 6(5): 585–600.

Mitchell, N. (2005) 'You betrayed us, Steve', *Herald-Sun*, 2 August.

Mitroff, I. (2003) 'Do not promote religion under the guise of spirituality', *Organization*, 10(2): 375–82.

Mole, G. (2004) 'Can leadership be taught?', in J. Storey (ed.), *Leadership in Organizations: Current issues and key trends*, London: Routledge, pp. 125–37.

Moreton-Robinson, A. (2000) *Talkin' Up to the White Woman*, Brisbane: University of Queensland Press.

Morley, K. (2005) *Leadership Index*, Carlton: Melbourne Business School.

Morley, L. (2002) 'Lifelong yearning: Feminist pedagogy in the learning society', in G. Howie and A. Tauchert (eds), *Gender, Teaching and Research in Higher Education*, Aldershot: Ashgate, pp. 86–98.

Mulholland, K. (1996) 'Entrepreneurialism, masculinities and the self-made man', in D. Collinson and J. Hearn (eds), *Men as Managers, Managers as Men: Critical Perspectives on Men, Masculinities and Managements*, London: Sage.

National College of Schools Leadership (2006) 'Synthesis of Leadership research outside education', a report prepared by A. Coleman, Lancaster: NCSL.

Nicholson, B. (2005) 'Slightly shirty, PM suits himself', *The Age*, 28 October.

O'Donnell, E. (2006) 'Twigs bent left or right', *Harvard Magazine*, February: 1.

O'Reilly, B. (2000) 'The power merchant', *Fortune*, 141(8), 17 April.

Perriton, L. and Reynolds, M. (2004) 'Critical management education: From pedagogy of possibility to pedagogy of refusal?', *Management Learning*, 35(1): 61–77.

Pfeffer, J. (1977) 'The ambiguity of leadership', *Academy of Management Review*, January: 104–12.

Pirola-Merlo, A. (2006) 'Moral Leadership is an Oxymoron', paper presented to the Monash-Melbourne Leadership Group, June.

Popper, M. and Mayseless, O. (2002) 'Internal world of transformational leaders', in B. Avolio and F. Yammarino (eds), *Transformational and Charismatic Leadership: The Road Ahead*, Oxford: Elsevier Science, pp. 203–30.

Porter, M. (2006) *The New Puritans*, Melbourne: Melbourne University Press.

Prabhavananda, S. and Isherwood, C. (1953, 1981) *How to Know God: The Yoga Aphorisms of Patanjali*, California: The Vedanta Society of Southern California.

Prenzler, T. (2004) 'Chief Commissioner Christine Nixon, Victoria: Australia's first female police chief', *Policy Practice and Research*, 5(4/5): 301–15.

Quinn, R. and Snyder, N. (1999) 'Advanced change theory', in J. Conger, G. Spreitzer and E. Lawler (eds), *The Leader's Change Handbook*, San Francisco: Jossey-Bass, pp. 162–94.

—— (2005) 'Moments of greatness: Entering the fundamental state of leadership', *Harvard Business Review*, 83(7): 75–83.

Raab, N. (1997) 'Becoming an expert in not knowing: Reframing teacher as consultant', *Management Learning*, 28(2): 161–75.

Ram-Prasad, C. (2005) *Eastern Philosophy*, London: Weidenfeld & Nicolson.

Rama, S. (1978) *Living with the Himalayan Masters*, Honesdale, PA: Himalayan Institute Press.

—— (1988) *Path of Fire and Light: Advanced Practices of Yoga*, Honesdale, PA: Himalayan Institute Press.

Rama, S., Ballentine, R. and Hymes, A. (1979) *The Science of Breath*, Honesdale, PA: Himalayan Institute Press.

Reynolds, M. (1999) 'Grasping the Nettle: Possibilities and pitfalls of a critical management pedagogy', *British Journal of Management*, 10(2): 171–84.

Richardson, R. (1995) *Family Ties that Bind: A Self-Help Guide to Change through Family of Origin Therapy*, North Vancouver, BC: International Self-Counsel Press.

Rickards, T. and Clark, M. (2005) *Dilemmas of Leadership*, New York: Routledge.

Rinpoche, S. (1992) *The Tibetan Book of Living and Dying*, ed. and trans. P. Gaffney and A. Harvey, London: Rider/Random House.

Ritzer, G. (2000) *The McDonaldization of Society*, Thousand Oaks: Pine Forge Press.

Roach, M. (2000) *The Diamond Cutter: The Buddha on Managing Your Business and Life*, New York: Doubleday.

Roberts, J. (2003) 'Agency without agents: Undoing our preoccupation with identity', unpublished paper presented at the 21st Standing Conference on Organizational Symbolism, 'Organisational Wellness', Cambridge, 9–12 July.

—— (2005) 'The power of the 'imaginary' in disciplinary processes', *Organization*, 12(5): 619–42.

Rose, N. (1989) *Governing the Soul: The Shaping of the Private Self*, London: Routledge.

—— (1996) *Inventing our Selves: Psychology, Power and Personhood*, Cambridge: Cambridge University Press.

—— (1999) *Powers of Freedom: Reframing Political Thought*, Cambridge: Cambridge University Press.

Sarra, C. (2003) 'Young and black and deadly: Strategies for improving outcomes for Indigenous students', Paper No. 5, Canberra: Australian College of Educators, Quality Teaching Series, Practitioner Perspectives: 6.

Schön, D. (1983) *The Reflective Practitioner: How Professionals Think in Action*, New York: Basic Books.

—— (1987) *Educating the Reflective Practitioner*, San Francisco: Jossey Bass.

Scott, S. and Morgan, D. (eds) (1993) *Body Matters*, London: Falmer Press.

Segal, Z., Williams, J. and Teasdale, J. (2002) *Mindfulness-based Cognitive Therapy for Depression: A New Approach to Preventing Relapse*, New York: Guilford.

Senge, P. (1990) *The Fifth Discipline: The Art and Practice of the Learning Organization*, Sydney: Random House.

Shand, A. (2005) 'The last laugh', *The Bulletin*, 123(1), 2 August.

Shklar, J. (1984) *Ordinary Vices*, Cambridge, MA: The Belknap Press of Harvard University Press.

Bibliography

—— (1990) *The Faces of Injustice*, New Haven, CN: Yale University Press.

Sinclair, A. (1992) 'The tyranny of a team ideology', *Organization Studies*, 13(4): 611–26.

—— (1994) *Trials at the Top*, Melbourne: The Australian Centre, University of Melbourne.

—— (1995a) 'Sex and the MBA', *Organization*, 2(2): 295–317.

—— (1995b) 'The seduction of the self-managed team and the reinvention of the team-as-group', *Leading and Managing*, 1(1): 44–62.

—— (1995c) 'Sexuality in leadership', *International Review of Women and Leadership*, 1(2): 25–38.

—— (1998) *Doing Leadership Differently: Gender, Power and Sexuality in Leading*, Melbourne: Melbourne University Press.

——(2000a) 'Teaching managers about masculinities', *Management Learning*, 31(1): 83–101; reproduced in edited form in *Impact*, 7(3) 2001: 50–3.

—— (2000b) 'Women within diversity: Risks and possibilities', *Women in Management Review*, extended special issue 15(5/6).

—— (2004a) 'Renewal', *Mt Eliza Business Review*, 7(1): 39–44.

—— (2004b) 'Journey around leadership', *Discourse: Studies in the Cultural Politics of Education*, 25(1): 7–19.

—— (2004c) *Doing Leadership Differently: Gender, Power and Sexuality in Leading*, 2nd edn, Melbourne: Melbourne University Press.

—— (2005a) 'Body and management pedagogy', *Gender, Work and Organization*, 12(1): 89–104.

—— (2005b) 'Critical diversity management practice in Australia: Romanced or co-opted', in A. Konrad, P. Prasad and J. Pringle (eds), *Handbook of Workplace Diversity*, Thousand Oaks: Sage, pp. 511–30.

—— (2005c) 'Body possibilities in leadership', *Leadership*, 1(4): 387–406.

—— (forthcoming) 'Seducing leadership: Stories of leadership development', *Gender, Work and Organization*.

—— (forthcoming) 'Teaching leadership critically to MBAs', *Management Learning*.

Sinclair, A. and Wilson, V. (2002) *New Faces of Leadership*, Melbourne: Melbourne University Press.

Smircich, L. and Morgan, G. (1982) 'Leadership: The management of meaning', *Journal of Applied Behavioural Science*, 18(2): 257–73.

Smith, F. (2006) 'Get in touch with your inner leader', *Australian Financial Review*, 7 November, p. 59.

Steinberg, B. (2001) 'The making of female presidents and prime ministers: The impact of birth order, sex of siblings and father–daughter dynamics', *Political Psychology*, 22: 89–114.

Stewart, L. (1992) *Changemakers: A Jungian Perspective on Sibling Position and Family Atmosphere*, London: Routledge.

Steyrer, J. (2002) 'Stigma, Charisma and the Narcissistic Personality', in B. Avolio and F. Yammarino (eds), *Transformational and Charismatic Leadership: The Road Ahead*, Oxford: Elsevier Science, pp. 231–54.

Still, L. (2006) *Corporate Elders*, Perth: University of Western Australia Press.

*Stogdill, R. (1974) *Handbook of Leadership: A Survey of Theory and Research*, New York: Free Press.

*Storey, J. (ed.) (2004) *Leadership in Organizations: Current issues and Key Trends*, London: Routledge.

Sulloway, F. (1996) *Born to Rebel: Birth Order, Family Dynamics and Creative Lives*, New York: Pantheon.

Sveiby, K. and Skuthorpe, T. (2006) *Treading Lightly: The Hidden Wisdom of the World's Oldest People*, Sydney: Allen & Unwin.

Swartz, M. with Watkins, S. (2003) *Power Failure: The Rise and Fall of Enron*, London: Aurum Press.

Tacey, D. (1996) *Edge of the Sacred*, London: HarperCollins.

—— (2003) *The Spirituality Revolution: The Emergence of Contemporary Spirituality*, Hove, East Sussex: Brunner-Routledge.

Thich, N.H. (1991) *The Path of Mindfulness in Everyday Life*, New York: Bantam Books.

—— (1999) *The Miracle of Mindfulness*, Boston, MA: Beacon Press.

Tonn, J. (2003) *Mary Parker Follet: Creating Democracy, Transforming Managers*, Boston: Yale University Press.

Tourish, D. and Vatcha, N. (2005) 'Charismatic leadership and corporate cultism at Enron: The elimination of dissent, the promotion of conformity and organizational collapse', *Leadership*, 1(4): 455–80.

Townley, B. (1994) *Reframing Human Resource Management: Power, Ethics and the Subject at Work*, London: Sage.

—— (1995) 'Know thyself: Self-awareness, self-formation and managing', *Organization*, 2(2): 271–89.

Trounson, A. (2005) 'ASX not "soft" on insider trading', *The Australian*, 1 August.

Trungpa, C. (1973) *Cutting Through Spiritual Materialism*, Boston, MA: Shambala Press.

Turner, B. (1984) *The Body and Society*, London: Sage.

Twemlow, S. (2000) 'The roots of violence: Converging psychoanalytic models and explanatory models for power struggles and violence in schools', *Psychoanalytic Quarterly*, 69(4): 741–85.

—— (2001) 'Training Psychotherapists in Attributes of "Mind" from Zen and Psychoanalytic Perspectives', Part 1 and Part 2, *American Journal of Psychotherapy*, 55(1): 1–21 and 22–39.

Van Nostrand, C. (1993) *Gender-Responsible Leadership: Detecting Bias, Implementing Interventions*, Newbury Park, CA: Sage.

Walkerdine, V. (1992) 'Progressive pedagogy and political struggle' in C. Luke and J. Gore (eds), *Feminisms and Critical Pedagogy*, London: Routledge, pp. 15–24.

Watson, D. (2003) *Death Sentence*, Sydney: Random House.

—— (2004) *Watson's Dictionary of Weasel Words, Contemporary Clichés, Cant and Management Jargon*, Milsons Point, NSW: Knopf.

Weber, M. (1968) *Max Weber on Charisma and Institution Building: Selected Papers*, ed. S. Eisenstadt, Chicago: University of Chicago Press.

Wheen, F. (2004) *How Mumbo-Jumbo Conquered the World: A Short History of Modern Delusions*, London: Fourth Estate.

Whyte, W. (1956) *The Organization Man*, New York: Simon and Schuster.

Williams, P. (2004) 'Heretic', *Australian Financial Review* magazine, September: 74.

Zaleznik, A. (1977) 'Leaders and managers: Are they different?', *Harvard Business Review*, 55(3): 67–78.

Zizek, S. (2001) *One Belief*, New York: Routledge.

Zohar, D. and Marshall, I. (2000) *SQ: Connecting with Your Spiritual Intelligence*, London: Bloomsbury.

—— (2004) *Spiritual Capital: Wealth We Can Live By*, London: Bloomsbury.

index

Index

Index